crazy about
cookies

crazy about cookies

300 Scrumptious Recipes for Every Occasion & Craving

Krystina Castella

STERLING

New York / London
www.sterlingpublishing.com

STERLING and the distinctive Sterling logo are registered trademarks of Sterling Publishing Co., Inc.

Library of Congress Cataloging-in-Publication Data

Castella, Krystina.
Crazy about cookies : 300 scrumptious recipes for every occasion & craving / Krystina Castella.
p. cm.
Includes index.
ISBN 978-1-4027-6913-9 (pb-with flaps : alk. paper) 1. Cookies. I. Title.
TX772.C385 2010
641.8'654—dc22
2009051115

2   4   6   8   10   9   7   5   3   1

Published by Sterling Publishing Co., Inc.
387 Park Avenue South, New York, NY 10016
© 2010 by Krystina Castella
Distributed in Canada by Sterling Publishing
c/o Canadian Manda Group, 165 Dufferin Street
Toronto, Ontario, Canada M6K 3H6
Distributed in the United Kingdom by GMC Distribution Services
Castle Place, 166 High Street, Lewes, East Sussex, England BN7 1XU
Distributed in Australia by Capricorn Link (Australia) Pty. Ltd.
P.O. Box 704, Windsor, NSW 2756, Australia

Printed in China
All rights reserved

Sterling ISBN 978-1-4027-6913-9

For information about custom editions, special sales, premium and
corporate purchases, please contact Sterling Special Sales
Department at 800-805-5489 or specialsales@sterlingpublishing.com.

Photography by Teri Lyn Fisher

For my parents, Marion and Michael Castella.
Thank you for all your support and encouragement.

Acknowledgments

Thank you to everyone whose help has crafted this book:

Jennifer Williams, my editor, for seeing the potential of this book from the onset, and for all of her support and insight throughout the process

The outstanding photographer Teri Lyn Fisher, for her professional demeanor and her commitment to bringing each cookie's personality to life through her spectacular images

Grace Cho, aka "Amazing Grace," the pastry chef, for her impeccable recipe-testing and cookie-making skills

Isaias Mendoza, the baker, for his creative enthusiasm

Adam C. Pearson, the food stylist, for his discerning eye and playful humor

Liana Krissoff, line editor

Rodman P. Neumann, project editor

Rachel Maloney, designer

Gavin Motnyk, for his help with the templates and other drawings

Elizabeth Mihaltse, cover art director

Eileen Chetti, copyeditor

Barbara J. Greenberg, proofreader

Jay Kreider, JS Editorial, LLC, indexer

Contents

Author's Note

Throughout the book you'll notice this icon ♥.

Each ♥ indicates a healthier (and equally delicious) option for a recipe, where there is less sugar (sweetened only with juices and honey), fruit and veggie (extra vitamins), energy cookies and bars (extra vitamins and full proteins), low fat (less fat and healthy fats), gluten-free (no wheat, barley, rye), and vegan (no animal products).

There was a 4-H commercial in the seventies that had a big impact on my perception of cookies as a kid. It took place inside a cookie factory where hundreds of cookies were shown coming off of conveyor belts. The jingle went something like this: "It takes a lot of work baking cookies, but you can buy them so easy in the store."

My eight-year-old mind thought, "Yeah, you know, they're right." And since there was no song like that for cupcakes, cakes, or ice pops, I decided to focus my young love for kitchen time on them. Every time I considered making cookies I thought of the commercial and figured, "I'll just buy them."

I focused my cookie-related energy on supporting my mission as a Girl Scout. I spent months going door-to-door in my neighborhood in Staten Island, New York, selling Thin Mints, Samoas, Do-Si-Dos, and Tagalongs. Each year when I would show up at the door, kids would tell their parents, "The cookie girl is here again!" I created ways of describing the tastes of each cookie, explaining why one is better for a particular time of day, snack, occasion, or holiday than another. Thin Mints were the Christmas cookie, Samoas were for summertime camping trips, and Tagalongs were the after-school cookie to enjoy with a tall glass of milk. When the cookies arrived I would package them nicely for each customer. Each year I topped my previous sales numbers, and I made people smile at the same time. I eventually got a badge for selling a thousand boxes of cookies.

For decades, the only cookies I made from scratch were chocolate chip cookies and oatmeal raisin cookies. As I got older I realized that, at least in those two cases, the commercials were wrong and homemade was better than store bought. I made those two recipes from the chocolate chip bag and the oatmeal canister over and over again. But I nursed a secret desire to venture further. I had amassed a huge collection of cookie cutters and decorating books but was not yet brave enough to take the leap into cookie decorating. I bought them because I liked the idea of it and thought maybe someday I could do it, but there was something about it that seemed intimidating. Even though I went to art school, drawing isn't my thing, so the idea of making perfect lines with icing seemed out of the question.

After the success of *Crazy about Cupcakes* and *Pops! Icy Treats for Everyone*, I was ready for a new challenge and decided it was time to give cookies a shot. I took out that big box of cookie cutters, collected recipes I loved from friends and family, played around in the kitchen, and changed them, tweaked them, and then started developing my own recipes and cookie ideas from scratch. As I got into it I realized that not only was I having fun; I was becoming downright obsessed. My years of fearing the cookie were over—in a big way.

COOKIES ARE STYLISH

Cookies can be edible art. Flavor, form, and technique all work together to make a supremely satisfying cookie. Shortbread and gingerbread are constructive building materials that allow shaping and decorating techniques that can be explored in no other medium.

COOKIES ARE AUTHENTIC AND INNOVATIVE

There is so much history surrounding cookies that sometimes a traditional cookie is just what is needed; other times a new cookie recipe and design are called for. Attention to the flavor can highlight a season or set a look or mood for a holiday occasion.

COOKIES HAVE PERSONALITY

As with cupcakes, a batch of cookies provides a multitude of blank slates for improvisation, with possibilities for incorporating many artistic styles. Each cookie can have a personality of its own, whether it's through varying flavors within a batch or decorating each cookie in a unique way. With a full-scale cake (although I love those, too), a bit more planning is involved, and you get only one shot per cake.

COOKIES ARE SIMPLE AND FRIENDLY

The fastest homemade baked treat to make if you are short on time? Cookies, of course. Kind of hip, kind of cool—and extremely fun. Whether they are rustic melt-in-your-mouth after-school snacks or casual dinner-party desserts, presentation is easy: Put them in a box for gifting or on a plate for serving. If the cookies look and taste good, that's all that's needed.

ABOUT THIS COOKBOOK

Let me tell you a little about the *Crazy about Cookies* adventure in which you're about to partake. There are more than three hundred and fifty cookie ideas and one hundred photos contained in five chapters: "Everyday Cookies," "Party Cookies," "Occasions Cookies," "Holiday Cookies," and "Christmas Cookies." I chose this structure because this is the way we experience cookies, and to me that is the most important part of the process. From baking to eating, the whole cookie experience is fun, but—like many people—I bake cookies for specific purposes and want to find the right cookie to make for each one, whether it's to serve as a simple snack or to present as a dessert that epitomizes a celebration or special event. I gave Christmas a chapter of its own because if people bake once a year, they bake for the holidays. And

I couldn't resist giving gingerbread and butter cookie constructions a section of their own. I have also included many healthful recipes for all of my vegan-, sugar-free-, low-fat-, and gluten-free-cookie-loving friends. And since there is not just one perfect way to make a cookie for many of the recipes, in most cases I give a main recipe with one or more variations.

If you want to learn more about ingredients, tools, cookie baking, and cookie classifications, take a look at "Cookies in the Know." Decorators wanting to expand their skills might want to read "Baking and Decorating Techniques," as well as the detailed instructions for making each cookie. For the creative innovator, I've provided suggestions for mix-ins and templates for cookie constructions.

The techniques, recipes, and design ideas in this book are here for you to re-create or use as a springboard for coming up with concepts for your own personalized cookies. Make your cookies as simple or complex as you like. Follow the recipes exactly or experiment. Whatever approach you choose, I hope you find that once you've begun to explore all the possibilities in the world of making cookies, there is defiantly no turning back. Happy baking and good eating!

—Krystina Castella
Crazyaboutcookiesbook.com
Glendale, California

Chapter 1

Cookies in the Know

As an industrial designer, I have designed many products for manufacturing, and I am very sensitive to the products designed for baking. I don't believe in purchasing the most expensive gear, just the *right* gear. Fancy prep, molding, and decorating equipment is fun, but if you have baking sheets made of the right materials, with proper insulation and reflective qualities, that's all you really need to turn out great cookies. If you're going to purchase new gear, look for these qualities in the baking sheets, and over time you can accumulate the rest.

BAKING EQUIPMENT

Aluminum Foil

Aluminum foil can be used to line baking sheets for ease of cleaning. It also works as an insulator to trap air, similar to double panning, but it captures more heat than parchment paper and may brown the bottoms of cookies faster.

Baking Molds

There are many types of shaped baking molds on the market: madeleine pans, springerle molds, shortbread molds, and a host of silicone molds. Ceramic molds need to be oiled and floured, while most silicone molds are fine left uncoated.

Baking Pans

Bar cookies and shortbread can be made in baking pans. The sides of the pan should be around 1½ to 2 inches high. For most bar cookies, square or rectangular, shiny, heavy-gauge aluminum pans are perfect. The size of the pan you need depends on the recipe. If you use a different pan size from the one specified in the recipe, you'll need to adjust the baking time. With a larger pan, the baking time will be shorter, and with a smaller pan the baking time will be longer.

Cake Pans

Cookie cupcakes, ice cream cookies, and large cookie cakes can be made in cupcake tins or cake pans. Springform pans work well for cookie cakes. Shortbread and cookie cakes can be made in a round baking pan, one with a removable bottom, or a springform pan. If you'll be storing the bar cookies or shortbreads in the pan you baked them in, choose one with a lid.

Cookie Cutters

Choose sharp metal or plastic cutters without rough edges. Cooking times will vary depending on the size of your shapes. Use less baking time when working with smaller shapes and more baking time for larger shapes. Dip the cutter in flour every time before using. Cut from the center of the rolled dough and work your way out, starting with larger cutters first, placed as close together as possible. To keep cookie cutters from rusting, wash them thoroughly; then place them in a 200°F oven for 10 minutes, until dried. Let cool, and store.

Cookie-Dough Cutter

Pizza cutters or pastry cutters can be used after the dough is rolled to create straight lines and freeform cuts.

Cookie Jars and Tall Airtight Containers

Most cookies will be eaten in a day or two, so beautiful ceramic cookie jars, even if not airtight, are fun ways to store them. Airtight jars are even better, because your cookies will last longer. If you are storing cookies for more than a week, I recommend tall airtight glass or plastic containers for easy stacking. Store with waxed or parchment paper between layers to prevent sticking.

Cookie Press or Spritz Gun

In a cookie press, dough is extruded through dies (aka disks) made of either metal or plastic. There are old-fashioned hand-cranked models and newer pressure-press and electric models. Most come with several disks to make different shaped cookies.

Cookie Sheets

Flat cookie sheets with no rims are best for most cookies because the cookies will slide off easily with a spatula. Choose a sheet with a lip on a short side for easy gripping. The material the cookie sheet is made from determines the success of your cookies. Invest in several good-quality shiny, heavy-gauge aluminum sheets. I like to work with four so I always have cool, clean pans ready for the next batch. Dark nonstick cookie sheets absorb the heat and may brown your cookies too much on the bottom. Measure the inside of your oven before purchasing. The cookie sheets need to be about 2 inches smaller than your oven on all sides so that heat can circulate around them.

A 12 x 15½-inch cookie sheet is a standard size that works well in most ovens. Insulated cookie sheets are excellent for soft cookies but don't work as well for crisp cookies. If you have only lightweight, noninsulated cookie sheets, create your own insulation by layering one cookie sheet on top of another.

Cooling Racks

Some cookies continue to bake if left on the cookie sheet after they are taken from the oven. Transfer them to a heavy-duty wire rack so that air circulates around them to allow for even cooling. Less-sturdy cookies will need to sit on the cookie sheets for 5 to 10 minutes to harden before transferring.

Double Boiler

A double boiler is good for melting chocolate, mixing fillings and icings, and preparing other ingredients that need to be cooked over low heat. You don't want the top pan to touch the water, so purchase one whose top is not too deep and don't fill the bottom with too much water. You can also make your own by setting a heatproof bowl over a saucepan.

Food Processor or Blender

A food processor is the best choice for grinding nuts, kneading some doughs, sifting flour, and combining dry ingredients. A blender can work as a substitute.

Hand and Stand Mixers

Although most cookie doughs can be mixed by hand, a handheld or stand mixer can make creaming butter and mixing stiff doughs easier. Cookies don't need rigorous mixing like many cakes do, so if you enlist help from an appliance, be sure not to overmix.

Measuring Cups and Spoons

Nested cups and spoons are best for dry ingredients so you can level off the top with a knife to get exact measurements. Glass cups are best for measuring liquids so you can read the measurements at eye level. Pour liquid ingredients into measuring spoons until full.

Mixing Bowls

Ceramic, glass, stainless-steel, and plastic bowls will work well as long as they are big enough to hold the ingredients.

Ovens

All ovens are different, so get to know your oven intimately by testing different recipes. Is it hotter or cooler than its thermometer indicates? Does the air circulate well, or is it hotter at the edges? Once you know your oven, adjust the timing, temperature, and placement of cookies on the sheets accordingly.

Parchment Paper

Parchment paper is an insulator that helps promote even baking without burning the bottoms of cookies. Large sheets can be folded into a double layer and then flipped over for a new batch, and small sheets can be cut to about the size of the cookie sheet. There is no need to butter the parchment paper unless the recipe suggests doing so. (Avoid baking on waxed paper; it makes a poor substitute for parchment paper and because the wax can melt you run the risk of turning out waxy cookies.) Templates can be drawn on parchment paper with a pencil. Dough can also be rolled out between two pieces of floured parchment paper.

Pastry Bag, Mechanical Piping Tools
For years I decorated cookies and cakes with plastic baggies with the corners cut off, and this method worked just fine, but a dedicated pastry bag can make piping a little easier. A pastry bag can be used for both forming and decorating cookies. A bigger bag with a large tip is best for shaping cookie dough. Don't overfill or the bag will be difficult to handle. Canvas bags with plastic lining are easy to reuse and clean. Cheaper disposable bags are useful if you will be decorating with several colors of icing. There are also mechanical pastry bags that control the flow of the icing and dough. To keep tips from rusting, wash them thoroughly, then place them in a 200°F oven for 10 minutes, until dried. Let them cool before you put them away.

Pastry Brush
Brushes are used to dust excess flour off of cookie molds, and to dust confectioners' sugar on fondant to keep it from sticking to tools when shaping. They are also used to apply egg wash to the tops of cookies, Buy a high-quality brush so you don't get bristles on the cookies.

Plastic Wrap
Plastic wrap is used to retain moisture; cover dough with plastic wrap when you put it in the refrigerator or freezer to chill.

Rolling Pins
Rolling pins are available in a variety of materials, including wood, plastic, and marble. I have a marble one that I love because the weight means I don't have to press too hard when rolling out cookies. Also, the marble stays cool, so when it is floured, the cookie dough never sticks to it. If you have a strong grip, plastic or wood will work for you if you press hard.

Rubber Spatulas, Wooden Spoons, Metal Spatulas

Stock an assortment of different sizes of rubber spatulas and wooden spoons for mixing, scraping bowls, and preparing fillings and frostings. A large offset metal spatula helps release the dough from the work surface when you are making rolled cookies. A small one helps release individual cookies. Thin metal spatulas are best for moving cutout cookies onto cookie sheets and removing baked cookies from sheets. Use the thinnest, flattest spatula that will support the weight of the cookies.

Ruler and Utility Knife

To measure cookies, use a ruler. Use a utility knife to cut freeform shapes from cookie dough with templates.

Silicone Cookie Sheet and Pan Liners

Silicone liners are placed on cookie sheets or in pans in cases where the cookies would otherwise stick even with liberal greasing. They are insulators as well. Know the dimensions of your cookie sheets and pans when purchasing liners.

Thermometers, Candy Thermometer

Place an oven thermometer in the oven so that you know your oven is the correct temperature (the built-in thermometers are not always accurate). Purchase a candy thermometer that can be clipped to the side of a saucepan for checking the temperature of liquid mixtures as they cook on the stovetop.

Timer

Cookies have a short cooking time, so it is best to keep on top of them with a timer because oven temperature varies. Set the timer to go off 2 to 3 minutes before the recommended baking time is up.

Waxed Paper

Dough can be rolled out between layers of waxed paper. Flouring the waxed paper before putting the dough on it will prevent sticking.

Wooden Strips

To save time when measuring dough thickness for cutout cookies, I cut strips of wood 18 inches long (the length of my work surface) and

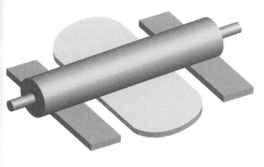

of various heights. I have two ⅛-inch strips, two ¼-inch strips, two ⅜-inch strips, and two ½-inch strips. I set one strip on either side of the dough and rest the rolling pin on them as I roll so that the dough is automatically rolled to the correct thickness. Wooden strips are available at hardware and hobby stores.

Work Surface

You will need a work surface for rolling out some cookies. It can be a wood or plastic cutting board, marble, granite, or a countertop. When cookies need to be chilled after they are rolled out, it is best to roll them out on a cutting board; you can put the cutting board right in the refrigerator.

Zester or Grater

These tools are used to grate the zest of citrus fruit. A good zester with small grates will grate the zest and not the white pith, which can be bitter. A grater can be used, but be gentle to avoid digging into the pith.

DECORATING TOOLS

Candy Molds

Form chocolate in plastic or silicone candy molds to create letters, numbers, leaves, and flowers. Candy for melting is also available in a variety of colors at craft and cake-decorating supply stores.

Cookie Cutters

Technically cookie cutters are forming tools; you can read more about them on page 2. In addition to cutting, though, they can be used for creating embossing lines and patterns.

Drinking Glasses

Dip the edge of a glass in flour and use it to cut out round cookies.

Knives and Spatulas

Frost cookies with a butter knife or small stainless-steel icing spatula. To speed up the process, reserve a separate spreading tool for each color.

Long-Handled Tweezers

Use tweezers for precise placement of tiny toppings.

Long Lollipop or Ice-Pop Sticks, Wooden Dowels

Lollipop sticks are good for drawing, and Popsicles sticks are good for spreading icing. Both of them, as well as dowels, can be used to make cookie pops. Insert sticks into cookie pops before baking. Wrap the sticks with foil while baking to keep them from burning and then remove before serving.

Parchment Paper and Plastic Baggies

Parchment can be rolled into a cone and made into a pastry bag. Cut the tip to size based on your desired flow. Plastic baggies can be used in the same way. Fill with icing and seal, and then cut a hole in one corner to pipe.

Pastry Bag, Couplers, Tips, and Twist Ties

In addition to shaping cookies, pastry bags are used to draw borders, sculpt and shape frosting, and add design details with icing. There are mechanical piping tools, and reusable cloth and disposable polyester bags. Even though I have them all, I use the disposable type when working with several colors. There are hundreds of tips available. To start, purchase a basic set or a few individual tips in popular shapes. Writing, round, and star-shaped tips are the most popular. Small tips are great for detailed designs and royal icing. Use larger tips for butter-cream icings and frosting. See the instructions for using a pastry bag on page 43. You will need couplers to secure the tips to the bag and twist ties to hold the bag closed.

Pastry Brush and Paintbrushes

Extra-fine high-quality pastry brushes, artist brushes, and household paintbrushes can be used to brush away extra sprinkles and sugars that don't stick. They can also be used to smooth out frosting or to paint cookies with food coloring or powders. Soft natural brushes will last forever and are superior to synthetic ones, though both work.

Piping Glue

This clear icing is sold in a prepackaged tube and is used to glue on decorations or build cookie constructions. I rarely use it because I prefer homemade icings but all homemade icings have color. If you prefer to purchase your icings this it is an amazing product because it is invisible and offers a clean look.

Plastic Squeeze Bottle

Squeeze bottles work well for piping a simple, clean line if you don't have a pastry bag. They are inexpensive, too, so you can put a different color in each bottle.

Stencils

Sold in stationery and office supply stores, premade stencils of letters, numbers, and hundreds of other shapes can be used to make designs with sifted cocoa powder or confectioners' sugar.

Straw

A straw is a great tool for punching holes in cutout cookies for hanging. Holes should be punched before baking. Boba straws are good for larger holes.

Toothpicks and Bamboo Skewers

Use round and flat toothpicks as drawing tools to create detailed designs with liquid icing, spreading icing into a corner, or picking off mistakes. Bamboo skewers do the same jobs and are easy to hold. No-bake cookies or cookies with a dense dough can be placed on bamboo skewers (see Rum, Mint, and Bourbon Ball Kabobs, page 140).

BAKING AND STORING COOKIES

Preparing for Cookie Making

- Arrange the racks close together in the center of the oven. Leave enough room to pull out the sheets and rotate positions while baking if necessary. Put a thermometer inside the oven.

- Preheat the oven 10 to 15 minutes before baking. Check the oven temperature with the oven thermometer and adjust the oven setting if necessary.

- Grease or cover the cookie sheets or baking pans with parchment paper or a silicone liner. No flour is necessary unless a recipe recommends it. Often when there is a lot of butter in the recipe, greasing or flouring is not necessary.

- Lightly sprinkle a work surface with 2 to 3 tablespoons of flour if necessary. Spread out any clumps of flour with a pastry brush to create an even surface.

Making Cookie Dough

- Measure accurately.

- Mix the dry ingredients; set aside.

- Cream the butter, with the sugar if indicated. Use a low mixer speed to start, and increase if needed. The mixture may look curdled, but when the flour is added it will even out. If you are mixing by hand, use a wooden spoon and beat at about 150 strokes per minute.

- Gradually add the dry ingredients to the wet ingredients. Do not overmix. The more you work it, the tougher the dough gets.

- Add the mix-ins (chips, nuts, berries) if indicated.

- If the dough is soft or the recipe requires it, wrap the dough tightly in plastic wrap and chill it in the refrigerator for 20 to 30 minutes. Chilling dough ensures that the butter does not melt too fast during baking, which can cause cookies to spread too much.

- Form the dough, drop the cookies, roll out the dough, or do whatever your cookie type requires for shaping. Make cookies the same size and shape for even baking, or place similar-size cookies on the same cookie sheets and adjust baking times accordingly. Make sure spacing on sheets is appropriate for your style of cookie. Drop cookies need more space than cutout cookies.

Baking Cookies

- Cookies bake quickly, so keep an eye on them and do not overbake. Check the cookies often and reverse placement of the cookie sheets on the racks or switch them front to back in the oven if necessary. Work quickly to avoid too much heat escaping when opening and closing the oven.

- Check the cookies a few minutes before the shortest baking time is up. Usually, the edges should be slightly golden, a bit darker than the center of the cookie. Lift the edges with a spatula to look underneath to make sure cookies are golden and not doughy.

- Most cookies are best when removed from the oven slightly before they are done to avoid drying them out. It keeps them chewy. Some recipes require cookies to be left in the oven. For these cookies, lower the oven temperature as directed in the recipe to cool them down.

Cooling Cookies

- Generally the rule is to remove cookies quickly from the cookie sheets to prevent them from overbrowning on the bottom and sticking to the sheet. Let cookie sheets cool; then wash and regrease them if necessary before using them for the next round of cookies. Cooling the sheets before reusing them prevents the next batch of cookies from spreading too much.

- Cool individual cookies on a cooling rack. Cool bar cookies in the pan, set on a cooling rack (or, if the pan was lined with parchment paper, remove the bar of cookies with the parchment paper and let cool on a rack). Bar cookies are best cut when cold or frozen. Most cookies can be eaten 10 minutes after they are removed from the oven. Cool completely before decorating unless noted in the recipe. Additional sprinkled toppings such as cinnamon sugar sticks best to warm cookies.

Storing Cookies

- There is nothing like fresh-baked cookies straight from the oven. The chocolate is melted and the dough is warm. In order to prevent myself from eating a whole batch in one sitting, this is what I do: I usually make a double batch of dough; I freeze half of one batch and refrigerate the other half so I can pull it out and bake cookies fresh another day. I bake one full batch, and then I freeze some baked cookies to take out later.

- Cool cookies completely before storing.

- Cream-filled cookies have a short shelf life and are best refrigerated, although refrigerating will dry out the cookies in a few days.

- Store crisp and soft cookies in separate containers to keep crisp ones from softening.

- Bar cookies and shortbread can be cut and stored in containers or stored in their baking pan. If you know you will be storing them, use a baking pan that has a lid.

- Separate layers of sticky, moist, or decorated cookies with waxed paper.

- If you need to store cookies for a few days before gifting, choose airtight gift containers or store the cookies in an airtight container, and then transfer them to the gift packaging at the last minute.

- Crisp cookies that have gone soft can be recrisped: Heat in a 300°F oven for 3 to 4 minutes.

- To moisten dry cookies, add a piece of fruit to the container. A slice of apple, pear, orange, lemon, or lime will work. Let stand for a day or two, and then remove the fruit. The cookies will pick up the flavor of the fruit, so choose complementary flavors. If you don't want to flavor the cookies, try putting a piece of fresh bread in the container instead of fruit.

Freezing Cookies

- Freeze cookies, icing, and filling separately. Assemble when ready to eat.

- When freezing baked cookies, keep them in airtight containers to prevent sogginess. Line the container with paper towels to absorb moisture. When you're ready to eat the cookies, remove them from the containers and let them thaw uncovered for 1 to 2 hours; after you've enjoyed your fill, return the leftovers to airtight containers.

- Most prepared cookie dough can be stored in the refrigerator for up to 2 weeks. If the dough contains eggs, or milk or cream, I usually play it safe and use it within 5 days.

- Frozen dough usually stays good for 3 to 4 months. I usually use it much sooner, because why freeze it for that long when I can eat it?

- Defrost the dough for 30 minutes before dropping or rolling it.

- Frozen icebox cookies can be sliced within 5 minutes of removing them from the freezer.

Scaling Cookies

When I write about scaling recipes, most of the time I mean *more cookies*. It is possible to scale down a recipe by cutting the ingredient amounts in half, but you're usually better off just making the whole batch and freezing half of it to bake later. Sometimes I do scale down if a recipe requires 2 eggs and I have only one and I really want that particular cookie.

When baking cookies for gifting or bake sales, you may want to scale up the recipes. If you are doubling or tripling the recipes, you can make several batches by multiplying the volume of ingredients. If you're scaling up more than that, reduce the amount of leavener, spices, and salt just a bit. For example, if you're making a quadruple batch (multiplying the amounts by four), you may want to reduce the baking powder by 1/4 to 1/2 teaspoon depending on how much is used in the recipe. (When you're scaling up by a factor of ten or more—which you need special equipment for—you will want to reduce the leavening by 50 percent.) When tripling a recipe, simply use slightly less spice and salt; when quadrupling the recipe, use only three times the spices and salt in the original recipe.

I like to bake large batches of cookies in rimmed cookie sheets stacked on top of each other in the oven. I set the oven rack slightly below the middle (and remove all of the rest) and stack the sheets, resting the rims on top of each other in a crosswise fashion. This method allows me to bake eight sheets at once.

Scaling a cookie can also mean making a small cookie into a large cookie, or a large cookie into a small cookie. To use a recipe developed for a small cookie to make a large cookie, increase the baking time. If you are making a *much* larger cookie, you may need to decrease the amount of fat and liquid in the dough a bit as well so that the cookie bakes evenly in the middle and around the edges. When making a smaller cookie, decrease the baking time. For cookies that are supposed to be baked for just 5 minutes, of course, this may be hard to do. Just keep an eye on them while baking.

TRANSPORTING COOKIES

Choosing the right cookies makes all the difference when mailing a care package to a friend or packing treats for a picnic. Drop, bar, and fruit-filled cookies, as well as biscotti, are all good, sturdy cookies. Avoid shaped cookies, square or rectangular cookies with pointed edges, and wafer-thin cookies.

GOOD COOKIES TO TRANSPORT
- Biscotti
- Shortbread, butter, and spritz cookies
- Gingerbread cookies
- Chocolate chip, oatmeal, peanut butter, and sugar drop cookies

High-Altitude Baking

All of the recipes in this book were tested and prepared in Los Angeles at sea level. Cookies are much less susceptible to fluctuations due to altitude than cakes are because of their low water content and high fat content. If you live in a high-altitude region, test the recipes once as written; make adjustments if needed. For delicate cookies, increase the oven temperature by 15°F to 20°F and use a slightly shorter baking time: Decrease by 5 to 8 minutes per 30 minutes of baking time. Leavening and evaporation occur more quickly at high altitudes, and a higher temperature will bind the cookies before they dry out. Since the oven is hotter, the cooking time needs to be shorter.

Your local agricultural extension office may have an adjustment chart on its Web site or at the office that gives advice specific to your region. Following are estimates for 3,000 and 10,000 feet. If you are at 5,000 or 7,000 feet, your measurements will lie in the middle. As a general rule, increase liquid slightly to help the dough come together and decrease the baking powder and soda.

- Flour is increased by the cup. Flour with a higher protein content (about 12 percent) yields better results. The higher the altitude, the more flour is needed. At 3,000 feet, add 1 tablespoon per cup; at 10,000 feet, add 2 to 4 tablespoons per cup.
- Baking powder and soda are decreased by the teaspoon. At 3,000 feet, subtract $1/8$ teaspoon per teaspoon. At 10,000 feet, subtract $1/2$ to $2/3$ teaspoon per teaspoon.
- Sugar is decreased by the cup. Increased evaporation increases sugar concentration, so not as much is needed. At 3,000 feet, subtract 1 tablespoon per cup. At 10,000 feet, subtract 3 to 4 tablespoons per cup.
- Liquid is increased by the cup. More liquid keeps cookies from drying out at higher temperatures. At 3,000 feet, add 2 tablespoons per cup. At 10,000 feet, add 3 to 4 tablespoons per cup.
- Butter and fats rarely need to change except at very high altitude. At 10,000 feet, subtract 1 to 2 tablespoons per cup.

- Waffle cookies
- Macaroons
- Madeleines
- Fruit cookies: rugelach, hamastachen, and fruitcake
- Pumpkin spice cookies
- Chinese almond cookies

MAILING COOKIES
- Wrap different textures separately to preserve their respective softness and crispness.
- Layer cookies in stacks, with the heaviest on the bottom.

Place back to back with the flat sides facing each other. Add wax paper in between to prevent sticking. Pack tightly. Fill gaps with crumbled wax paper in the container to prevent the cookies from moving around.

- Heat seal or shrink-wrap cookies in stacks if necessary.
- Choose the best available shipping method. I like Priority Mail flat-rate boxes.
- Mark the shipping box as fragile.

COOKIE INGREDIENTS

Cookies take just minutes to put together when you have all of the ingredients on hand. Since most cookies include butter, sugar, flour, eggs, baking powder, and baking soda, always keep these stocked for when you have the urge to bake. The proportions of these ingredients are what give the cookie its texture, from soft and chewy to crackly and crunchy. Butter tenderizes the cookie, eggs bind it, and flour gives it structure. Some cookie recipes exclude ingredients entirely—the flour, the butter, or the leavener—to produce unique tastes and textures. Contrasting textures and flavors with mix-ins such as extracts, cocoa powder, chocolate chips, nuts, and spices, as well as toppings and fillings, also boost the flavor. If you like to experiment, many ingredients can be substituted for others to create new flavors or textures and meet dietary requirements.

Dairy
BUTTER
To me, butter gives cookies a homemade taste. I prefer to eat one cookie made with butter than two made with shortening, margarine, or oil. I believe butter produces the richest cookie. Butter contributes to the golden cookie color, adds moisture, and creates a smooth texture. When creamed with sugar, butter traps air bubbles that help the dough rise while baking. It adds its own sweet flavor, as well as picking up flavors of the other ingredients. Many of the recipes in this book are made with unsalted butter because I prefer adding my own amount of salt

than starting with salted butter. Sweet butter made from sweet cream can be used to yield a sweeter flavor. In cookies, the amount of butter used determines how much they will spread, since butter melts during baking. Butter is also used in icing and for coating the pan to make the cookies easy to remove. Cooking sprays can also be used to "butter" the pan.

Butter for cookies is almost always used at room temperature or softened. This takes 20 to 30 minutes depending on the room temperature. To speed the softening process, cut the butter into small cubes. Softening the butter will make it easier to cream and combine with the other ingredients. Be careful, though, not to oversoften. The cookies will spread too much and the butter will melt out of the cookies. I choose a brand that has measuring lines on the wrapper. Whipped butter has more air, and you will need to use 15% to 20% more whipped butter than called for in the recipe to achieve the same texture.

CREAM CHEESE, SOUR CREAM, AND YOGURT
Cream cheese adds tang and gives cookie dough a creamy texture. Sour cream makes cookies sour, and yogurt makes cookies tangy. You can use low-fat versions of any of these dairy ingredients.

MILK AND CREAM
Since cookies are made from dough and not batter, not much liquid is necessary. Whole milk and creams are used only in small amounts, if at all. Milk and cream are more often used in toppings and fillings. Heavy or whipping cream should be used when cream is required. Milk and cream work best at room temperature. I use whole milk and heavy cream, but you can substitute low-fat, skim, or buttermilk. This will change the flavor and texture of the recipe slightly.

Other Fats
MARGARINE
You are welcome to substitute margarine for butter. Margarine is made from oil and milk. Use it if you prefer, though the flavor will be different.

VEGETABLE SHORTENING

I rarely use shortening because I don't like the taste. Shortening does have benefits over butter, though. It melts at a higher temperature so the dough holds its shape longer in the oven and doesn't spread as much. A good shortening melts after the cookie has risen and set. I tend to sacrifice this factor a bit because I prefer the flavor of butter over that of shortening. Most store-bought cookies and bakery cookies are made with vegetable shortening because it is a cheap alternative to butter. Sometimes both shortening and butter are used: butter for flavor and shortening as a stabilizer. The recipes in this book use butter although it always colors icings and frostings yellow so some people prefer to substitute shortening to keep the color white.

VEGETABLE AND NUT OILS

Oils are used to produce a cookie with monounsaturated fats. Canola is an all-around good oil. Olive, peanut, walnut, sesame, and other oils can be swapped for some of the canola oil measurements or used in small amounts to change flavors.

EGGS

Eggs are a fat and protein that thicken and bind ingredients together. They give cookies a silky texture, color, and structure. They are used for leavening and when whipped produce a tender, airy cookie. They also extend the shelf life by adding moisture. Whites are used as a glaze and are brushed on cookie tops to produce browning during baking.

Most of the recipes in this book call for large eggs. Brown or white are the same in flavor; the breed of hen is what affects the shell color. Grade A eggs are fresher, B grade older. Egg substitutes are suitable for many recipes.

If separating eggs, keep in mind that cold eggs separate best, but they should be added to the dough at room temperature.

EGG REPLACEMENTS FOR ICING

When making royal icing, some people prefer to use egg-white replacements to keep uncooked icing fresh. Powdered egg whites, liquid pasteurized egg whites, and meringue powder are included in some recipes for royal icing.

Dry Ingredients

FLOUR

Flour provides substance and structure and holds ingredients together. Combined with liquid, flour creates gluten, which allows the mixture to hold air and rise. Unbleached or bleached all-purpose flour is used in most recipes. All-purpose flour is made from a blend of hard and soft flour and is the best flour for cookies. Bleached flour will give you a lighter-colored cookie. When dusted on a work surface or on a cookie sheet, flour helps keep the dough from sticking.

Pastry and cake flour is too soft for cookies and only used when trying to achieve a cake texture like the black and white anisette cookies (page 194). Self-rising flour has baking powder and salt added, and it is hard to know how much, so check a substitution chart on the package if you use it.

Sifting to remove lumps lightens and aerates the flour. Lighter flour blends better with the other dry ingredients. To tell you the truth, though, most of the time I don't sift unless there are big lumps in the flour because I think it's boring. I usually avoid the need for sifting by buying small packages of flour and baking often so the flour is not lingering long enough in my cupboard to accumulate lumps.

Wheat flour can be substituted for white all-purpose flour. It is coarser and has more nutritional value. It adds a toasted flavor and produces denser, heavier cookies. When using wheat flour, sift it though a fine sieve before measuring.

Rice flour is used in Chinese cookies, graham flour is used for graham crackers, and cornmeal is used for corn cookies.

Flour should be measured in cups. Scoop or spoon flour into the measuring cup, and level off with a knife.

BAKING POWDER, BAKING SODA, AND YEAST

Baking powder and baking soda are chemical leaveners that make cookies rise. One of the most common mistakes in baking is to mistake baking soda for baking powder. They behave and taste differently. Baking soda is four times stronger and metallic tasting. Pay close attention when selecting these ingredients for the dough. Both ingredients should be stored in sealed containers because they absorb odors, which will be transferred to your cookies.

Baking powder is made with baking soda and other ingredients. It is used when the dough contains mostly nonacidic ingredients. The recipes in this book use double-acting baking powder. It reacts twice—once when mixed with liquid and again when heated.

Yeast is rarely used in cookies; I have used it in the doggie cookie recipes for added flavor. Make sure the yeast is active and foaming before you add it to the dough.

SALT
Salt contrasts with the sweetness of sugar in cookies. The most common type of salt used in cookies is table salt because it is fine grained. Kosher and sea salts can be substituted, but they have larger grains and will offer different textures in some recipes.

CREAM OF TARTAR
Cream of tartar is used to stabilize egg whites as they are whipped so they rise to full volume. It is also used to stabilize icing.

OATMEAL, GRANOLA, AND CEREAL
Oatmeal gives cookies a rich flavor and texture. Use old-fashioned rolled oats, not instant or quick oats. Steel-cut oats can be used too: They are less absorbent and produce a cookie with a crunchy texture. They must be softened before adding to the dough. Plain unflavored granola was used in the cookie recipes in this book. To vary the

flavors, add flavored granola or granola with added fruits. Cereals can be added to cookies for different textures.

Sweeteners

SUGAR

Most cookie recipes call for sugar for sweetness, moisture, and tenderness. When whipped with eggs, sugar stabilizes the eggs to hold air. When creamed with butter or fats, it is evenly distributed to create smoothness. It offers color through browning and caramelizing while baking. Sugar is a preservative and prolongs the life of cookies. It is used in fillings and icings. Sugar can be added as a decoration before or after baking. Always measure sugar in measuring cups by scraping overflow from the rim back into the container.

CORN SYRUP

Corn syrup, a sweetener made from cornstarch, provides moisture. It is resistant to crystallization. It is available in a light version, for a lighter flavor, and a dark version, for a stronger flavor. It has about the same sweetness intensity as granulated sugar.

HONEY

Honey is a sweetener available in a variety of flavors depending on the flowers the bees pollinate. Hints of orange, sage, lavender, and blackberry can be added to the cookies through your honey choices. Honey adds sweetness, prevents sugar from crystallizing, and is a good preservative.

MOLASSES

Molasses, a sweetener that provides moisture, is a product of the sugar-making process. It is available in both light and dark varieties; the flavor of dark molasses is preferable for baking. Sulfured molasses is more flavorful but sometimes too strong, so unsulfured is better for baking. It is the major sweetener in many gingerbreads.

MAPLE SYRUP

Pure maple syrup is the boiled sap of the sugar maple tree. It is graded according to color and flavor. AA is delicately flavored; A has a strong flavor, B stronger flavors, and C even stronger flavors. When it comes

Types of Sugar

- **Granulated or white sugar** is highly refined. A large amount of granulated sugar produces a crackly, crunchy cookie. Unbleached cane sugar is not as refined. It can be used interchangeably with granulated sugar.

- **Superfine sugar** is more finely granulated and dissolves easily during baking. Make your own by processing granulated sugar in a food processor before measuring.

- **Organic sugar** is not processed as much as granulated sugar and has larger grains. Grind organic sugar in a food processor before measuring.

- **Dark** and **light brown sugars** are moist and have a rich flavor. Brown sugar absorbs moisture and helps cookies remain soft over time. Dark brown sugar has more molasses and light has less. Brown sugars can be substituted for each other, although the flavor and moisture content will change. Brown sugars sometimes harden in their containers, so you might need to regrind the sugar in a food processor or heat it in the oven for a few minutes at 350°F to soften. Always pack the sugar for accurate measuring.

- **Confectioners' sugar** and **powdered sugar** are the same ingredient, made from powdered granulated sugar and 3 percent cornstarch. Confectioners' sugar is best used in icings and fillings. Because of its light density, measuring confectioners' sugar is not an exact science. Use measuring cups, but be aware that you still might need to adjust the recipes by adding a little more sugar or liquid to reach your desired spreading consistency.

- **Coarse** and **crystal sugars** are the sugars you find on the tops of cookies. The extra-large decorative grains are up to six times the size of those of granulated sugar. The sugar catches the light and is reflective. It is available in numerous colors. You can make your own colored sugars by mixing in a few drops of food coloring to the sugar.

- **Muscovado sugar** has large grains and high molasses content. It is good for topping cookies.

- **Turbinado** or **raw sugar** is slightly brown because it contains a bit of molasses, and it has larger grains than granulated sugar. It holds more moisture than granulated sugar and can be a substitute for light brown sugar. It can also be used on cookie tops for decoration.

- **Sugar substitutes** are sugar extracts from fruits or chemicals that simulate a sweet taste. I have not been able to get them to react well in baking, so I avoid them.

to cookies, if you want delicate, choose grade A, and if you want strong, choose grade B. Imitation maple syrup is either a combination of maple syrup and corn syrup or imitation maple–flavored corn syrup. It is fine to use it in a pinch, but amber pure maple syrup is better.

Flavorings, Spices, and Mix-ins

EXTRACTS

Vanilla and other extracts, including rose water, peppermint, anise, and almond, offer additional opportunities for flavoring cookies. They do not store for very long, so buy the smallest bottle available and close it tightly to keep the alcohol from evaporating. Vanilla extract is the most commonly used flavoring in cookies. It is available in natural and artificial varieties. Pure vanilla tastes better than artificial vanilla, but it is much more expensive and sometimes less available than the artificial version. Choose whichever you prefer.

LIQUORS, LIQUEURS, AND WINES

Liquors, liqueurs, and wines are also excellent flavorings. Some of the alcohol evaporates, while the flavor remains. For an extra boost of flavor, glaze cookies with liquor toppings. If you do not like the taste, you can leave it out of the recipe and prepare the rest of the recipe as directed. Liqueurs keep for a long time, but if you will not be using them often, buy small, airline-size bottles.

HERBS AND SPICES

I have an herb garden and use fresh herbs and spices such as lavender, rosemary, and ginger all the time to add rich flavor to cookies. Dried spices such as cinnamon, ginger, nutmeg, and cloves loose intensity over time so purchase in small containers to use up quickly. Different brands have very different prices. Sometimes there is a huge taste disparity and other times there is none. I start with the most afford-able brand and, if I like it, I stick with the same brand over time. If not, I upgrade the next time around. Store them in a cool, dark place.

COFFEE

When adding coffee flavor, go for strength. Instant coffee granules or double- or triple-strength espresso will give you a rich coffee flavor.

ZESTS

Lemon, lime, orange, or other citrus zests give a flavor punch without the added liquid. Sugar absorbs the oils in zest spreading the flavor throughout the cookies.

CHOCOLATE AND COCOA POWDER

Those who know me or who have read any of my books know that chocolate is my thing. Dark, milk, white, semisweet, German, unsweetened, bittersweet—there are so many kinds to love. Chocolate comes in numerous shapes—bars, chunks, and chips, to name the most common—each giving a different texture. You may substitute your favorite chocolate in a recipe to suit your taste. For example, chocolate chunks can be substituted for chocolate chips, and white chocolate can be substituted for semisweet. It's all good.

WORKING WITH CHOCOLATE

- Chop chocolate on a cutting board with a large knife.
- To grind chocolate, chop it first; then put it in a food processor with the other dry ingredients.
- Melt chopped chocolate in a double boiler over low heat, stirring constantly until melted. Try not to get water in it.
- Shave chocolate with a grater or knife.
- Create chocolate curls with a vegetable peeler.

Dutch-processed or regular cocoa powder work well for the recipes in this book. In a bind I have also substituted high-quality cocoa mix or Mexican chocolate, which are presweetened. If you choose to do this, remember to scale down the amount of other sugars in the recipe.

FRESH FRUITS AND VEGETABLES

Fresh carrots, zucchini, apples, bananas, and berries keep cookies moist and soft. Fresh are better than frozen fruits, which tend to release more water. If you are using frozen, defrost before using and drain off the excess water; also decrease the amount of liquid in the recipe. Berries such as cranberries and blueberries are only around or cost-effective for a month or two every year, so you

might consider buying them when they are available and freezing them for baking.

DRIED AND CANDIED FRUITS, COCONUT

Whole, chopped, and pureed dried fruits add chewiness to cookies. Raisins are the most popular dried fruit, but also try golden raisins, dried cranberries, dried cherries, and dried currants for different tastes. Dried pineapple, figs, and apricots are sweet and add an interesting texture to cookies. To soften dried fruits, soak them in rum or boiling water.

Candied fruits are preserved with sugars and are sweeter than dried fruits. Candied ginger, cherries, and—around the holidays—fruit mixtures are readily available.

Whole coconuts are available fresh and can be shredded on a grater or in a food processor. Dried or desiccated coconut is available in both shredded and flaked forms. Shredded coconut is more common than flaked, but either can be used in these recipes. Dried coconut comes both sweetened and unsweetened, though sweetened is more common. Both can be used; if using sweetened, you might scale down the sugar used in the recipe, depending on your sweet tooth. Toasting coconut radically changes the flavor. It tastes great both ways. Frozen shredded or flaked coconut can also be used in any of these recipes.

NUTS AND SEEDS

Nuts work really well sliced, whole, chopped, and toasted for flavoring and decorating cookies. Nuts are perishable, so store them in airtight bags in the freezer. Defrost nuts before chopping them. Chop nuts on a cutting board with a large, sharp knife. The size of the pieces does not need to be exact. To grind nuts, place the nuts and either the sugar or flour in the recipe in a food processor and pulse. The sugar or flour will absorb the flavors of the nut oil and distribute it throughout the cookie.

To toast nuts, preheat the oven to 325°F. Spread the nuts in a baking dish or on a baking sheet in a single layer. Bake for 5 to 7 minutes; then stir and toast for 3 more minutes. You can also stir the nuts around for 5 to 7 minutes in a frying pan over medium heat.

Nuts are a very common allergen, so consider your guests when deciding whether to include them in your cookies. You might want to divide the dough and make some cookies with and some without nuts. Just make sure not to cross-contaminate the nut-free batch with a bowl or spoon used to make a nut batch.

Seeds are full of intense, nutty, spicy flavors. Poppy, sunflower, sesame, and caraway all will toast while baking. They toast quickly so keep your eye on cookies topped with seeds to make sure they don't burn.

JAMS AND PRESERVES

When fruits are readily available, I make my own jam and preserves; when they are not, I use store-brought jams and preserves. Choose good-quality brands because they contain more fruit. Heating jam with a little water makes a great glaze, filling, or frosting for your cookies.

DECORATING INGREDIENTS

FOOD COLORINGS

Food coloring can be added to frosting, icing, and cookie dough to transform the colors for decorating. Liquid food coloring is available at most grocery stores. Start with white frosting or icing. To achieve light colors, add a few drops; to make deep colors, add several drops. Adding food coloring will thin the frosting or icing, so you may need to add more confectioners' sugar to reach the desired consistency.

Gel and paste food coloring are highly concentrated; you need only a little bit to achieve dark or bright colors. You can find these products online or in cake-decorating supply stores. If you want to make black or dark-colored frosting, start with chocolate frosting and add coloring gels.

Powdered food coloring can be brushed on for deep colors. Combine powders with water or lemon extract for painting. You can purchase powdered food coloring in metallic, iridescent, and deep colors.

Colored icing and decorating gels are available in many

Cookie Mix-ins and Fillings

DRIED AND CANDIED FRUIT MIX-INS

Apple rings
Apricots
Banana chips
Bing cherries
Candied cherries (red and green)
Candied ginger
Candied orange peel
Candied mixed peel
Cranberries
Currants
Dates
Figs
Ginger slices
Guava slices
Mango slices
Papaya slices
Peaches
Pineapple
Prunes
Raisins (golden or brown)
Shredded or flaked coconut
Toasted coconut

FRESH FRUIT MIX-INS

Apples
Apricots
Bananas
Black cherries
Blueberries
Cranberries
Figs
Fruit cocktail
Kiwis
Mandarin oranges
Mangoes
Maraschino cherries

Papayas
Peaches
Pears
Pineapple

CANDY MIX-INS

Caramels
Carob-covered raisins
Chocolate chunks
Chocolate-covered espresso beans
Chocolate-covered raisins
Chocolate sprinkles
Chopped candy bars
Colored sprinkles
Fruity cereal
Ground butterscotch candies
Ground citrus candies
Ground peppermint candies
Ground root beer candies
Marshmallows
Peanut brittle
Popcorn
Puffed rice cereal
Taffy
Turkish delight
Yogurt-covered raisins

JAM AND PRESERVE FILLINGS

Apple butter
Apricot
Apricot pineapple
Blackberry
Black cherry
Black currant
Blueberry
Boysenberry

Cherry
Ginger
Grape
Kiwi
Lemon curd
Mint
Orange curd
Orange marmalade
Peach
Pineapple
Plum
Raspberry
Raspberry curd
Strawberry
Strawberry curd
White grape

NUT AND SEED MIX-INS

Almonds
Brazil nuts
Caraway seeds
Cashew butter
Cashews
Fennel seeds
Hazelnuts
Honey-roasted peanuts
Macadamia nuts
Party mix
Peanut butter
Peanuts
Pecans
Pine nuts
Poppy seeds
Pumpkin seeds
Roasted chestnuts
Sesame seeds
Sunflower seeds
Walnuts

supermarkets, cake-decorating, and crafts stores. The packaging of these products eliminates the need for a pastry bag. They come ready to use.

CANDY TOPPINGS

The list of candy toppings for decorating is endless—including snowflakes, stars, hearts, flowers, dots, balls—you name it. They stick to wet icing, making frosting the easiest way give a cookie a theme. Sprinkles are tiny candies available in dozens of colors. They will stick to wet icing, ice cream, and creamy fillings. Nonpareils are even tinier candy dots available in an assortment of colors.

SUGARS

Coarse sugar with large granules is used as a decoration on cookie tops. It's available in every color imaginable and in different grain sizes, from a fine dust to large rock-candy chunks.

LUSTER DUST AND PEARL DUST

These toppings produce a metallic finish. Dissolved in vodka, they give a shiny glow.

COOKIE TYPES AND TECHNIQUES

Cookies are classified by how they are made. Drop cookies are dropped, pressed cookies are pressed, hand-formed cookies are shaped by hand, and rolled cutout cookies are—you guessed it—rolled and cut out. Here are the different types of cookies you will find in this book, along with tips for making each kind.

Drop Cookies

Nostalgic and with a homemade feel, drop cookies are soft and chewy and are the easiest type to make in large batches. Chocolate Chip Walnut Cookies (page 72), Oatmeal Raisin Cookies (page 82), Old-Fashioned Peanut Butter Cookies (page 79), and Snickerdoodles (page 77) are all drop cookies, made from soft, sticky dough that is dropped onto the cookie sheets by the spoon or a scoop that looks like a mini–ice cream scoop. Some cookies with denser dough are formed into balls. Although usually made from a free-form piece of dough, drop cookies without mix-ins can be piped from a cookie press or

pastry bag. The butter-based dough spreads as it bakes. The shape of drop cookies cannot be tightly controlled, but most flatten evenly into a round shape. Drop cookies can be prepared in silicone or baking molds to control the shape. The dough can also be refrigerated for 3 to 6 hours and formed using the icebox cookie method.

TIPS FOR MAKING DROP COOKIES

- Butter the cookie sheet or line it with parchment paper to prevent sticking.

- Drop the cookie dough (or form it into balls if directed). For bigger cookies, drop the dough by the tablespoon or two, for smaller cookies by the teaspoon. Leave 1½ to 2½ inches of space between the mounds so the cookies have room to spread. Balls can be flattened with the bottom of a drinking glass if desired.

- The dough can be chilled for 20 to 30 minutes after the cookies are dropped so the butter hardens and does not melt fast and spread too quickly.

- Check the cookies often as they bake to make sure the edges are golden but not brown.

- After baking, let the cookies cool on the pans for 3 to 5 minutes; then remove to a wire rack and let cool for 10 minutes before eating.

- Drop-cookie dough can be refrigerated for up to 2 days.

- Most drop cookies are good for at least 5 days after baking.

- Freeze drop-cookie dough in an airtight container for up to 2 months.

Rolled Cutout Cookies

Rolled cookies are great because the basic doughs provide many creative opportunities for decorating. Rolled cookies are made with stiffer dough than drop cookies. After it is rolled out, the dough can be chilled to get a clean cut with a cutter. Additional flour can be added to many drop cookie recipes so that they can be prepared as cutout cookies.

TIPS FOR MAKING ROLLED CUTOUT COOKIES

- Divide the dough in half and flatten each half into a disk before wrapping in plastic wrap. Smaller batches will chill faster and be easier to roll.

- Chill wrapped dough for 30 minutes to several hours depending on the recipe. Test by pressing your finger in the dough to see whether it is ready. If your finger leaves a dent, it is not ready to roll out.

- Dust the work surface or parchment paper and rolling pin with flour. Avoid pressing hard, or roll out using risers (page 6) the height of the desired dough thickness. If the dough sticks to the work surface, loosen it occasionally with a spatula. Roll particularly sticky dough out between 2 sheets of plastic wrap or waxed paper.

- Dip the cookie cutter in flour to keep it from sticking. Cut shapes from the center out. Start with larger cutters and use smaller cutters for areas around the edges.

- Remove the scraps (the negative space around the cookies) so the cookie shape will be easy to pick up. Use a thin spatula to transfer the shapes to lined cookie sheets and place them 1½ inches apart. Cutout cookies usually don't spread too much. Place the cutout cookies in the refrigerator for 20 to 30 minutes to harden the dough so they will keep their shape as they bake. Combine the scraps and roll the dough out again to the desired thickness, and cut more cookies.

- After baking, decorate with royal icing, drizzle with chocolate, top with candies and sprinkles, and so on.

- Rolled-cookie dough can be refrigerated for up to 2 days.

- Most cutout cookies are good for at least 5 days after baking.

- Freeze rolled-cookie dough in an airtight container for up to 2 months.

Icebox (Refrigerator) Cookies

Made in advance, icebox cookies can be stored in the icebox (refrigerator or freezer) and cut into perfect cookie shapes right before baking. The dough is stiff and then made stiffer through chilling. The dough is often shaped into cylinders or blocks, which are sliced into round, square, or rectangular cookies before baking. The logs can be patterned with spirals (page 244), stripes (page 212), waves and checkerboards to create interesting designs in the cut cookies. Make two batches and keep one in the freezer for unexpected guests.

TIPS FOR MAKING ICEBOX COOKIES

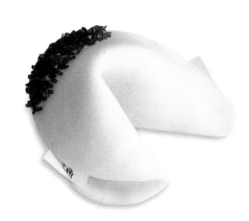

- Roll the dough into a log that is about 2 inches in diameter or the size specified by the recipe.

- Wrap the log tightly in plastic wrap and refrigerate or freeze. You can also form the log in a paper towel roll to make a perfectly round shape. Slit down one side of the tube and line it with parchment or waxed paper. Fill it with dough, wrap it in plastic wrap, close and secure the roll with rubber bands, and chill it in the refrigerator or freezer.

- When ready to bake the cookies, let the roll sit for a few minutes to soften; then unwrap it and slice, using a sharp knife, into rounds the thickness specified in the recipe.

- Transfer to cookie sheets, spacing the cookies 1 to 1½ inches apart. Icebox cookies usually don't spread too much.

- Store at room temperature for 2 weeks, or freeze for up to 2 months.

Hand-Shaped Cookies

Formed cookies are made from a stiff dough that is molded into balls and flattened or molded by hand into other shapes. Some cookies, such as cones (page 132, step 5) and fortune cookies (page 195), are formed after baking. These cookies are relatively thin and waferlike and are shaped while hot; they hold their shape when cool. Hand-formed cookies have personality and character with a homemade feel. My favorite hand-shaped cookies are thumbprints (page 198, step 5), crescents, biscotti (page 63), braids, logs, rings, pretzels (page 170), and pinwheels (page 210).

TIPS FOR MAKING HAND-SHAPED COOKIES

- The majority of hand-shaped cookies are most easily worked if the dough is formed into individual balls, chilled for 20 to 30 minutes, and then shaped.

- Store at room temperature for 2 weeks, or freeze for up to 2 months.

MOLDED AND STAMPED COOKIES, AND COOKIE CAKES

Cookies with stiff dough can be baked and shaped in molds. Springerle (page 256) can be made with either a mold or a special rolling pin. Little fluffy cakey cookies that have a springy texture can also be made in molds. Madeleines (page 114) are made in a shell-shaped mold. Detailed designs can also be pressed into the cookie with cookie stamps, rubber stamps, or cookie tiles; the cookies are then baked on a cookie sheet.

TIPS FOR MAKING MOLDED COOKIES

- Coat the mold with vegetable oil spray. Wipe out excess oil with a paper towel if necessary. Dust with flour. Brush off excess flour with a pastry brush.

- Press the dough into the mold, spreading it into all the crevices. Add additional dough in pieces if needed to fill the mold completely.

- Prick the surface of the dough with the tines of a fork to allow air to escape. This prevents the dough from buckling.

- Place the mold on a cookie sheet and bake. Check frequently. When done, remove the cookie sheet and mold from the oven and let the cookies cool in the mold for 1 to 2 minutes. Turn the cookies out of the mold onto a rack to cool completely.

- Spray stamps or tiles with vegetable oil spray, and dust with flour. Brush off excess flour with a pastry brush. Add more flour (but not oil) after stamping each cookie.

- For stamped cookies, roll the dough into balls about 2½ inches in diameter on a floured surface. Put the balls 4 inches apart on a greased cookie sheet. Press each ball firmly with the stamp, and cut off the excess dough.

- For tile cookies, roll the dough into a shape to accommodate the tile. Place the shapes 4 inches apart on a greased cookie sheet. Press the tile into the cookie, and trim off the excess.

FILLED AND SANDWICH COOKIES

These cookies are filled with jam, ice cream, fruit, dried fruit, cream cheese, candy, or nuts. Some, such as rugelach (page 226) and thumb-print cookies (page 197), are charmingly old-fashioned. Wafers, floren-tines (page 258), tulles, and lace cookies are thin and delicate cookies; they can be shaped straight from the oven by laying the warm cookies over molds, then cooled and filled with cream, ice cream, or fruit.

Sandwich cookies are made from two or more baked and cooled cookies that are assembled into a sandwich with filling in the middle. Frosting, icing, ice cream, and jams are just some fillings used to fill the cookies. Soft cookies make the best sandwiches.

TIPS FOR MAKING FILLED COOKIES

- Prepare the filling first and set it aside. Then concentrate on the cookie dough and producing cookies with consistent, accurate dimensions.

- Sandwich cookies are easiest to make consistent with a cookie cutter. If you want to top the cookies with candy or sugar, do so before baking or filling.

- When the filling and dough will be baked together, try to make the filling and the dough a similar consistency and temperature so they bake evenly.

- Store in a cool place to keep the filling from melting or softening.

Fried Cookies

Fried cookies are made in many regions of the world. Bow ties (page 193) are my favorite fried cookie. Most cookie doughs can be fried instead of baked, if you would like to experiment.

TIPS FOR MAKING FRIED COOKIES

- Fry in 3 to 4 inches of oil in a large, heavy pot. Consistent heat is crucial. Heat the oil and take its temperature with a candy thermometer. Test the oil by putting a scrap of bread in the oil; if it browns quickly, the oil is hot enough.

- Turn the cookies with tongs as they fry to brown both sides evenly.

- Drain the finished cookies first with a slotted spoon, then on paper towels.

- Fried cookies taste best soon after they are made. They should be eaten the day they are prepared.

Pressed or Piped Cookies

Soft dough is extruded and formed into incredible shapes using a cookie press or pastry bag. When you are making pressed or piped cookies, the temperature of the dough is everything. Refrigerate the dough for about 1 hour, place it in the press, and let it warm slightly. If the dough is too cold and hard, it will be difficult to extrude; if it's too warm and soft, the cookie will not keep its form while coming out of the press and while baking. Spritz cookies (page 262), meringues (page 120), and some drop-cookie doughs can be piped through a pastry bag. Pressed cookies can also be formed in a waffle iron or pizzelle press.

TIPS FOR MAKING PRESSED COOKIES

- Make a test batch of 4 or 5 cookies. If they don't work, refrigerate the dough further to harden or leave for a few minutes to soften.

- Bake the cookies for the recommended time, and test for doneness.

- Cool the cookies for 5 to 7 minutes on a wire rack before eating.

TIPS FOR MAKING PIPED COOKIES

- Spoon the dough into a pastry bag fitted with a large tip, filling no more than half full.

- Squeeze from the top down onto parchment-lined cookie sheets.

- Bake. When ready, transfer the parchment paper and cookies to a wire rack and let cool.

- Store at room temperature for 2 weeks or freeze for up to 2 months.

Bars

Easy-to-prepare bars are made like a cake but with cookie dough. The dough is pressed into the pan to bake in one big sheet. Sometimes I press it into mini–muffin pans. The sheet is then layered with other doughs, mix-ins, and toppings. After it is baked, the sheet is cut into cookie-size squares, diamonds, or rectangles. Brownies (page 185), rice treats (page 58), and protein bars (page 94) are my favorite bar cookies.

TIPS FOR MAKING BAR COOKIES

- Try to use the pan size called for in the recipe. The size of the pan affects the size, shape, and texture of the finished cookies. If you can't, adjust the baking time to be longer for a smaller pan or shorter for a larger pan.

- Prebake layers as called for in the recipe.

- Cool in the pan or on a wire rack until warm before cutting unless directed otherwise in the recipe. Many bar cookies will crumble if you cut them while they are hot.

- To make cutting easier, remove the sheet of cookies from the pan first: Line the pan with aluminum foil or parchment paper, leaving a 2-inch overlap on the sides. Pull the corners up first to remove the sheet from the pan.

- Store bar cookies in a flat, airtight container.

Cookie Architecture and Constructions

Cookie architecture is almost too good to eat. But that's part of the thrill. Don't keep your creativity on a pedestal to throw away later. Take tons of pictures, and then indulge. See chapter 6 for examples of cookie architecture.

TIPS FOR MAKING COOKIE ARCHITECTURE

- Test your cookie architecture by cutting templates from cardboard and taping the pieces together. Remember to make pieces smaller than your cookie sheets. If your model stands up, your cookie architecture probably will work too.

- Choose a heavy base made from plywood, thick corrugated cardboard, or a large cookie sheet.

- For large houses, roll the dough out to ⅜ inch thick. For houses about 6 inches tall, roll the dough out to ½ inch thick, and for small houses, roll the dough out to ¼ inch thick.

- Align the seams, apply icing glue by putting one stripe of icing on the edge of each piece to be joined, press together and let the icing harden for 30 minutes. Then add a generous amount of icing down the center of the seam to fill the gaps , and let dry. Clean up with a damp paper towel.

- To decorate apply additional icing with a piping bag, and add candies. Hold heavier candies in place until dried.

Cookie Cakes and Pies, and Ice Cream Cookies

Cookies can be crushed to be used in cakes as a cookie crust, as in the cheesecake bites (page 147), or as a crunchy layer in ice cream cakes (page 160). They can also be made larger and with a different ratio of ingredients to make gooey pies, like the Crusted Cookie Dough Pie (page 136), and cookie-flavored cupcakes (page 182) and ice cream sandwiches and cream pie (pages 178 and 138).

No-Bake Cookies

Some cookies, like the Rum, Mint, and Bourbon Ball Kabobs (page 140), don't need to be baked. The dough is chilled and cookies are formed at room temperature.

Cake-Mix Cookies

Using cake mix as a base reduces the number of ingredients for a recipe and makes the cookies easier to make. I chose this method for the Red Velvet Cookies with Cream Cheese Filling (page 200) and Coconut Bars (page 209) for those who are just starting to bake.

DECORATING TECHNIQUES

I find designing cookies to be a lot like designing products. I think about the use, taste, form, color palette, and appearance to create the perfect cookies for the occasion. I also decide on a production method: Is crafting one at a time better than using an assembly-line technique?

First I choose the taste of the cookie; then I plan the form and choose the color palette and details. If I will be decorating with royal icing, I choose a cutout cookie with a uniform thickness that will produce a flat top, such as shortbread butter cookies (page 271). To create a perfectly shaped cookie, first I draw the design on card stock the actual size of the cookie, then cut them out to make templates. I place the templates on the top of the rolled out dough, and I cut around the edges with a utility knife. I reference the drawn details on the template and fill in with my chosen technique. If I am making a

10 Troubleshooting Solutions

1. **The bottoms burn while the tops are not yet cooked**
You need an insulator. Use an insulted baking pan or parchment paper, or stack two pans together to create a double layer. Make sure the cookie sheet is placed in the middle of the oven.

2. **Cookies are too flat**
Too-soft butter was the most likely culprit. Next time, refrigerate the dough for 20 to 30 minutes before baking.

3. **Cookies look fine in the oven but flatten out when removed**
Too much air was beaten into the dough while creaming. Don't worry; they will still taste good.

4. **Rolled-cookie dough is too sticky to roll**
Remember that the dough will also pick up flour from the work surface and rolling pin. If that won't be enough, chill the dough for 1 hour and see whether that helps. If not, then add a bit more flour to reach the desired consistency.

5. **Cookies are too hard**
Soften in an airtight container with a piece of bread or fresh sliced apple. The cookies will absorb the moisture.

6. **Cookies are overbaked**
Make small test batches. Prepare 4 or 5 cookies at the preheated temperature and test the dough consistency and baking times. Adjust for the full batches.

7. **Cookies are too dry and crumbly**
This is something you can observe when the dough is prepared. There might be too much flour or too little liquid or shortening in the dough. Don't pack the flour in the measuring cups. If you have this problem in the dough again, add more butter or a few tablespoons of milk next time.

8. **Sides of the cookies fuse together**
Leave more space between them on the pans: 1 inch for cutout cookies, at least 2 inches for drop cookies. No harm will be done if you leave more space than you think you need.

9. **Cookies stick to the cookie sheet**
The cookie sheet was not adequately greased or the cookies were left on the sheet to cool too long. Next time use parchment paper or grease. For now, reheat the cookies at the recipe baking temperature for 2 to 3 minutes and remove.

10. **Cookies baked unevenly**
The dough is not thoroughly mixed, the cookies are different sizes, or there are hot spots in the oven. Mix dough thoroughly, make cookies the same size, and rotate sheets in the oven.

hand-formed cookie, I choose a dough that will hold its shape as it bakes, such as the pretzel (page 170). With all of these variables, it is easy to use many of the cookies in this book as a base to create your own. Here are some basic decorating tips to get started.

Prebaking Techniques

COLORING DOUGH

Colors can be used straight from the bottle or can be combined to make new colors in small containers. See the color wheel and color key on page 41 for suggestions. Remember that as it bakes the dough color will shift in tone, intensity, and saturation, depending on the color of the original dough. Yellow dough will result in yellower hues, and white dough will make the colors more pastel. Color the dough by adding food coloring a little bit at a time. For stickier dough, stir the coloring in with a spatula; for denser dough, knead it in with your hands.

EMBOSSING

Dense dough holds embossed lines, patterns, and imprinted images better than sticky dough. Emboss with cookie cutters, rubber stamps, toothpicks, or the back of a knife. Freeze or let the dough dry out before baking, depending on the recipe. See Thank-You Cookies (page 208) Springerle (page 256) and Midcentury Gingerbread House (page 244) for examples of embossing.

ADDING DIMENSION

Dough and cutout pieces can be stacked before and after baking to make a more dimensional cookie. They can also be folded into shapes; see Fourth of July Pinwheels (page 210), Hamantaschen (page 228), and Sugar-and-Spice Cinnamon Butterflies (page 186) for examples of not-so-flat cookies.

HOLES

Holes should always be made before baking. If the cookies are meant to hang—such as the Saffron Heart Necklaces (page 199)—or be inserted on a cocktail stirrer—see Cornmeal Olive Cookies (page 140)—holes are easiest to cut out with a straw. If larger holes are needed, they can

Making a Stencil

Here's how to make and use a stencil:

1. Cut a circle a little larger than the cookies from a piece of poster board.

2. Draw a pattern on the stencil and cut it out with a utility knife. You can also fold the circle into quarters or eighths and cut out shapes as if you were creating a paper snowflake.

3. Put confectioners' sugar or cocoa powder in a fine-mesh sieve. Hold the stencil over the cookie, and sift the sugar or cocoa powder lightly over the stencil. Carefully lift the stencil straight up to reveal the pattern.

be cut with a boba straw or a utility knife. Small holes are best drilled after baking, since they will close up in the baking process. Drill with a small new clean drill bit or cut by punching the cookie with a utility knife and rotating it to create a circular opening.

CUTOUTS, WINDOWPANES

Cutting out windows—see Stained-Glass Ornament Cookies (page 240) and Fifth-Wheel Trailer (page 248)—is best done with a utility knife or cookie cutters. Use a ruler to guide the knife when making straight lines. Place the cookie on parchment, not directly on the cookie sheet. Fill the holes with crushed hard candy to the top of the dough and brush off any extra candy from the surface of the cookie with a pastry brush. Check the cookies while they bake and the candy melts; you may want to add more candy halfway through to thicken the windows. Let the cookies cool completely before peeling off the parchment.

To cut out patterns using templates, print the template actual size on paper or clear acetate. Place the template on the chilled dough, and cut out the shape with a utility knife.

SUGARING AND SPRINKLING

Sugar and sprinkles added before baking stick best with egg wash. Brush some on the cookies before sprinkling. Stencils can be used to create sugar shapes and patterns such as stars, hearts, and paisley. Cut out the stencil so that it masks the cookie where you don't want the sugar to fall, and sprinkle the sugar over it.

Postbaking Techniques

DUSTING WITH SUGAR OR COCOA

Stenciling is an easy and quick method for assembly line style decorating. Confectioners' sugar or cocoa powder can be dusted on frosted or unfrosted cookies.

SUGARING

To sugar cookies after they are baked, brush the cookies with corn syrup and sprinkle with sugar. Try to cover the corn syrup completely with the sugar or the cookie will be sticky.

Frosting Color Wheel and Palettes

This color wheel is a chart for mixing food coloring to achieve desired colors. The color palettes are suggestions of color schemes to help produce an occasion-specific look for your cookies.

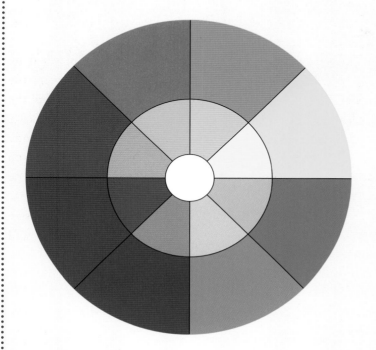

COLOR KEY

- Red and yellow make orange
- Yellow and blue make green
- Blue and green make turquoise
- More blue and less red make purple
- More red and less blue make violet
- Blue and orange or red and green make brown
- Red and white make pink
- Orange and white make peach
- Yellow and white make lemon
- Green and white make mint
- Turquoise and white make sea green
- Blue and white make light blue
- Purple and white make lavendar
- Brown and white make light brown
- To make black frosting start off with chocolate frosting and add black coloring gel.

DRIZZLING WITH GLAZE OR CHOCOLATE

Place the cookies on a cookie sheet and drop glaze or melted chocolate from a height with a spoon, moving slowly and steadily over
the cookie. Thin icing and chocolate can also be put in a pastry bag
and squeezed onto the cookie. Allow the chocolate to harden for
30 minutes.

DIPPING COOKIE IN CHOCOLATE

Hold the cookie on one side and dip it halfway into melted chocolate.
For complete coverage, dip the face of the cookie first, then the back
side.

ATTACHING TOPPINGS AND STACKING

Royal icing is the best glue for attaching toppings such as nuts, and
for building dimensional cookies. Most icings that dry hard will also
work.

Decorating with Frosting

Frosting must be the correct consistency to create shapes. If it is too firm, it will be hard to push through the tip on the pastry bag; if it is too soft, it will not hold its shape on the cookie. Add a little confectioners' sugar if it is too thin. If it is too thick, add a little liquid such as milk or water.

HOW TO USE A PASTRY BAG

1. Choose your tip shape and place the tip on the bag, securing it with a coupler.

2. Fill the bag one-half to two-thirds full with frosting. Fold over the edges to prevent the frosting from drying and hardening.

3. Tightly squeeze the sides of the bag until the frosting emerges from the tip onto the cookie. Control the flow of the frosting to create the desired shape. Different shaped tips will require you to hold the bag straight or at an angle.

4. Practice by making shapes on a plate; then scoop the frosting up to reuse it once you have perfected your technique.

5. If you make a mistake on the cookie scrape it off with an icing spatula and start over.

Here are different piping techniques that can be achieved with the many tips available.

LINES, LOOPS, ZIGZAGS, AND TRELLISES

The smaller the hole on a writing tip, the finer the line. Rest the tip on the cookie at your starting point. Hold the bag at an angle and pipe out a little frosting, lifting the bag slightly above the surface as you continue. Do not pull on the line, or it will break. When you reach the end of the line, release the pressure. Create loops, zigzags, and curves with your lines. You can also create a grid or trellis by overlapping lines.

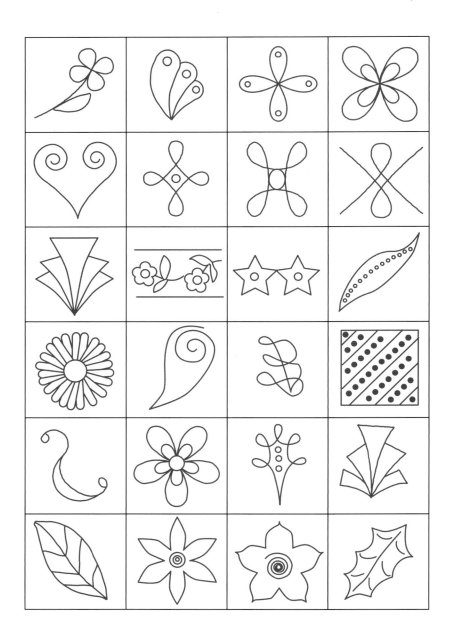

DOTS

Use a pastry bag with a writing tip and hold the bag over the area you wish to decorate. Press out the frosting so it forms a dot. Release the pressure on the bag and detach the tip from the dot. Flatten the points with a damp paintbrush. For a playful design, make large dots with a large tip, and overpipe them with smaller dots using a small tip.

STARS

Choose a star-shaped tip in the size that best suits your design. Holding the piping bag upright, gently squeeze the bag to release the frosting and form a star. Pull the bag away quickly to make a neat point on the star.

SHELLS

Use a star tip, and press the tip on the surface of a cookie at your starting point. Gently squeeze the bag and lift it up, then down, returning to the surface of the cookie every ½ to 1 inch and pulling the tip off to release the frosting from the tip.

WORDS

Words are created like doodling. To create cursive writing, use a small writing tip to pipe a continuous flow of frosting. To create individual letters, start piping at the beginning of each letter and pull the tip away from the cookie at the end of each letter.

FLOWERS

Use a petal tip. Pipe about five flat petals in a circle so they overlap each other. Pipe different colored dots in the centers of the flowers.

LEAVES

It is nice to add leaves to your flowers because it will make them look more like flowers. Hold the bag at a 45-degree angle to the surface of the cookie. Without moving the tip, squeeze the bag and allow the frosting to fan out. Lessen your pressure as you pull the tip away to a point.

Working with Royal Icing

The key to working with royal icing is getting the consistency right for the desired effect. Thin icing is used as a glue to attach photo transfers (page 191, step 4), toppings, or parts of dimensional cookies.

It is also used when you want the icing to flow (spread) to the borders of the cookie, as in Baby Toys (page 173). Thick icing is used to pipe borders as in the "Grad Cookies" (page 191), and write messages as in the "Valentine's tattoos" (page 200). Extra-thick icing is used to pipe flowers or stars as in the "Party at My Crib" Baby Invite (page 171).

TIPS FOR USING ROYAL ICING

- Set out one pastry bag, parchment cone, or squeeze bottle for each color you will be piping. Each color should have its own container.

- Premix custom colors in small bowls first. Add a little icing at a time and stir after each addition until the icing reaches the desired consistency. Try to avoid making the colors too dark. I usually leave a little white icing in a bowl on the side in case I do make it too dark; I can stir the white in later to lighten it.

- If the icing is too thick, add water; if it is too thin, add confectioners' sugar a little at a time until it reaches the desired consistency. Keep in mind that the icing is going to thicken as it sits in the bowl as you are decorating, so you'll probably have to refresh the batch as you work.

- Put the icing in the pastry bags (page 43). Funnels are handy for putting the icing in squeeze bottles.

- Hover about ¼ inch from the surface; don't touch the cookie while piping.

- The tips chosen and pressure applied will determine the line thicknesses.

- Pipe all of the outlines first and let them dry. The outlines will hold the thinner "flood" icing.

- Pipe inside the hardened outlines with thinner, flood icing. Do not touch the outlines while piping. Push the icing to the borders with a toothpick or the tip of the pastry bag until the space is filled. If the icing does not spread smoothly, it is too thick. Scrape it off, thin icing and start over.

- Wet piping, a technique where you pipe wet icing on top of wet icing, is used to create eyes or polka dots or patterns. This will dry into a completely flat surface. For a dimensional look cover the cookie surface with flood icing; then drop a dot on top.

- Attach sugars and candies to the icing while it is still wet.

- Store royal icing in the refrigerator, in an airtight container. I don't store icing that contains raw egg white for more than a day.

Piping Buttercream Frostings

Buttercream is thicker than royal icing, so you will need a larger pastry-bag tip. When filling cookies with buttercream or chocolate, such as in thumbprints (page 197), put the filling in a pastry bag to control the amount added.

Chocolate Techniques

MELTING CHOCOLATE

The best way to melt chocolate is in a double boiler. If you don't have one, create a double boiler by placing a heatproof bowl over a saucepan filled with simmering water. Do not allow the bowl to touch the water. Also make sure that the bowl or pan you'll use for the chocolate is absolutely dry; even a drop of water can damage the chocolate.

1. Break or chop the chocolate into small pieces or use chocolate chips. Put them in the top of a double boiler over simmering water. Slowly melt the chocolate, stirring occasionally.

2. When almost completely melted, remove the chocolate from the heat and stir until smooth.

Chocolate can also be melted in a microwave oven, although the timing is hard to control.

1. Place the chocolate in a microwave-safe bowl and heat on high for 30 seconds. Check to see whether the chocolate is melted. If not, heat on low for another

30 seconds. Continue reheating using smaller time increments until the chocolate is melted.

2.   When it is melted, remove the chocolate from the microwave and stir.

PIPING CHOCOLATE DESIGNS

Use these piping designs to pipe melted chocolate directly onto cookies. You can pipe white, milk, or dark chocolate using a pastry bag with a small writing tip. Let it cool to set.

PIPING CHOCOLATE DESIGNS ON COOKIES

1.   Melt the chocolate, and let it cool slightly. You will need to decorate quickly because the chocolate will cool and set before you know it. Make sure the chocolate is the right consistency—not too runny, or it will not hold its shape.

2.   Fit the piping bag with a small writing tip and fill with chocolate.

3.   Pipe your favorite design in a continuous line directly onto the cookies.

Working with Marzipan, Sugar Paste Icing, Fondant

Marzipan, sugar paste, and fondant are all pastes that are similar in texture to clay and can be formed into shapes and used to decorate cookies. I have gone into detail in the specific recipes on how to make marzipan fruit (Marzipan Fruit Cookies, page 115) or cover cookies with sugar paste or fondant (Girls on the Verge Cookies, page 188).

TIPS FOR USING MARZIPAN, SUGAR PASTE ICING, AND FONDANT

•   To color marzipan, divide the batch into balls, one for each color. Flatten each ball and add a few drops of food coloring to the center. Knead the marzipan until the color is evenly absorbed. Continue to add food coloring until the desired color is achieved.

•   To decorate a whole cookie with marzipan or fondant, roll the marzipan or fondant out to ⅛ inch thick with a rolling pin. For a topped cookie, cut it with the same cookie cutter you used for the cookie. For a cookie with both the tops and sides covered, cut the marzipan or fondant with a cutter that is larger than the cookie. Attach the marzipan or fondant to the cookie with royal icing or corn syrup.

- Imprint with cookie cutters or rubber stamps to create images and patterns.

- Use to sculpt forms and shapes such as basket weaves, bows, and fruit.

Making Photo Transfers

Create the artwork ¼ inch smaller than your cookie size. E-mail or take the file or printout of the image to a decorating shop that produces edible frosting transfers. Have the shop print your file or scan your image to print. Edible transfers are available in sizes up to 8½ x 11 inches. If you have small designs and order the 8½ x 11 size you can fit several designs on one page, then cut the frosting yourself. Cut to size and freeze the transfer for 20 minutes so it hardens and peels off easily from the backing. Place over a thin coating of royal icing.

Using Edible Markers and Painting on Icing

Cookies can be drawn on or painted after they are baked, or iced with edible markers and paints. Food coloring can be used as paint. Place a few drops in a palette with some water, and brush it on just like you would watercolors. Edible markers can be used to create interesting shading or line work. Powdered tints are also available for painting.

1. Allow the sugar paste icing or marzipan to dry on the cookies before painting.
2. Draw your design on the cookie with an edible marker or emboss the design on with cookie cutters. You can also use stencils cut out of card stock.
3. Dilute the food coloring with water. Mix the colors you would like to use in small cups or a plastic palette.
4. With a brush, paint your designs in food coloring or powdered tints. Add highlights and shading with markers.

Everyday Cookies

BREAKFAST AND BRUNCH COOKIES

Good morning! I am a big fan of lazy Saturday mornings eating cookies for breakfast and spending hours in the kitchen baking sweet treats for the coming week. Not only does the house smell excellent, but baking is super-relaxing. Inspired by the sweet and energizing flavors of breakfast, I have transformed waffles, cereal, and cinnamon rolls into cookies that are great choices for a not-so-fussy weekend brunch, and the Cereal Killer Cookies and Lemon Poppy-Seed Cookies are perfect choices to grab for breakfast on the go with a latte or with yogurt and fruit.

Cinnamon Swirls

Type of cookie: Icebox

24 cookies

> Inspired by my favorite breakfast pastry, these are the icebox cookie counterpart. The thinner you roll the dough, the tighter the circles. When the dough is sliced you'll have very pretty concentric circles. Drizzle with thin Cream Cheese Icing for that authentic cinnamon-roll flavor.

Left: Cinnamon Swirls, Waffle Cookies, and Lemon Poppyseed Cookies.

Cookie Dough

2 cups all-purpose flour

1/4 cup granulated sugar

1 cup (2 sticks) butter, cubed

1/4 cup maple syrup, plus more for brushing

2 tablespoons apple juice

3 large egg whites, beaten

Pecan Filling

1/4 cup brown sugar

1 1/2 tablespoons ground cinnamon

3/4 cup ground pecans

Topping

Cream Cheese Icing (page 275)

Cinnamon Swirls continued

1. Make the dough: Put the flour, sugar, and butter in a food processor or blender. Pulse until the dough gathers into little pieces.

2. Add the 1/4 cup syrup and the apple juice and pulse to form into a ball.

3. Divide the dough into two batches, flatten, and wrap in plastic wrap. Refrigerate for 2 hours.

4. Make the filling: Combine the brown sugar, cinnamon, and pecans in a small bowl; set aside.

5. When the dough is chilled, roll one batch on a floured work surface to 1/8 inch thick and roughly 10 inches wide by 15 inches long. Brush with egg white (this will hold the roll together). Sprinkle half the filling on the dough. Starting with a short side, roll the dough up into a tight log. Repeat with the other piece of dough. Wrap each log in plastic wrap and refrigerate for 1 hour.

6. Preheat the oven to 325°F. Line 2 cookie sheets with parchment paper.

7. Once the logs are chilled, cut them into 1/4-inch slices. Do not slice them too thin, or the cookies will break apart while baking. Place the cookies on the cookie sheets 1 1/2 inches apart, and brush the tops with syrup. Bake for 20 to 25 minutes, until lightly golden. Remove from the oven and arrange close together on a rack to cool.

8. Put the icing in a pastry bag with a small writing tip. Hold the bag 6 inches over the cookies and squeeze. Allow the icing to drizzle onto the cookies, and move back and forth to create lines.

Waffle Dough

⅔ cup all-purpose flour

½ teaspoon baking powder

½ teaspoon ground cinnamon

⅛ teaspoon salt

¼ cup (½ stick) butter, softened,
   plus more for the iron

¼ cup granulated sugar

1 large egg

1 tablespoon maple syrup

Topping

2 tablespoons confectioners' sugar

Waffle Cookies

Type of cookie: Drop

30 cookies

The most memorable baking epiphany I have had was when I put cookie dough in the waffle iron and it cooked so fast and had the added bonus of the iconic waffle texture. If you have a standard waffle iron, drop the dough by the 1½ rounded teaspoon; if you have a Belgian iron, drop the dough by the 1½ rounded tablespoon. Serve these cookies dusted with sugar, drizzled with maple syrup, or made into sandwiches with Strawberry Cream Cheese Filling (page 275).

1. Preheat a waffle iron and brush it with butter.

2. Combine the flour, baking powder, cinnamon, and salt in a medium bowl; set aside.

3. Beat the butter and sugar until light and fluffy. Add the egg and syrup and beat until blended.

4. Gradually add the flour mixture, stirring until just mixed.

5. Drop 1½ teaspoon or tablespoon mounds of dough into the hot waffle iron 2 inches apart. Close the lid and cook for 1½ to 2 minutes, until firm. Lift the cookies with a fork and set them on a rack to cool. Dust with confectioners' sugar.

Variation

Chocolate Waffle Cookies: Add 2 tablespoons cocoa powder, 1 teaspoon vanilla extract, and 1 tablespoon milk at the same time as the egg and syrup.

Lemon Poppy-Seed Cookies

Type of cookie: Drop

36 cookies

2½ cups all-purpose flour
1½ cups granulated sugar
2 teaspoons baking soda
¼ teaspoon salt
¾ cup vegetable oil
Freshly squeezed lemon juice from
   6 medium lemons
3 tablespoons grated lemon zest
   from 2 medium lemons
2 teaspoons vanilla extract
⅛ cup poppy seeds

Intensely lemony poppy-seed cookies have a tang that really grows on you. Try preparing orange or lime cookies by substituting the juice and zest. For an all-around good citrus butter cookie, just omit the poppy seeds.

1. Preheat the oven to 350°F. Line 2 cookie sheets with parchment paper.

2. Combine the flour, sugar, baking soda, and salt in a medium bowl.

3. Stir in the oil, lemon juice, lemon zest, vanilla, and poppy seeds; blend well.

4. Drop 1-teaspoon mounds of dough on the cookie sheets 2 inches apart. Bake for 8 to 10 minutes, until the edges are golden. Transfer to a rack to cool.

Variation

Lemon-Filled Thumbprints: After dropping the cookies, press into thumbprints and fill each cookie with 1 tablespoon of lemon filling (page 120, Lemon-Filled Meringues recipe).

Cereal Cookie Base

1¼ cups all-purpose flour

½ teaspoon cream of tartar

½ teaspoon baking soda

½ cup (1 stick) butter, softened

½ cup granulated sugar

½ cup brown sugar

1 large egg

½ teaspoon vanilla extract

Add-ins

1½ cups cornflakes

¾ cup semisweet chocolate chips

Cereal Killer Cookies

Type of cookie: Drop

24 cookies

We all have favorite, kind of offbeat cereal combos. My husband thinks I am nuts to put chocolate chips in my cornflakes, but I think it's weird that he adds sugary, fruity cereals to his healthful ones to sweeten them. Somehow by converting these combos into cookie form, they become even tastier and more acceptable. Try adding your favorites to this cookie-dough base.

1. Preheat the oven to 375°F.

2. Line 2 cookie sheets with parchment paper.

3. Combine the flour, cream of tartar, and baking soda in a medium bowl; set aside.

4. Beat the butter and both sugars until light and fluffy. Add the egg and vanilla and beat well.

5. Gradually add the flour mixture to the butter mixture until blended. Stir in the cornflakes and chocolate chips.

6. Drop rounded-tablespoon mounds of dough on the cookie sheets 2 inches apart. Bake for 10 to 12 minutes, until the edges are golden. Remove from the oven and let cool for 2 minutes. Transfer to a rack to cool.

Variations

Whole-Grain Fruit Cookies: Instead of the cornflakes and chocolate chips add ¾ cup whole-grain cereal and ¾ cup dried cranberries and apricots to the cereal cookie base.

Fruity Cereal Cookies: Instead of the cornflakes and chocolate chips, add 1 cup fruity cereal to the cereal cookie base.

Right: Cereal Killer Cookies, Rice Cereal Marshmallow Sandwiches.

Cookie Base

¼ cup (½ stick) butter

3 cups minimarshmallows

1 teaspoon vanilla extract

4 cups puffed rice cereal

Marshmallow Filling

¾ cup marshmallows

2 tablespoons butter

¼ cup confectioners' sugar

Rice Cereal Marshmallow Sandwiches

Type of cookie: Bar sandwich

24 cookies

It seems sinful to eat marshmallow sandwiches for breakfast, but why not? Especially when they meet the requirement of the perfect breakfast on the go. If you absolutely have no guilt, indulge in the chocolate ones.

1. Butter a 9 x 13-inch baking dish.

2. Make the cookie base: Melt the butter in a double boiler over low heat.

3. Add the marshmallows and stir until completely melted. Remove from the heat and stir in the vanilla. Add the cereal and stir until well coated. Press into the prepared pan and let cool.

4. Make the marshmallow filling: Melt the marshmallows and butter together in a double boiler over low heat. Remove from the heat and stir in the confectioners' sugar.

5. Remove the cookie base from the pan by flipping on to a cutting surface using a spatula to loosen if necessary. Cut into 3-inch squares. Spread the filling on half of the squares and sandwich with remaining squares.

Variation

Chocolate Rice Marshmallow Treats: Add 1 cup chocolate chips to the rice cereal mixture. After assembling the sandwiches with filling melt 1 cup chocolate chips in a double boiler and spread on top of the rice cereal sandwich bars. Let cool to harden.

1 cup all-purpose flour
¾ cup rolled oats (not instant)
½ teaspoon ground cinnamon
½ teaspoon baking powder
½ teaspoon baking soda
¼ teaspoon salt
½ cup (1 stick) butter, softened
½ cup light brown sugar
½ cup mashed banana
1 large egg
1 teaspoon vanilla extract
¼ cup dried banana chips

Banana Oatmeal Cookies

Type of cookie: Drop

30 cookies

After a morning workout, wholesome banana oatmeal cookies are my reward breakfast of choice—much better than a bowl of oatmeal. I usually pair them with a cup of herbal tea.

1. Preheat the oven to 350°F. Butter 2 cookie sheets.

2. Combine the flour, oats, cinnamon, baking powder, baking soda, and salt in a medium bowl; set aside.

3. Beat the butter and sugar in a medium bowl until light and fluffy. Beat in the banana, egg, and vanilla.

4. Add the flour mixture and mix until blended.

5. Drop 1-tablespoon mounds of dough on the cookie sheets 2 inches apart. Bake for 5 minutes; then press a banana chip onto the top of each cookie. Continue to bake for 5 to 6 minutes more, until the cookies are golden. Let cool for 5 minutes before transferring to a rack to cool completely.

Variations

Banana Oatmeal Raisin Pecan Cookies: Add ¾ cup raisins and ¾ cup chopped pecans after the dry and wet ingredients are combined.

Banana Oatmeal Chip Cookies: Add ¾ cup chocolate chips after the dry and wet ingredients are combined.

Crust Dough

¾ cup (1½ sticks) butter, softened

¼ cup confectioners' sugar

¼ teaspoon salt

2 large egg yolks

1 teaspoon vanilla extract

1½ cups all-purpose flour

Filling

1 cup blueberry jam

1 cup blueberries

2 large egg whites, lightly beaten

Crumble Topping

3 tablespoons all-purpose flour

3 tablespoons brown sugar

2½ tablespoons butter

⅛ teaspoon salt

2 tablespoons ground pecans

Blueberry Crumble Pockets

Type of cookie: Rolled cutout

24 cookies

Ring up your pals to come over for brunch to share these flaky blueberry crumble cookies. Inspired by my favorite blueberry pie recipe with crumb topping, they are filled with fresh blueberries and blueberry jam. For variation, the cookie crust can also be flavored with spices such as ground ginger or cinnamon and filled with strawberry, raspberry, or other jam and fruit combinations. Check out the Pomegranate Pillows recipe (page 62) as an example.

1. Make the crust dough: Cream the butter, sugar and salt until light and fluffy. Mix in the egg yolks and vanilla.

2. Gradually add the flour. Form the dough into two flattened disks, wrap it in plastic wrap, and refrigerate for 1 hour.

3. Preheat the oven to 325°F. Butter 2 cookie sheets.

4. Once the dough is chilled, roll one disk on a floured work surface to ¼ inch thick. Cut the dough into 3-inch circles with a ravioli cutter or cookie cutter. Place half of the circles on the cookie sheets 1½ inches apart. Repeat with second disk.

5. Fill the cookies: Put 1 teaspoon blueberry jam and a few blueberries in the center of each circle on the cookie sheets. Top with the remaining circles. Press the top and bottom edges of the cookies together with your fingers or the tines of a fork. Brush the tops with the egg whites.

6. Make the crumble topping: Mix the flour, brown sugar, butter, salt, and pecans until blended. Press onto the tops of the cookies. Bake for 12 to 15 minutes, until the edges are golden. Let cool for 5 minutes. Transfer to a rack to cool completely.

Pomegranate Pillows, Blueberry Crumble Pockets.

Pomegranate Filling

2 cups pomegranate juice

2½ cups granulated sugar

½ teaspoon cornstarch

1½ cups pomegranate seeds

½ cup golden raisins, chopped

1 teaspoon orange juice

Crust Dough

Crust dough (page 61, Blueberry
   Crumble Pockets dough)

1 teaspoon grated orange zest

¼ teaspoon ground ginger

Pomegranate Icing

1½ cups confectioners' sugar

1 teaspoon orange juice

¼ cup pomegranate juice

Pomegranate Pillows

Type of cookie: Rolled cutout

30 cookies

Fill these puffy pillow cookies with a fresh jam of pomegranate, the fruity flavor of the decade. To bring out more of the pomegranate flavor, top the cookies with pomegranate icing.

1. Make the filling: Combine the pomegranate juice and sugar in a saucepan over high heat and stir until the sugar is dissolved. Sift in the cornstarch and continue stirring until the mixture has thickened slightly. Add the pomegranate seeds, raisins, and orange juice and cook, stirring occasionally, for 20 to 30 minutes, until very thick. Chill the jam in the refrigerator for at least 2 hours.

2. Make the crust dough, adding the orange zest with the wet ingredients and the ginger with the dry ingredients. Form the dough into two flattened disks, wrap it in plastic wrap, and refrigerate for 1 hour.

3. Preheat the oven to 375°F. Butter 2 cookie sheets.

4. Remove the doughs from the refrigerator and roll one disk out on a floured work surface and cut out 2 inch squares with a cookie cutter. Spoon ½ teaspoon filling onto half the squares. Top with remaining squares and pinch all edges together tightly with your fingers or the tines of a fork. Place on the cookie sheets 1½ inches apart and repeat with remaining disk.

5. Bake for 12 to 15 minutes, until golden. Let cool on the cookie sheets for 10 minutes. Transfer to a rack to cool completely.

6. Make the pomegranate icing: Put the confectioners' sugar in a small bowl. Gradually add the orange and pomegranate juices, stirring, until the icing is the desired consistency. Drizzle the icing on the cooled cookies.

Biscotti

⅔ cup whole almonds

1 tablespoon anise seeds

2 tablespoons sambuca

2 cups all-purpose flour

1½ teaspoons baking powder

¼ teaspoon salt

½ cup (1 stick) butter, softened

¾ cup sugar

2 large eggs

Topping

2 cups semisweet chocolate chips

Chocolate-Coated Anise Almond Biscotti

Type of cookie: Hand shaped

36 cookies

My father's side of the family is from Sicily and follows the breakfast tradition of dunking anise-flavored biscotti in coffee with hot milk. These great-tasting small oblong wafers are twice baked, once as a loaf and then as individual cookies, making them ultracrisp. Try some of my variations on the classic recipe.

1. Preheat the oven to 325°F. Butter 2 cookie sheets.

2. Toast the almonds on a cookie sheet for 8 to 10 minutes. Rub the nuts between paper towels to remove the skins. Let cool.

3. Combine the anise seeds and sambuca in a small microwave-safe bowl. Cover and cook in the microwave for 15 seconds; set aside.

4. Combine the flour, baking powder, and salt in a large bowl; set aside.

5. Cream the butter and sugar until light and fluffy. Beat in the eggs and anise mixture.

6. Gradually stir in the flour mixture.

7. Divide the dough in half and shape it into 2 logs about ¾ inch thick, 1½ inches wide, and 3 inches long. Place on the cookie sheet 2 inches apart. Bake for 18 to 22 minutes. Let cool for 5 minutes.

8. With a serrated knife, slice ½-inch cookies. Place upright on the cookie sheets and bake for 10 minutes. Transfer to a rack to cool completely.

9. Melt the chocolate in a double boiler over low heat. Brush the tops of the logs with the chocolate and let cool to harden.

Clockwise from the top: Raspberry Almond, Chocolate Chip, and Chocolate-Coated Almond Biscotti

Variations

Orange Chocolate Chip Biscotti: Replace the anise seeds and sambuca with 2 tablespoons freshly squeezed orange juice and 1 tablespoon grated orange zest. Replace the almonds with ⅔ cup chocolate chips.

Raspberry Almond Biscotti: Omit the sambuca and anise. Use 1¼ cups sliced almonds instead of whole almonds. Add ⅔ cup to the recipe and reserve the rest for topping. After the dough is thoroughly mixed, gently fold in ¾ cup raspberry jam to create swirls. Brush an egg wash on the logs and top with coarse sugar and sliced almonds before baking.

Pistachio Lime Biscotti: Replace the anise seeds and sambuca with 1 tablespoon grated lime zest and 2 tablespoons freshly squeezed lime juice. Replace the almonds with pistachios.

Pignoli Biscotti: Replace the anise seeds and sambuca with 1 tablespoon grated lemon zest and 2 tablespoons freshly squeezed lemon juice. Replace the almonds with pine nuts.

Low-Fat Chocolate Biscotti ♥

Type of cookie: Hand shaped

30 cookies

1 cup whole-wheat flour
¾ cup all-purpose flour
¼ cup sugar
½ cup cocoa powder
1 teaspoon ground espresso beans
1 teaspoon baking soda
¼ teaspoon salt
3 large eggs
1 teaspoon vanilla extract
¼ cup chopped chocolate chips

Bravo for these chocolate biscotti in which no butter at all is added! Flecked with just enough ground espresso and chocolate chips, they make the perfect accompaniment to breakfast cappuccino or brunch dessert wine.

1. Preheat the oven to 300°F. Butter 2 cookie sheets.

2. Combine the flours, sugar, cocoa powder, espresso beans, baking soda, and salt in a medium bowl; set aside.

3. Beat the eggs and vanilla in a large bowl. Stir in the chocolate chips.

4. Add the flour mixture to the egg mixture and stir until blended.

5. Divide the dough in half and shape into two logs about

¾ inch thick, 1½ inches wide, and 6 inches long. Place on the cookie sheets 2 inches apart and bake for 50 minutes. Let cool for 5 minutes.

6. With a serrated knife, slice ½-inch cookies. Lay them flat on the cookie sheets, bake for 10 minutes, then flip the cookies and bake for 10 more minutes. Transfer to a rack to cool completely.

Variation

White Chocolate Hazelnut Biscotti: Replace the cocoa powder with melted white chocolate and the chips with white chocolate chips. Toast ¾ cup hazelnuts in a cookie sheet for 8 to 10 minutes. Rub the nuts between paper towels to remove the skins. Let cool. Add the nuts to the dough.

TOTALLY CHOCOLATE COOKIES

I love chocolate! It is the only food that I eat every day. Long before me, the Aztecs and Maya indulged in its seductive qualities. The Spanish were the first to see chocolate's sweet potential, and eventually the world saw bittersweet, white, milk, and many more varieties of chocolate. Here I offer cookies that take chocolate to new heights: the nostalgic Milk Chocolate Icebox Cookies, chewy-gooey candy bar cookies, elegant molded chocolate cookies, and melt-in-your-mouth white chocolate cookies.

Milk Chocolate Icebox Cookies

Type of cookie: Icebox

24 cookies

Lovers of milk chocolate will get their fix with these smooth, foolproof cookies. Icebox cookies are super-easy to make if you allow them time to freeze. Dress them up by adding some milk chocolate glaze on the top and sprinkles on the sides. I like to serve them dipped in my favorite rocky road milk chocolate pudding parfait (page 278).

Milk Chocolate Cookies

4 ounces milk chocolate
1⅔ cups all-purpose flour
¼ cup cocoa powder
1 teaspoon baking powder
½ teaspoon baking soda
¼ teaspoon salt
¾ cup (1½ sticks) butter, softened
½ cup light brown sugar
½ cup granulated sugar
1 large egg
1 teaspoon vanilla extract
1 large egg white, beaten
1 cup milk chocolate sprinkles

Milk Chocolate Glaze

3 ounces milk chocolate
3 tablespoons butter
1½ cups confectioners' sugar
¼ teaspoon salt

1. Make the milk chocolate cookies: Melt the chocolate in a double boiler and set aside to cool.

2. Combine the flour, cocoa powder, baking powder, baking soda, and salt in a medium bowl; set aside.

3. Beat the butter and sugars in a large bowl until fluffy. Add the whole egg and vanilla. Stir in the melted chocolate.

4. Gradually add the flour mixture and stir until blended.

5. Divide the dough in half. Shape the dough into logs 2 inches wide by 9 inches long. Wrap in plastic wrap and freeze for 2 hours.

6. Preheat the oven to 350°F. Line 2 cookie sheets with parchment paper.

7. Unwrap the logs and let them soften a bit. Brush the logs with egg white, and then roll them in the sprinkles. Slice into ¼-inch cookies. Place on the cookie sheets 1½ inches apart, and bake for 8 to 10 minutes, until the edges are lightly browned. Transfer to a rack to cool completely.

8. Make the milk chocolate glaze: Melt the chocolate and butter together in a double boiler. Stir in the confectioners' sugar and salt. Spread the glaze on top of the cookies and let set.

Variation

White Chocolate Icebox Cookies: Omit the cocoa powder from the cookie dough and increase the flour by ¼ cup. Replace the milk chocolate with white chocolate in the dough and in the glaze.

White Chocolate Macadamia Cream Cookies

Type of cookie: Drop
30 cookies

In the mood to bake something sweet for a white chocolate fan? This dough is flavored with white chocolate, and the variations have you covered—from minisandwiches made with minichips

White Chocolate Cookie Dough

2¼ cups all-purpose flour

¾ teaspoon baking soda

½ teaspoon salt

14 tablespoons (1 stick and 6 tablespoons) butter, softened

1½ cups brown sugar

3 large eggs

1½ teaspoons vanilla extract

4 ounces white chocolate (before melting), melted and cooled to room temperature

¾ cup coarsely chopped white chocolate

1 cup macadamia nuts

White Chocolate Cream

4 ounces white chocolate (before melting), melted and cooled to room temperature

1¾ cups confectioners' sugar

¼ cup milk

1 teaspoon vanilla extract

⅛ teaspoon salt

6 tablespoons butter, softened

¼ cup coarsely chopped white chocolate

to extra-large sandwiches made with macadamia nuts and white chocolate chunks. The medium-size ones are left to enjoy plain.

1. Preheat the oven to 350°F. Butter 2 cookie sheets.

2. Make the white chocolate cookie dough: Combine the flour, baking soda, and salt in a medium bowl; set aside.

3. Cream the butter and brown sugar in a large bowl until fluffy. Beat in the eggs and vanilla until blended. Stir in the melted white chocolate and chopped white chocolate, then the nuts; then gradually add the flour mixture.

4. Drop 1½-tablespoon mounds of dough on the cookie sheets 2 inches apart. Bake for 10 to 12 minutes, until golden around the edges. Remove from the oven and let cool for 5 minutes. Transfer to a rack to cool completely.

5. Make the white chocolate cream: Combine the melted white chocolate and confectioners' sugar in a medium bowl and stir until blended. Stir in the milk, vanilla, and salt.

6. Beat in the butter and fold in the white chocolate chunks. Refrigerate for 15 to 20 minutes to thicken. Spread the white chocolate cream between 2 cookies.

Variation

Triple Chocolate Sandwiches: Keep the melted white chocolate in the dough. Replace the white chocolate chunks in the cookies with bittersweet chocolate. Replace the white chocolate in the cream with milk chocolate.

German Chocolate Cookies

2 cups all-purpose flour
1 teaspoon baking powder
¼ teaspoon salt
½ cup cocoa powder
½ cup butter, softened
1 cup granulated sugar
½ cup grated German chocolate
½ cup ground pecans
1 teaspoon vanilla extract
2 large egg whites

Coconut Pecan Filling

2 large egg yolks
¾ cup evaporated milk
2 ounces German sweet chocolate, chopped
1 teaspoon vanilla extract
¾ cup sugar
⅓ cup butter
1 cup sweetened shredded coconut
1 cup chopped pecans

German Chocolate Cookies with Coconut Pecan Filling

Type of cookie: Rolled cutout sandwich

12 sandwiches

A riff on the famous cake originally from the southern United States, these German chocolate sandwich cookies are made with coconut pecan filling in the middle. The scalloped edge is cut with the edge of a mini–tart pan that I made into a cookie cutter. They can also be prepared without the filling as drop cookies with icing on top.

1. Preheat the oven to 350°F. Line 2 baking sheets with parchment paper.

2. Make the German chocolate cookies: Combine the flour, baking powder, salt, and cocoa powder in a medium bowl; set aside.

3. Beat the butter, sugar, chocolate, pecans, and vanilla in a large bowl until blended.

4. Add the flour mixture, alternating with the egg whites, stirring until the dough comes together.

5. Divide the dough in 4 and roll each batch out on a floured work surface to ¼ inch thick. Using a cookie cutter with scalloped edges, cut into 3-inch rounds. Place on the cookie sheets 1 inch apart and bake for 8 to 10 minutes, until lightly browned. Let cool for 5 minutes. Transfer to a rack to cool completely.

6. Make the coconut pecan filling: Heat the egg yolks, evaporated milk, chocolate, and vanilla in large saucepan over medium heat, beating with a whisk until blended.

7. Add the sugar and butter and cook, stirring, for 10 to 12 minutes, until thickened. Remove from the heat. Stir in the coconut and pecans and refrigerate for 30 minutes.

8. Spread the filling between the cookies to make sandwiches.

Variations

Chocolate Hazelnut Cookies: Prepare the dough with hazelnuts instead of pecans. Omit the filling.

Semisweet Chocolate Cookies: Prepare the dough with semisweet chocolate and omit the nuts.

Chunky Candy Cookies

Type of cookie: Drop

12 large cookies

Chunky Candy Cookies are a chocolate candy bar lover's version of happiness. Extra large and packed with chocolate, nuts, raisins, toffee, and caramel, they are chocolaty and chewy at the same time. Try substituting some of the ingredients with your favorite candies.

1 cup all-purpose flour
⅔ cup cocoa powder
1½ teaspoons baking powder
½ teaspoon salt
¾ cup (1½ sticks) butter
9 ounces semisweet chocolate, chopped
1 teaspoon vanilla extract
3 large eggs
1 cup granulated sugar
⅓ cup light brown sugar
1⅓ cups semisweet chocolate chips
1 cup walnut halves
6 ounces white chocolate chips
¾ cup raisins
¼ cup coarsely crushed toffee

1. Preheat the oven to 325°F. Butter 2 cookie sheets.

2. Combine the flour, cocoa powder, baking powder, and salt in a medium bowl; set aside.

3. Stir the butter and chocolate in a double boiler over simmering water until melted. Remove from the heat and stir in the vanilla; set aside.

4. Beat the eggs and sugars in a bowl until creamy. Beat in the melted chocolate mixture.

5. Gradually add the flour mixture until just blended.

6. Stir in the chocolate chips, nuts, white chocolate, raisins, and toffee.

7. Drop 2-tablespoon mounds of dough on the cookie sheets 2 inches apart, and flatten slightly. Bake for 15 to 18 minutes, until slightly cracked on top. Transfer to a rack to cool.

Left: Chunky Candy Cookies.

Chocolate Cookie
Dough (page 271)

Topping

1 cup green molding chocolate
1 cup orange molding chocolate
1 cup semisweet chocolate chips

Molded Chocolate Cookies

Type of cookie: Rolled cutout

20 cookies

"Extravagant" is the right description for these beautiful, rich chocolate cookies topped with molded candies. This technique is a simple method to decorate cookies for those without the skill or will to pipe designs. There are many types of shaped candy molds available, so have fun with it. Here I used colored molding chocolate and formed it in leaf-shaped silicone molds; then I attached each candy to the cookie with a pool of melted semisweet chocolate.

1. Wrap the Chocolate Cookie dough in plastic wrap and refrigerate for 30 minutes. Then roll the dough out on a cutting board to ¼ inch thick and refrigerate for 1 hour.

2. Preheat the oven to 350°F. Line 2 cookie sheets with parchment paper.

3. Cut the chilled dough with cookie cutters (here I used an oval tartlet pan). Place on the cookie sheets 1½ inches apart. Bake for 7 to 10 minutes, until lightly browned. Transfer to a rack to cool completely.

4. Make the toppings: Melt the green chocolate in a double boiler over simmering water, stirring until smooth. Pour into a squeeze bottle and squeeze into candy molds; scrape any excess from the top of the mold. Tap the mold on the countertop to pop any air bubbles. Let the chocolate sit for 1 hour to harden. Repeat with the orange chocolate.

Below: Molded Chocolate Cookies.

Chocolate Mint Cookies

2½ cups all-purpose flour

⅓ cup cocoa powder

½ teaspoon salt

1 cup (2 sticks) butter, softened

1 cup sugar

1 large egg

½ teaspoon vanilla extract

½ teaspoon peppermint extract

Mint Cream

6 tablespoons butter, softened

3 cups confectioners' sugar

2 tablespoons milk

¼ teaspoon peppermint extract

3 drops green food coloring

5. Melt the semisweet chocolate chips in a double boiler and spoon with a teaspoon onto the tops. While wet use as glue to attach the molded chocolate to the cookies.

Mint Chocolate Creams

Type of cookie: Rolled cutout

15 cookie sandwiches, or 30 piped cream cookies

Mint and chocolate are two of the simple pleasures in life, especially gratifying when eaten together. Prepare these cookies as sandwiches filled with the mint cream, or pipe the cream on top of single cookies for a more elegant look.

1. Preheat the oven to 350°F. Line 2 cookie sheets with parchment paper.

2. Make the chocolate mint cookies: Combine the flour, cocoa powder, and salt in a medium bowl; set aside.

3. Cream the butter and sugar until fluffy. Add the egg and vanilla and peppermint extracts and beat until blended.

4. Transfer the dough to a floured work surface and divide it into two batches. Roll one batch to ¼ inch thick then roll out the second batch. Cut with 2½-inch cookie cutters. Place on the cookie sheets 1½ inches apart and bake for 10 to 12 minutes, until the cookies brown lightly around the edges. Let the cookies sit for 5 minutes. Transfer to a rack to cool completely.

5. Make the mint cream: Beat the butter and confectioners' sugar until fluffy. Add the milk, peppermint extract, and food coloring. Beat until smooth. Spread the cream between the cookies.

Variation

Mint Chocolate Ice Cream Sandwiches: Prepare the cookies and make sandwiches with chocolate ice cream instead of mint cream.

SNACK CLASSIC COOKIES

When I think comfort food I think classic cookies. Milk and cookies have long been associated with kids, but most adults would admit that they too love the nostalgic chewy, gooey, crunchy, and melt-in-your-mouth flavors and textures. Everyone has a favorite snack classic cookie, and a particular way they like them: soft and chewy, crisp and crunchy, vegan, low fat, or sugar free. Here you will find the most requested old-fashioned cookie-jar cookies in America. Chocolate chip and peanut butter cookies are homespun American cookies. Snicker-doodles, oatmeal raisin cookies, and gingersnaps were reinvented in America based on European classics.

Chocolate Chip Walnut Cookies

Type of cookie: Drop

30 cookies

No one knows exactly who baked the first chocolate chip cookie, but Americans credit Ruth Wakefield from the toll inn in Whitman, Massachusetts, with the addition of chocolate chips sometime in the 1930s. They soon became an instant snack classic. These easy-to-make cookies are great anytime, each bite prompting consumption of another morsel.

1. Preheat the oven to 375°F. Butter 2 cookie sheets.

2. Combine the flour, baking powder, and salt in a medium bowl; set aside.

3. Cream the butter and sugars together until light and fluffy. Add the eggs and vanilla, and beat well.

4. Gradually add the flour mixture until blended. Stir in the chocolate chips and walnuts.

5. Drop heaping-tablespoon mounds of batter on the cookie sheets 2 inches apart. Bake for 10 to 12 minutes, until lightly browned. Transfer to a rack to cool.

2¼ cups all-purpose flour

1 teaspoon baking powder

½ teaspoon salt

1 cup (2 sticks) butter, softened

¾ cup dark brown sugar

¾ cup granulated sugar

2 large eggs

1 teaspoon vanilla extract

1 cup semisweet chocolate chips

1 cup chopped walnuts

Variations

Chocolate Chip Raisin Cookies: Replace the walnuts with 1 cup raisins.

Chocolate Chocolate Chip Cookies: Reduce the flour to 2 cups and add ⅓ cup cocoa powder to the dry ingredients.

Chocolate Chunk Yogurt Cookies ♥

Type of cookie: Drop

30 cookies

2 cups whole-wheat flour
1 teaspoon baking soda
¼ teaspoon salt
½ cup (1 stick) margarine, softened
3 large egg whites
1 teaspoon vanilla extract
1 cup plain unsweetened nonfat yogurt
1¼ cups sugar free chocolate chunks
1¼ cups dried cranberries
1¼ cups chopped pecans

Intensely fruity, chewy, chocolaty—and sugar free. The yogurt adds tartness and cranberries sweetness, and the whole-wheat flour makes them earthy. Can you stop at just one?

1. Preheat the oven to 375°F. Line 2 cookie sheets with parchment paper.

2. Combine the flour, baking soda, and salt in a medium bowl; set aside.

3. Beat the margarine until fluffy. Beat in the egg whites, vanilla, and yogurt.

4. Gradually add the flour mixture until blended. Stir in the chocolate chunks, dried cranberries, and pecans.

5. Drop heaping-tablespoon mounds on the cookie sheets 2 inches apart. Bake for 12 to 15 minutes, until golden. Transfer to a rack to cool.

Variation

Chocolate Walnut and Raisin Yogurt Cookies: Replace the dried cranberries with raisins and the pecans with walnuts.

Gluten-Free Chocolate Chip Apricot Cookies

Type of cookie: Drop

24 cookies

I came up with this chocolate chip recipe when I was baking cookies as a gift for a friend who eats gluten free. Gluten is a

1¾ cups buckwheat flour

1¼ cups millet flour

1 tablespoon arrowroot

1½ teaspoons baking soda

1½ teaspoons xanthan gum

1 tablespoon cocoa powder

1 teaspoon salt

½ cup (1 stick) butter, softened

1 large egg

1 tablespoon vanilla extract

½ cup agave nectar

¼ cup apple juice

1 cup semisweet chocolate chips

½ cup chopped walnuts

¾ cup chopped dried apricots

Gluten-Free Baking

Gluten is made of proteins found in wheat, rye, and barley. It structures cookies by making dough stretchy and, in yeast doughs, holding the carbon dioxide produced by the yeast to allow for rising. Gluten-free cookies are made with nut, rice, and bean flours and other ingredients that don't contain gluten.

protein found in wheat, rye, and barley products. Some people are allergic to it; others think it is healthier not to eat it. Agave nectar and apricots are used as the sweeteners.

1. Combine the flours, arrowroot, baking soda, xanthan gum, cocoa powder, and salt in a medium bowl; set aside.

2. Beat the butter, egg, and vanilla until mixed.

3. Add the flour mixture, alternating with the agave nectar and apple juice, until blended.

4. Stir in the chocolate chips, walnuts, and apricots. Gather the dough into a ball and chill for 30 minutes.

5. Preheat the oven to 325°F. Line 2 cookie sheets with parchment paper.

6. Drop 1-tablespoon balls of the dough on the cookie sheets 2 inches apart; do not flatten. Bake for 15 to 18 minutes, until golden. Let cool on a rack for 15 minutes. Serve warm.

Variations

Gluten-Free Chocolate Spice Cookies: Add 1 teaspoon ground cinnamon, ¼ teaspoon freshly grated nutmeg, and ½ teaspoon ground ginger to the dry ingredients.

Gluten-Free Mocha Chip Cookies: Replace the apple juice with double-strength espresso.

Toffee Chip Cookies

Type of cookie: Drop

24 large cookies

Toffee and cookies are an unbeatable match. You can buy toffee prepackaged to add to these cookies or, if you would like to make your own, use my favorite homemade recipe, below, which yields enough toffee for several batches of cookies.

Toffee

¾ cup granulated sugar

¾ cup brown sugar

1 cup (2 sticks) butter

¼ cup water

⅛ teaspoon salt

1 teaspoon vanilla extract

Cookies

1⅓ cups all-purpose flour

1 teaspoon baking powder

⅛ teaspoon salt

⅓ cup butter, softened

½ cup granulated sugar

½ cup light brown sugar

1 large egg

1 teaspoon vanilla extract

½ cup semisweet chocolate chips

1½ cups whole-wheat flour

½ teaspoon baking soda

½ teaspoon cream of tartar

¼ teaspoon salt

½ cup (1 stick) butter, softened

¾ cup light brown sugar

1 large egg

1 teaspoon vanilla extract

¼ cup granulated sugar

2 tablespoons ground cinnamon

Left: Toffee Chip Cookies, Snickerdoodles, Brownie Cookies, Peanut Butter Cookies

1. Butter a 9 x 13-inch baking pan.

2. Make the toffee: Combine the sugars, butter, water, and salt in a saucepan. Stir over low heat until it reaches the light-crack stage (310°F on a candy thermometer). Remove from the heat and stir in the vanilla.

3. Pour the mixture into the baking pan. Let cool for 1 hour; then cover and refrigerate for 1 more hour. Remove from the pan and crack into pieces.

4. Preheat the oven to 375°F. Butter 2 cookie sheets.

5. Make the cookies: Combine the flour, baking powder, and salt in a medium bowl; set aside.

6. Cream the butter and sugars together until light and fluffy. Beat in the egg and vanilla.

7. Gradually add the flour mixture until blended. Stir in 1 cup of the toffee (reserve the rest for another batch) and the chocolate chips.

8. Drop 2-tablespoon mounds of dough on the cookie sheets 2½ inches apart. Bake for 12 to 15 minutes, until lightly browned. Transfer to a rack to cool.

Snickerdoodles

Type of cookie: Drop

24 cookies

The whimsical name of this cookie has no particular origin or purpose except for the fact that it is fun to say and makes people smile. The cookies' surface is characteristically cracked and coated with cinnamon sugar.

1. Preheat the oven to 375°F. Line 2 cookie sheets with parchment paper.

2. Combine the flour, baking soda, cream of tartar, and salt in a medium bowl; set aside.

3. Beat the butter and brown sugar until fluffy. Beat in the egg and vanilla.

4. Gradually add the flour mixture to the butter mixture until well mixed.

5. Stir the sugar and cinnamon together in a small bowl. Shape the dough into 2-inch balls. Roll the balls in the sugar-cinnamon mixture. Place the balls on the cookie sheets 2 inches apart and lightly flatten them.

6. Bake for 12 to 14 minutes, until light golden. Transfer to a rack and top with additional cinnamon sugar. Let cool.

Brownie Cookies

Type of cookie: Drop

18 large cookies

These cookies push the concept of the brownie further into the cookie world. They're delicious plain, but with the addition of walnuts they are nutty, chewy, and chocolaty all at once.

½ cup all-purpose flour
¼ teaspoon baking powder
¼ cup (½ stick) butter
12 ounces bittersweet chocolate
¾ cup light brown sugar
2 teaspoons vanilla
2 large eggs
1¼ cups walnut halves
(optional)

1. Combine the flour and baking powder in a small bowl; set aside.

2. Heat the butter and chocolate in a double boiler over simmering water, stirring constantly until melted.

3. Remove from the heat, and stir in the brown sugar and vanilla. Let cool for 5 minutes. Transfer to a large bowl and blend in the eggs and walnuts, if using.

4. Gradually add the flour mixture. Cover and refrigerate for 20 minutes.

5. Preheat the oven to 350°F. Line 2 baking sheets with parchment paper.

6. Drop 2-tablespoon mounds of dough on the cookie sheets 2½ inches apart and bake for 12 to 16 minutes,

until set around the edges and soft in the center.
Transfer to racks to cool.

Variations

Marshmallow Walnut Brownie Cookies: Add an additional 1 cup
walnuts and 2 cups minimarshmallows to the dough after the wet
and dry ingredients have been combined.

Toffee Brownie Cookies: Replace the walnuts with ¾ cup toffee chips
and ¾ cup chocolate chunks.

Chocolate Cream Cheese Brownie Cookies: After dropping the cookies
on the cookie sheet, press down in the middle to make a well in each
cookie. Fill with Cream Cheese Filling (page 275) and bake.

Old-Fashioned Peanut Butter Cookies

Type of cookie: Drop

18 cookies

2½ cups all-purpose flour
1 teaspoon salt
1 teaspoon baking powder
1 teaspoon baking soda
1¼ cups creamy peanut butter
1 cup vegetable shortening
1 cup granulated sugar
1 cup light brown sugar
1 teaspoon vanilla extract
2 large eggs

Just a glance at the cracked surface of these cookies is all it takes
to identify the flavor: You know they're peanut butter cookies.
These cookies are a bit crisp, and chewy on the inside. Make
sure to take a moment to pause and smell the nutty sweetness as
they bake.

1. Combine the flour, salt, baking powder, and baking soda
   in a large bowl; set aside.

2. Blend the peanut butter, shortening, and sugars in a large
   bowl with a mixer until fluffy. Beat in the vanilla and eggs.

3. Gradually add the flour mixture, mixing until the dough
   is firm. Refrigerate for 15 minutes.

4. Preheat the oven to 350°F. Ready 2 cookie sheets.

5. Shape the dough into 2-inch balls. Place the balls on
   ungreased cookie sheets 2½ inches apart. Bake for 12 to
   16 minutes, until light golden brown. Let cool on a rack
   for 10 minutes before serving.

Variations

Crisscross Chocolate Peanut Butter Cookies: Add 1 cup finely chopped chocolate to the dough after mixing the wet and dry ingredients. After making the balls, press each cookie down with a fork in two directions to make a crisscross pattern.

Peanut Chip and Peanut Cookies: Add ¾ cup peanut chips and ½ cup chopped peanuts to the dough after mixing the wet and dry ingredients.

Chunky Nutty Cookies: Add ¾ cup roasted peanuts to the dough after mixing the wet and dry ingredients.

Sugar-Free Peanut Butter and Jam Cookies ♥

Type of cookie: Rolled cutout

24 cookies

These "sandwich" cookies are so cute, nobody will ever guess they're sugar free (note these do include honey). Spread with peanut butter topping and sugar-free jam, they can be made into large open-faced cookies or smaller closed sandwiches. Prepare the homemade jam in advance. If you are looking for a quick alternative, use store bought jam and prepare as thumbprint cookies (see page 197).

1. Make the jam: Put the strawberries, apple juice, gelatin, cornstarch, and lemon juice in a saucepan over medium heat and cook, stirring, for 15 to 17 minutes, until thickened. Chill until cold, about 4 hours.

2. Make the cookies: Combine the flour, baking powder, and baking soda in a medium bowl; set aside.

3. Beat the applesauce, juice, honey, and peanut butter until smooth.

4. Add the flour mixture and blend until just mixed. Stir in the peanuts. Wrap the dough in plastic wrap and chill for 1 hour.

5. Preheat the oven to 350°F. Line 2 cookie sheets with parchment paper.

Sugar-Free Peanut Butter Cookies

3½ cups all-purpose flour
1 teaspoon baking powder
½ teaspoon baking soda
½ cup unsweetened applesauce
½ cup sugar-free apple juice
¾ cup honey
¾ cup sugar-free peanut butter
¼ cup ground peanuts

Sugar-Free Strawberry Jam

3 cups sliced strawberries
¼ cup sugar-free apple juice
6 ounces unflavored gelatin
1 tablespoon cornstarch
1 teaspoon lemon juice

Topping

1 cup sugar-free strawberry jam
1 cup sugar-free peanut butter
6 tablespoons cream cheese
Black food coloring

Above: Peanut Butter and Jam Cookies.

6. Roll the dough out on a floured work surface to ¼ inch thick. Cut out toast shapes with a knife. Put the shapes on the cookie sheets 1 inch apart and bake for 15 to 17 minutes, until the edges are golden. Transfer to a rack to cool.

7. Spread the jam on half of the cookies and peanut butter on the other half.

8. Put 4 tablespoons of the cream cheese in a pastry bag with a fine tip and pipe the mouth and the white of the eyes. Color the remaining cream cheese black with food coloring. Put it in a pastry bag and pipe the pupils and the eyelashes.

Variations

Almond Butter Cookies: Replace the peanut butter with almond butter and the peanuts with almonds.

Cashew Butter Cookies: Replace the peanut butter with cashew butter and the peanuts with cashews.

2/3 cup all-purpose flour

1 teaspoon ground cinnamon

1/2 teaspoon salt

1/2 teaspoon baking soda

3/4 cup (1 1/2 sticks) butter, softened

1/2 cup granulated sugar

1 large egg

2 tablespoons apple juice

1 teaspoon vanilla extract

3 cups rolled oats (not instant)

1 cup raisins

1 cup walnuts

Oatmeal Raisin Cookies

Type of cookie: Drop

24 large cookies

If you like oatmeal cookies, this may be the most satisfying of the snack classic recipes. It is my idea of a baking chameleon: Swap out the raisins with other dried fruits such as cranberries and apricots, or chocolate chips and toffee, to create an infinite number of flavor variations. To add a delicious dimension to these cookies, top them with Lemon Icing (page 276).

1. Preheat the oven to 350°F. Butter 2 cookie sheets.

2. Combine the flour, cinnamon, salt, and baking soda in a medium bowl; set aside.

Right: Oatmeal Raisin Cookies.

3. Cream the butter and sugar until fluffy. Beat in the egg, then the apple juice and vanilla.

4. Gradually add the flour mixture until well blended. Stir in the oats, raisins, and nuts.

5. Drop 2-tablespoon mounds of dough on the cookie sheets 2½ inches apart. Bake for 10 to 12 minutes, until the edges are golden. Let cool on the pans for 2 minutes. Transfer to a rack to cool.

Variations

Oatmeal Cranberry Molasses Cookies: Replace the apple juice with molasses. Replace the raisins with dried cranberries.

Oatmeal Chocolate Pineapple Cookies: Replace the raisins with chopped dried pineapple and the walnuts with chocolate chips.

Oatmeal Apricot Cookies: Replace the walnuts with chopped dried apricots.

Oatmeal Mango Macadamia Nut Cookies: Replace the raisins with dried mango and the walnuts with chopped macadamia nuts.

Sugar-Free Carob Oatmeal Clusters ♥

Type of cookie: Drop

36 cookies

A friend challenged me to develop an all-natural chocolaty oatmeal cookie with no sugar. Carob is naturally sweeter and lower in cholesterol than chocolate, making it a good substitute in sugar-free recipes. These taste just as good as classic chocolate oatmeal cookies, but slightly different.

1¼ cups all-purpose flour
¼ cup unsweetened carob powder
¼ teaspoon baking soda
½ cup mashed banana
⅓ cup vegetable oil
¼ teaspoon vanilla extract
2 large eggs
¼ cup milk
⅔ cup rolled oats (not instant)
¼ cup unsweetened carob chips
1 cup walnuts, chopped

1. Preheat the oven to 350°F. Grease 2 baking sheets with oil.

2. Combine the flour, carob powder, and baking soda in a medium bowl; set aside.

3. Beat the banana, oil, vanilla, eggs, and milk until creamy.

4. Stir in the flour mixture, then the oats, carob chips, and walnuts.

5. Drop 1-teaspoon mounds of dough on the cookie sheets 2 inches apart. Bake for 8 to 10 minutes, until firm. Let cool on the pans for 5 minutes. Transfer to a rack to cool completely.

Variation

Oatmeal Raisin Clusters (Sugar Free): Omit the carob powder and increase the flour by ¼ cup. Replace the carob chips with raisins.

Vegan Oat Chocolate Chip Cookies ♥

Type of cookie: Drop

24 cookies

Today there is so much interest in vegan baking that vegan cookies appeal to vegans and nonvegans alike. A blend between oatmeal and chocolate chip cookies, these oatmeal chip cookies use banana as the egg substitute, which also adds moistness and richness of the flavor. For more elaborate cookies, top them with Vegan Chocolate Icing.

1. Preheat the oven to 350°F. Line 2 cookie sheets with parchment.

2. Make the oatmeal chip cookies: Combine the banana, oil, orange zest, and vanilla until creamy.

3. Add the flour, oats, chocolate chips, and walnuts and mix well.

4. Drop 1-tablespoon mounds of dough on the cookie sheets 2 inches apart. Bake for 7 to 10 minutes, until the cookies are browned around the edges. Transfer to a rack to cool.

5. Make the vegan chocolate icing: Mix the sugar, cornstarch, cocoa powder, and salt in a medium saucepan. Whisk in the water and cook over medium heat, stirring constantly, until the mixture thickens and comes to a boil. Boil for 1 to 2 minutes, until the icing reduces a bit; then immediately remove from the heat. Stir in the oil and vanilla. Let cool before icing the cookies.

Oatmeal Chip Cookies

½ cup mashed banana
¼ cup vegetable oil
1 teaspoon grated orange zest
½ teaspoon vanilla extract
1 cup all-purpose flour
1 cup rolled oats (not instant)
¾ cup chocolate chips
½ cup walnuts

Vegan Chocolate Icing

1 cup vegan granulated sugar
6 tablespoons cornstarch
4 tablespoons cocoa powder
½ teaspoon salt
1 cup water
2 tablespoons vegetable oil
½ teaspoon vanilla extract

Variations

Oat Raisin Pistachio Cookies: Replace the chocolate chips with raisins
and the walnuts with pistachios.

Oat Cranberry Almond Cookies: Replace the chocolate chips with
chopped fresh cranberries and the walnuts with sliced almonds.

Vegan Ginger Cookies ♥

Type of cookie: Drop

24 cookies

2¼ cups all-purpose flour
2 teaspoons ground ginger
2 teaspoons baking soda
½ teaspoon salt
1 cup dark brown sugar
⅔ cup vegetable oil
¼ cup molasses
½ banana, mashed
1½ tablespoons grated fresh ginger
½ cup diced crystallized ginger

It is very hip to be vegan. I am not a vegan, but I do enjoy
vegan cookies. Vegans tend to admit that their baked goods are
an acquired taste, but I got hooked on them right away. These
banana and ginger cookies have what I call flavor harmony. Their
tropical tastes work great together. Made with three kinds of
ginger, these cookies have depth of flavor and a melt-in-your-
mouth texture. If you prefer sandwich cookies, fill them with the
Vegan Cream Cheese Frosting or Vegan Berry Icing (page 275).
For a ginger-chocolate flavor, top them with Vegan Chocolate
Icing (page 84).

1. Combine the flour, ground ginger, baking soda, and salt
    in a medium bowl; set aside.

2. Beat the brown sugar, oil, molasses, and banana in a
    medium bowl until blended.

3. Stir in the flour mixture until well blended.

4. Add the fresh and crystallized ginger. Refrigerate for at
    least 2 hours.

5. Preheat the oven to 300°F. Grease 2 cookie sheets with oil.

6. Shape the dough into 1-inch balls. Place the balls on
    the cookie sheets about 2 inches apart. Bake for 8 to
    10 minutes, until browned. Let cool on the pans for 5
    minutes. Transfer to a rack to cool completely.

Vegan Substitutes

Vegans don't eat animal products, including milk, butter, eggs, and sometimes honey. Most cookie recipes contain butter (to give them a rich flavor and texture) and eggs (to hold them together). These are replaced with ingredients such as vegetable oil or palm oil and mashed bananas. Milk is replaced with soymilk or coconut milk and juice. Honey is replaced with molasses, maple syrup, or sugar. Cream fillings and icings are made with soymilk, coconut milk, or vegetable shortening. Nut butters, chocolate, nuts, seeds, and dried and fresh fruits are all fine to use in vegan cookies.

Above: Vegan Ginger Cookies.

Variations

Orange Ginger Cookies: Reduce the fresh ginger to 1½ teaspoons. Add 1½ teaspoons grated orange zest. Reduce the crystallized ginger to ¼ cup, and add ¼ cup candied citrus peel; add after the wet and dry ingredients have been mixed.

Ginger Banana Chip Cookies: Delete the crystallized ginger and add ¾ cup chocolate chips to the cookie dough after the wet and dry ingredients have been mixed.

1 cup (2 sticks) butter, softened
1½ cups granulated sugar
1 large egg
¼ cup molasses
2¼ cups all-purpose flour
2 teaspoons baking soda
⅛ teaspoon salt
4½ teaspoons ground ginger
1½ tablespoons grated fresh ginger

Gingersnaps

Type of cookie: Drop

40 cookies

As ginger bakes, it transforms into something truly amazing. These classic small ginger drop cookies are filled with both fresh and ground ginger for a double dose of flavor. To make them extra special, dip them in melted chocolate.

1. Preheat the oven to 350°F. Line 2 cookie sheets with parchment paper.

2. Beat the butter and sugar with a mixer on medium speed until light and fluffy. Mix in the egg and molasses.

3. Add the flour, baking soda, salt, ground ginger, and fresh ginger. Beat on low speed until just combined.

4. Shape the dough into 1-inch balls. Place the balls on the cookie sheets 2 inches apart. Bake for 11 to 14 minutes, until flattened and brown. Let cool completely before removing from the pans.

Variations

Chocolate-Dipped Gingersnaps: Line a cookie sheet with waxed paper. Melt 8 ounces semi-sweet chocolate in a double boiler over simmering water, and whisk until smooth. Dip the gingersnaps halfway into the chocolate. Sprinkle the chocolate with crystallized ginger. Place on the cookie sheet and refrigerate until set.

Gingersnap Raspberry Sandwiches: Spread raspberry jam between the gingersnaps to make sandwiches.

Low-Fat Ginger Cookies ♥

Type of cookie: Drop

30 cookies

In these flavorful low-fat ginger cookies, apple butter—like a highly concentrated applesauce—replaces the butter and also adds a nice texture and flavor.

1. Preheat the oven to 350°F. Line 2 cookie sheets with parchment paper.

2. Combine the flour, baking soda, salt, ginger, cinnamon, cloves, mace, and nutmeg; set aside.

3. Beat the apple butter and sugar until fluffy. Beat in the egg, molasses, and vanilla.

4. Stir in the flour mixture until mixed.

5. Shape 1-inch balls of dough and roll them in the sugar

2 cups all-purpose flour
2 teaspoons baking soda
½ teaspoon salt
1 tablespoon ground ginger
2 teaspoons ground cinnamon
½ teaspoon ground cloves
¼ teaspoon ground mace
¼ teaspoon freshly grated nutmeg
¾ cup apple butter
½ cup brown sugar
1 large egg
¼ cup molasses
1 teaspoon vanilla extract
⅓ cup coarse sugar

to coat lightly. Place the balls on the cookie sheets 2 inches apart. Bake for 8 to 10 minutes, until browned. Let cool on the pans for 3 minutes. Transfer to a rack to cool completely.

Variations

Ginger White Chocolate Chunk Cookies: Add 1 cup white chocolate chunks after the wet and dry ingredients have been mixed.

Ginger Raisin Cookies: Add 1 cup raisins after the wet and dry ingredients have been mixed.

Sugar-Free Butter Cookies ♥

Type of cookie: Drop

24 cookies

2 1/2 cups almond flour
1/2 teaspoon baking powder
1/2 teaspoon salt
1/2 cup (1 stick) butter, cubed
1/4 cup sugar-free apple juice
1 tablespoon vanilla extract

Don't let the name fool you: Sugar-free cookies are not only inherently healthful, but tasty, too. For a sugar-free cookie that's also gluten free, use gluten-free baking powder (page 91); they will be a bit less fluffy, but still delicious. Here they are made plain, but you can make sandwiches by filling them with sugar-free cream cheese filling (page 275).

1. Preheat the oven to 325°F. Line 2 cookie sheets with parchment paper.

2. Combine the almond flour, baking powder, and salt in a food processor or blender, and pulse to mix.

3. Add the butter, juice, and vanilla. Pulse until blended.

4. Drop 1½-tablespoon mounds of dough on the cookie sheets 2 inches apart. Bake for 6 to 8 minutes, until light golden. Transfer to a rack to cool.

Variations

Sugar-Free Cutout Cookies: Increase the almond flour to 3 cups, flatten the dough into a disk and wrap in plastic wrap and refrigerate the dough

Low-Fat Cookies

Cookies can be low in fat and high in scrumptiousness. The goal with low-fat cookies is to cut down on saturated fats. Fruit purees that contain high amounts of pectin are often used in low-fat recipes. These include mashed bananas, applesauce, and pumpkin and prune purees. Pectin behaves similarly to fats by shortening gluten strands and helping the dough rise by trapping air; it delays moisture loss and keeps cookies fresh. Before eliminating all fats in a recipe, try using low-fat versions of cream cheese, peanut butter, and milk. Reducing the number of egg yolks and replacing baking chocolate with cocoa powder are good starts. Unsaturated vegetable oil and nut oils are good lower-saturated-fat alternatives to butter and shortening.

Above: Sugar-Free Butter Cookies.

for 2 hours. Roll out the batch of dough on a work surface dusted with almond flour to ⅛ inch thick. Using a 2-inch round cookie cutter, cut out cookies and place on the cookie sheets 1½ inches apart. Bake as above.

Sugar-Free Orange Butter Cookies: Replace the apple juice with orange juice. Add the grated zest of 1 orange at the same time as the juice.

Low-Fat Lemon Sugar Cutout Cookies ♥

Type of cookie: Rolled cutout

36 cookies

Whipped eggs replace the butter in these lemony sugar cookies. They can be used as a low-fat alternative for any of the cutout cookies in this book.

5 cups all-purpose flour
1¼ tablespoons baking powder
½ teaspoon salt
½ teaspoon ground mace
5 large eggs
1½ cups sugar
1 cup brown sugar
Grated zest of 1 lemon
1 teaspoon lemon juice
Confectioners' sugar
2 large egg whites, beaten

1. Combine the flour, baking powder, salt, and mace in a large bowl; set aside.

2. Beat the eggs with an electric mixer for 3 to 5 minutes, until thick.

3. Add the sugars a little at a time until blended; then beat for an additional 7 to 10 minutes, until fully blended. Add the lemon zest and juice.

4. Gradually add the flour mixture until combined.

5. Divide the dough in half, and wrap in plastic wrap. Refrigerate for 4 to 6 hours.

6. Preheat the oven to 325°F. Line 2 cookie sheets with parchment paper.

7. Unwrap one of the batches of dough and roll it out on a work surface dusted with confectioners' sugar to ⅛ inch thick.

8. Cut the cookies with cookie cutters, and place on the cookie sheets 1½ inches apart. Repeat with second batch of dough.

9. Brush with the egg whites and bake for 12 to 15 minutes, until light golden. Transfer to a rack to cool.

Variations

Chocolate Cutout Cookies: Reduce the flour to 4½ cups. Add ½ cup cocoa powder to the dry ingredients.

Lemon Nut Cookies: Reduce the flour to 4 cups. Add 1 cup ground nuts to the dry ingredients.

Lime Cookies: Replace the lemon zest and juice with lime zest and juice.

Sugar-Free Baking

Sugar serves three purposes in cookies: It sweetens them, it attracts water to give cookies a tender, moist texture, and it helps cookies spread (with the exception of confectioners' sugar, which contains cornstarch and prevents spreading). When less or no sugar is used, you run the risk of dry, crumbly cookies, so the balance of the other ingredients is most important. When I am lowering the sugar content, I prefer to sweeten cookies with natural sweeteners such as honey, maple syrup, fruit juices, and fruits. They are moister and sweeter then sugar replacements.

Cookies

2 cups brown rice flour, or more
   as needed
1½ cups sweet rice flour
1 cup potato starch
1 tablespoon xanthan gum
1½ tablespoons baking powder
1 teaspoon salt
½ cup confectioners' sugar
1 cup granulated sugar
½ cup vegetable shortening
½ cup (1 stick) butter, softened
3 large eggs
6 tablespoons vanilla extract

Topping

Royal Icing (page 274)

How to Make Gluten-Free Baking Powder

Combine:
2 parts cream of tartar
1 part baking soda
1 part cornstarch

Gluten-Free Sugar Cookies ♥

Type of cookie: Rolled cutout

20 cookies

These are the first gluten-free cookies I learned how to make. I experimented a bit with the balance of flours, sugars, and fat and got to this versatile rolled cookie dough. Sometimes I add chocolate chips, nuts, or dried fruit and shape the cookies into balls or make the dough into thumbprint cookies or top them with icing. The baking time for these cutout cookies will depend on the size of the shapes.

1. Combine the rice flours, potato starch, xanthan gum, baking powder, and salt in a medium bowl; set aside.

2. Cream the sugars, shortening, and butter until fluffy. Beat in the eggs and vanilla.

3. Gradually add the flour mixture until combined.

4. Knead the dough on a floured work surface. If it is too sticky, add more brown rice flour; if it is dry, add some water.

5. Divide the dough into 2 balls, wrap in plastic wrap, and refrigerate for 1 hour.

6. Preheat the oven to 325°F. Line 2 cookie sheets with parchment paper.

7. Roll out the dough on a work surface dusted with brown rice flour to ¼ inch thick. Cut out with cookie cutters. Place on the cookie sheets 1½ inches apart. Bake for 8 to 10 minutes, until golden.

8. Decorate with royal icing.

Variations

Gluten-Free Maple Walnut Drop Cookies: Add 2 tablespoons maple syrup along with the eggs and vanilla. Mix with a mixer instead of kneading. Add 1 cup chopped walnuts and to the dough after the wet and dry ingredients have been mixed. Top with cream cheese icing after baking.

Gluten-Free Fruitcake Cookies: Mix with a mixer instead of kneading. Add 1 cup chopped dried fruits to the dough after the wet and dry ingredients have been mixed.

Gluten-Free Pineapple Thumbprints: Shape the dough into 1-inch balls. Press each ball with your thumb to make an indentation. Fill with Pineapple Filling (page 127) and then bake.

Butterscotch Icebox Cookies

Type of cookie: Icebox

28 cookies

Butterscotch flavor develops when butter and brown sugar fuse. These icebox cookies have extra flavor in the form of butterscotch chips and hard butterscotch candy. For the topping, I pool on white chocolate, then pipe on melted butterscotch and semisweet chocolate. When they're finished, choose the fattest one—with the thickest topping—for yourself.

1. Make the cookies: Combine the flour, baking soda, and salt in a medium bowl; set aside.

2. Cream the butter and brown sugar with an electric mixer until fluffy. Beat in the egg and vanilla.

3. Gradually add the flour mixture until well blended.

4. Stir in the butterscotch chips and crushed candy.

5. Shape the dough into a log about 2½ inches in diameter, and wrap in plastic wrap. Chill in the refrigerator for 1 hour.

6. Preheat the oven to 350°F. Butter 2 cookie sheets.

7. Slice the log into ¼-inch disks; then place the cookies on the cookie sheets and chill for 20 minutes. Bake for 12 to 15 minutes, until lightly browned. Transfer to a rack to cool.

2 cups all-purpose flour

1 teaspoon baking soda

½ teaspoon salt

¾ cup (1½ sticks) butter, softened

1 cup light brown sugar

1 large egg

1 teaspoon vanilla extract

1¼ cups butterscotch chips, chopped

¼ cup hard butterscotch candy, crushed

Topping

1 cup white chocolate chips

¾ cup butterscotch chips

¾ cup semisweet chocolate chips

8. Make the topping: Melt the white chocolate chips in a double boiler over simmering water and spoon it onto the tops of the cookies. Melt the butterscotch chips in a double boiler, transfer to a pastry bag with a fine tip, and pipe stripes over the white chocolate. Melt the semisweet chocolate chips in a double boiler, transfer to a pastry bag, and pipe in crosshatched stripes over the butterscotch. Let the cookies sit for 30 minutes to harden.

Variations

Butter Rum Cookies: Replace the vanilla extract with 3 tablespoons rum.

Butterscotch Pecan Cookies: Replace the butterscotch candy with ground pecans. Add ½ cup chopped pecans to the dough along with the butterscotch chips.

Old-Fashioned Butterscotch Cookies: Omit the butterscotch chips and candy. Top the cookies with ½ teaspoon brown sugar before baking. Omit the other toppings.

ENERGY COOKIES AND BARS

In this busy world, it is often hard to sit down for proper meal, so what do we rely on to enrich us? Snacks. These energy cookies and bars are more than just cookies; they are formulated to give you that boost that you need from a snack. Unlike store-bought alternatives, homemade energy cookies and bars are fresh, and *you* get to choose the ingredients. Grains, nuts, and seeds give a protein boost for long-lasting energy, and sweeteners give that quick kick needed to jump-start it.

Wild Honey Bran Protein Bars ♥

Type of cookie: Bar

18 bars

"Don't get love sick." What does that have to do with protein bars? Well, it's a mnemonic for the formula I use when preparing recipes for our backpacking trips to make sure we get enough protein. Take the first letter of each word and apply it to a food category: *D* for dairy, *G* for grain, *L* for legumes (nuts are legumes), and *S* for seeds. If your recipe contains items from any two categories that are next to each other, it is a full protein. These protein bars have grains and nuts, and nuts and seeds—so they're a double full protein. Wrap them up in parchment and take them on the trail.

1. Preheat the oven to 350°F. Grease a 9 x 13-inch baking dish with vegetable oil.

2. Combine the flour, cinnamon, allspice, baking soda, salt, and cereal in a large bowl; set aside.

3. Combine the raisins, apricots, cranberries, almonds, sunflower seeds, and sesame seeds in a medium bowl; set aside.

4. Beat the oil, brown sugar, egg, applesauce, vanilla, and honey until combined.

5. Gradually add the flour mixture until just blended; then stir in the fruit and nut mixture until combined.

6. Spread the dough in the pan and bake for 35 to 40 minutes, until golden. Let cool in the pan; then cut into bars.

1½ cups all-purpose flour

1½ teaspoons ground cinnamon

¼ teaspoon ground allspice

1 teaspoon baking soda

½ teaspoon salt

2½ cups bran or bran oat multi-grain cereal, uncooked

½ cup golden raisins, chopped

¼ cup dried apricots, chopped

¼ cup dried cranberries, chopped

½ cup blanched almonds

¼ cup sunflower seeds

¼ cup sesame seeds

½ cup vegetable oil

⅔ cup brown sugar

1 large egg

1 cup unsweetened applesauce

1 tablespoon vanilla extract

1 tablespoon honey, heated in the microwave for 10 to 15 seconds to thin.

Variation

Tropical Protein Bar: Replace the apricots and cranberries with dried pineapple and mango. Replace the almonds with macadamia nuts and the cinnamon with ground ginger.

Granola Fruit Nut Stars ♥

Type of cookie: Molded or drop

40 cookies

Homemade granola cookies are surprisingly easy to make. First you make the granola, and then you add it to the cookie dough. Here the cookies are bite-size, formed in silicone molds to make a healthful and playful energy pick-me-up. If you don't have shaped molds, prepare these as drop cookies.

1. Preheat the oven to 325°F. Butter a large cookie sheet.

2. Make the granola: Heat the honey, oil, brown sugar, and vanilla in a small saucepan until the sugar is dissolved. Put the oats in a medium bowl and add the honey mixture, tossing to coat.

3. Spread in the baking dish and bake for about 30 minutes, stirring every 10 minutes, until crisp. Let cool.

4. Preheat the oven to 375°F. Ready 2-inch baking molds.

5. Make the cookies: Combine the granola, raisins, apricots, peanuts, almonds, wheat germ, and coconut in a bowl; set aside.

6. Combine the butter and brown sugar in a medium bowl and beat with an electric mixer for 2 minutes.

7. Add the egg, salt, cinnamon, cloves, and allspice, and mix until blended.

8. Gradually add the flour and granola mixture until combined.

9. Dust your hands with flour, and pack tablespoons of

Granola

4½ tablespoons honey

4 tablespoons olive oil

4½ tablespoons brown sugar

2 teaspoons vanilla extract

3 cups rolled oats (not instant)

Cookies

⅓ cup raisins

⅓ cup chopped dried apricots

½ cup peanuts, chopped

½ cup almonds, chopped

⅓ cup wheat germ

½ cup sweetened shredded coconut

14 tablespoons (1 stick plus 6 tablespoons) butter, softened

¾ cup light brown sugar

1 large egg

½ teaspoon salt

1 teaspoon ground cinnamon

¼ teaspoon ground cloves

¼ teaspoon ground allspice

1 cup whole-wheat flour

dough into the molds, or shape into balls. Place the molds on the cookie sheets, or, if you prepared balls, place them on the cookie sheets 2 inches apart. Bake the cookies for 10 to 12 minutes, until golden but not firm. Let cool in the molds or on the pans for 5 minutes. Transfer to a rack to cool completely.

Variations

Granola Seed Nut Cookies: Omit the raisins and apricots and add ⅓ cup chopped walnuts and ⅓ cup sunflower seeds.

Tropical Granola Cookies: Replace the raisins and apricots with dried pineapple and mango and the peanuts with macadamia nuts.

Berry Cashew Granola Cookies: Replace the raisins and apricots with dried cranberries and blueberries. Replace the peanuts with cashews.

Sugar-Free, Low-Fat Cashew Sesame Flax Cookies ♥

Type of cookie: Drop

24 cookies

2 cups cashews
⅓ cup sesame seeds
¼ cup honey
1 cup all-purpose flour
2 teaspoons baking powder
2 tablespoons flaxseed
4 large eggs
3 tablespoons apple juice
1 teaspoon vanilla extract

Honey, sesame, and cashews are natural partners, so if you are looking for a cookie that is a full protein and is sugar free and low fat, I think you will agree that these cookies are winners. The honey sweetens them, and the sesame seeds and flaxseed up the nutty flavor and contribute to a tender texture.

1. Preheat the oven to 200°F for toasting.

2. Combine 1½ cups of the cashews, ¼ cup of the sesame seeds, and the honey in a small bowl, and stir to coat. Spread on a baking sheet and sprinkle with the remaining sesame seeds. Toast for 4 to 7 minutes, until light golden.

3. Preheat the oven to 375°F for baking. Line 2 cookie sheets with parchment paper.

4. Grind the remaining cashews in a food processor or blender. Combine the flour, baking powder, ground cashews, and flaxseed in a medium bowl; set aside.

5. Beat the eggs, juice, and vanilla in a medium bowl.

6. Add the flour mixture to the egg mixture and stir to combine. Stir in the toasted cashew mixture.

7. Drop 1-teaspoon mounds of dough on the cookie sheets 2 inches apart. Press down with a spoon. Bake for 7 to 10 minutes, until firm but not browned. Let cool for 5 minutes before devouring.

Variation
Peanut Flaxseed Cookies: Replace the cashews with peanuts.

Right: Cashew Sesame Flax Cookies.

Dough

1½ cups all-purpose flour

½ teaspoon baking soda

¼ teaspoon salt

¼ cup (½ stick) butter, softened

¼ cup light brown sugar

1 large egg

¼ cup honey

1 teaspoon vanilla extract

Filling

1½ cups pineapple juice

¼ cup light brown sugar

⅓ cup dates, pitted and chopped

⅓ cup fresh or dried figs

⅓ cup walnuts, chopped

Date-Fig-Nut Bites ♥

Type of cookie: Bar

24 cookies

Many of the world's figs and dates are grown about a hundred miles from my house, here in the Southern California desert. I am always developing recipes using the fresh and dried sweets I pick up from local farms. One of these date-fig-nut cookies could easily be a meal in itself. The outer honey cookie dough is filled with dates, figs, and nuts soaked in pineapple juice. For added sweetness, top them with Lemon Icing (page 276).

1. Make the dough: Combine the flour, baking soda, and salt in a medium bowl; set aside.

2. Beat the butter and brown sugar with an electric mixer until fluffy. Add to flour with with egg, honey, and vanilla. Form the dough into a ball, and divide it into two 6-inch-long logs. Wrap in plastic wrap and refrigerate for 1 hour.

3. Make the filling: Put the pineapple juice and brown sugar in a saucepan and heat to dissolve the sugar. Add the dates and figs, and simmer until almost all of the juice is absorbed or evaporated. Let cool. Put in a food processor or blender along with the nuts, and puree until smooth.

4. Preheat the oven to 325°F. Butter 2 cookie sheets.

5. Roll a dough log on a floured work surface to 12 inches long. With a rolling pin, roll to ¼ inch thick, 5 inches wide, and 16 inches long. Spread half of the filling over the dough and roll the dough around it tightly, pressing the edges to seal. Cut the log in half, and transfer to a cookie sheet. Repeat with the second log.

6. Bake for 18 to 22 minutes, until golden. Let cool on the pans for 5 minutes. Transfer to a rack to cool for 20 minutes. With a sharp knife cut the rolls into 1-inch cookies.

Variations

Apricot-Pineapple-Macadamia-Nut Bites: In the filling, replace the dates and figs with dried apricots and pineapple. Replace the walnuts with macadamia nuts.

Chocolate-Date-Fig Bites: In the dough, reduce the flour to 1¼ cups and add ¼ cup cocoa powder. Add 1 cup chocolate chips to the filling along with the dates and figs.

Left: Date Nut Fig Bites.

Zucchini Bites ♥

Type of cookie: Molded or bar

30 minibars

You will be surprised with the cookie possibilities of the zucchini. Prepare this zucchini batter as mini–bar bites, or bake it in a pan as bar cookies. Adding walnuts, coconut, or garden-grown zucchini flowers to the top brings out the healthful flavors baked inside.

1. Preheat the oven to 350°F. Ready a 2-inch silicone mini-bar tray.

2. Combine the flour, oats, salt, baking soda, and nutmeg in a medium bowl; set aside.

3. Blend the butter, oil, brown sugar, honey, and vanilla. Beat in the eggs.

4. Gradually add the flour mixture until combined. Stir in the raisins, coconut, zucchini, and walnuts.

Batter

1¼ cups whole-wheat flour

¾ cup quick oats (not instant)

½ teaspoon salt

1 teaspoon baking soda

¼ teaspoon freshly grated nutmeg

½ cup (1 stick) butter, melted

½ cup vegetable oil

1 cup light brown sugar

½ cup honey

1 teaspoon vanilla extract

2 large eggs, beaten

1 cup raisins

1 cup sweetened shredded coconut

2½ cups shredded zucchini

1 cup walnuts

Topping

Lemon Icing (page 276)

Chopped walnuts

Unsweetened shredded coconut

Veggie Cookies

A good way to sneak veggies into a kid's diet is to include them in cookies. I treat a vegetable like a starch, to structure the cookie. Zucchini, carrots, and sweet potatoes are healthful additions to cookies.

5. Drop the batter into sections of a minibar tray. Bake for 15 to 20 minutes, or until a toothpick inserted in the center comes out clean. Let cool in the pan; then pop out of the tray and top with Lemon Icing, walnuts, and coconut.

Variations

Chocolate Chip Zucchini Bars with Cream Cheese Frosting: Add 1½ cups chocolate chips to the batter after the walnuts. To make bars, butter and flour a 9-inch square baking pan. Spread the mixture evenly in the baking pan. Bake for 35 to 40 minutes. Let cool. Cut into 3-inch squares. Top with Cream Cheese Icing (page 275) instead of Lemon Icing.

Cranberry Zucchini Bars: Add 1 cup chopped cranberries to the batter after the walnuts.

Curry Apple Zucchini Bars: Replace the 1 cup coconut with 1½ cups chopped apples. Add ½ teaspoon curry powder to the dry ingredients. Omit the coconut topping.

Chapter 3

Party Cookies

DINNER PARTY COOKIES

Dinner parties are a lot of fun, but the pressure is always on to shine, especially when it comes to baking. These dinner party cookies are the perfect solution because they are all impressively beautiful and can be prepared ahead of time—so you can enjoy the party. The cookie cups with fresh berries and the ladyfinger cookie trifles and tiramisu are complete desserts on their own. The macaroons and pistachio cookies with rose water work well with pudding, fresh fruit, or ice cream.

Cookie Cups with Cream and Raspberries

Type of cookie: Molded

12 cookie cups

If you're looking for an idea for a dinner party dessert cookie, this is one of your best bets. These almond-flavored cookie cups are filled with berries and whipped cream. They can also be filled with gelato, ice cream, or sorbet. They are baked at a high temperature, so keep an eye on them in the oven to make sure they don't overbake.

1. Put the flour, almonds, and sugar in a food processor or blender and pulse until finely ground.

Cookie Cups

1¼ cups all-purpose flour

⅓ cup almonds

2 tablespoons sugar

½ cup (1 stick) butter, cubed

2 large egg yolks

1 teaspoon almond extract

1 tablespoon cold water

Filling

Whipped Cream (page 275)

1 cup raspberries

2. Add the butter and pulse 4 to 6 times, until the butter is incorporated.

3. Combine the egg yolks, almond extract, and water in a small bowl; then add to the flour mixture and pulse until the mixture forms a ball. Form the dough into 2 disks, wrap in plastic wrap, and refrigerate for 1 hour.

4. Preheat the oven to 400°F. Butter and flour the back side of a cupcake pan.

5. Remove the dough from the refrigerator. If it is too hard to roll out, let it sit for a few minutes. Roll the dough out on a floured surface to ⅛ inch thick. Using a 5-inch round cookie cutter (or a drinking glass), cut out circles.

6. Drape the circles over the cups of the inverted muffin pan. Bake for 6 to 8 minutes, until golden. Let cool on the pan.

7. Prepare the whipped cream and dollop it into the cookie cups. Top with berries. Serve on a plate with a spoon.

Ladyfingers, Peach Berry Trifles, Tiramisu

Type of cookie: Piped

24 ladyfingers, or 12 trifles, or 1 pan of tiramisu

It is no secret that ladyfingers are delicious cookies on their own, but their versatility in other desserts is sometimes overlooked. I like to use them in dinner party desserts to make individual deconstructed fresh fruit trifles and tiramisu. Here I have provided both recipes; you choose. For an extra-chocolaty tiramisu, prepare it with chocolate ladyfingers. The success of your cookie depends on retaining the air bubbles in the mixture. Don't let the dough sit too long from the time it is mixed to the time it is baked or the ladyfingers will spread instead of rise.

1. Preheat the oven to 425°F. Fit a ½-inch tip in a pastry bag. Cut 2 sheets of parchment paper to the size of the cookie sheets and draw lines lengthwise 2½ inches apart. Flip the paper over and put it on the cookie

Ladyfingers

5 large egg yolks

¾ cup granulated sugar

6 large egg whites

1 cup all-purpose flour

¼ cup confectioners' sugar

Trifles

2 cups blueberries

Whipped Cream (page 275)

4 peaches, sliced

Tiramisu

3 large eggs, separated

¼ cup granulated sugar

1 (8-ounce) container mascarpone
  cheese or cream cheese

¼ cup coffee liqueur or amaretto

¼ cup double-strength brewed
  espresso

4 ounces bittersweet chocolate,
  finely chopped

Above right: Peach Berry Trifles.

sheets. You should see the lines through the paper; if you don't, darken them.

2. Make the ladyfingers: Beat the egg yolks and 2 tablespoons of the granulated sugar with an electric mixer for 2 minutes, or until well blended.

3. In a separate bowl with a clean mixer on high speed, beat the egg whites until they form stiff peaks. Gradually add the remaining granulated sugar to the whites and beat until firm peaks form. Fold the egg whites into the egg yolk mixture. Gradually fold in the flour.

4. Put half of the batter into the pastry bag and pipe strips along the lines on the paper 1 inch wide, 4 inches long, and ¾ inch high. Continue with the remaining batter. Dust with confectioners' sugar. Bake for 8 to 10 minutes, until golden. Slide the parchment paper onto racks and let cool.

5. For trifles: Put 2 tablespoons of the blueberries in each of 12 trifle glasses and fill halfway with whipped cream. Add the peaches and more berries on top. Stick two ladyfingers into each glass. There will be extra ladyfingers. If you want to use all the ladyfingers, first line the glasses with ladyfingers, and then put the whipped cream and fruit in the center.

6. For tiramisu: Beat the egg yolks and sugar with an electric mixer until fluffy. Add the cheese and beat until smooth. Stir in 2 tablespoons of the liqueur.

7. In a separate bowl with a clean mixer on high speed, beat the egg whites until stiff and shiny. Fold the egg whites into the cheese mixture.

8. Combine the remaining liquor with the coffee in a small bowl.

9. Line the bottom of a 5 x 11-inch rectangular serving dish with ladyfingers. Brush with the coffee mixture; then spoon one-third of the cheese mixture over the cookies and sprinkle with one-third of the chocolate. Repeat these layers 2 more times. Cover and refrigerate for 2 hours before serving.

Variation

Chocolate Ladyfingers: Reduce the flour by ⅛ cup. Add ¼ cup Dutch-process cocoa powder to the dry ingredients. Dust with cocoa powder instead of confectioners' sugar.

Macaroons

3 large egg whites

½ teaspoon cream of tartar

⅓ cup sugar

1 teaspoon ground ginger

1 tablespoon grated fresh ginger

⅛ teaspoon salt

2 teaspoons vanilla extract

1½ cups sweetened shredded coconut

Topping

1½ cups chopped dark chocolate

2 tablespoons butter

Ginger Chocolate-Dipped Macaroons

Type of cookie: Piped

24 macaroons

The coffee cart at the college where I teach sells macaroons like these that I buy so often, I decided it was time to re-create them at home. I boosted them up a notch to a dinner party treat by adding ginger. These dense, moist, and sweet coconut macaroons are the type you will most commonly find in the United States, although they are originally from Scotland. A slightly different style of macaroon is a common Jewish treat for Passover because it is leavened with only egg whites (page 228). French and Italian macaroons are more like meringues (page 120). If you are lucky enough to own a 1-inch or larger star piping tip, you can pipe the cookie mixture from a pastry bag so the macaroon has a patterned surface. If not, drop the mixture from an ice cream scoop into mounds.

1. Preheat the oven to 325°F. Line 2 cookie sheets with parchment paper.

2. Beat the egg whites until foamy. Add the cream of tartar and continue to beat until soft peaks form.

3. Gradually add the sugar 1 tablespoon at a time until all the sugar is incorporated and the peaks are shiny and stiff.

4. Gently stir in the ground and fresh ginger, salt, vanilla, and coconut, being careful not to deflate the egg whites.

5. Put half of the mixture in a piping bag with a large star tip and pipe onto the baking sheets into 2-inch-wide, 1-inch-tall mounds. Bake for 18 to 22 minutes, until golden brown. Keep an eye on them, being careful not to overbake. Transfer to a rack to cool.

6. Heat the chocolate and butter in a double boiler over simmering water, stirring constantly until melted. Dip the macaroons halfway into the chocolate. Place on waxed paper until set.

Variations

Australian Macaroons: Pipe some of the batter into a mound; then spoon raspberry jam into the center. Pipe more batter over the jam to conceal it. Bake as above.

Almond Coconut Macaroons: Reduce the coconut to 1¼ cups. Add ½ cup ground almonds to the dry ingredients. After dipping the macaroons in chocolate, top with ½ teaspoon sliced almonds while chocolate is still wet.

Vegan Coconut Pistachio Macaroons with Chocolate Icing ♥

Type of cookie: Drop

24 macaroons

These vegan macaroons combine the enticing flavors of coconut, pistachios, banana, and chocolate. They are fantastic on their

Dough

1 large banana, mashed

3 tablespoons sugar

1 teaspoon vanilla extract

1½ cups unsweetened shredded coconut

¼ cup pistachio nuts, chopped

Vegan Chocolate Icing

1 cup vegan sugar

6 tablespoons cornstarch

¼ cup cocoa powder

½ teaspoon salt

1 cup water

2 tablespoons vegetable oil

½ teaspoon vanilla extract

own or dipped in chocolate icing. In this recipe a mashed banana replaces eggs. Since bananas vary in size, if the mixture is too gooey to form into a lump, add more coconut. If it is too firm, add more banana.

1. Preheat the oven to 325°F. Line 2 cookie sheets with parchment paper.

2. Make the dough: Beat the banana, sugar, and vanilla until blended.

3. Stir in the coconut and pistachios to create a moist dough.

4. Drop 1-tablespoon mounds of dough on the cookie sheets 1½ inches apart and bake for 10 to 12 minutes, until light golden around the edges. Transfer to a rack to cool.

5. Make the icing: Combine the sugar, cornstarch, cocoa powder, salt, and water in a medium saucepan. Stir over medium heat until the mixture thickens and starts to boil. Boil for 1 to 2 minutes, until golden. Remove from the heat and stir in the oil and vanilla. Let cool for 5 minutes. If the icing is not of dipping consistency, add more water. Dip the cookies one at a time halfway into the icing and transfer to the rack to harden.

Variations

Vegan Cherry Macaroons: Replace the pistachios with ¼ cup chopped dried cherries.

Vegan Orange Macaroons with Chocolate Orange Icing: Add 1 tablespoon grated orange zest to the dough after the vanilla. In the icing, replace the water with no pulp orange juice.

4 cups all-purpose flour
1 teaspoon salt
½ teaspoon ground cardamom
2 cups (4 sticks) butter, softened
6 ounces cream cheese
1½ cups granulated sugar
1 tablespoon vanilla extract
1 tablespoon rosewater
1 teaspoon lime juice
2 cups chopped pistachios
½ cup Rosewater Icing
¼ cup whole pistachios
Candied Rose Petals (optional)

Pistachio Cookies

Type of cookie: Drop

36 cookies

Rose water gives these pistachio cookies a part Middle Eastern, part Indian flavor. It was the most popular flavoring for cookies in America and Europe, too, before it fell out of fashion and vanilla became widely available in the nineteenth century. This cream cheese dough is also flavored with lime and cardamom and studded with pistachios. I top the cookies with just a bit of Rosewater icing to attach whole nuts after they are baked. For a dinner party, serve the cookies to guests with a bowl of pistachio ice cream. For Valentine's Day, enhance the roses and the Rosewater Icing (page 276) with a topping of Candied Rose Petals (page 277).

1. Combine the flour, salt, and cardamom in a large bowl; set aside.

2. Cream the butter and cream cheese with a mixer until fluffy. Add the sugar, vanilla, rosewater, and lime juice.

3. Gradually add the flour mixture until combined. Stir in the chopped pistachios. Divide the dough into 2 disks, wrap in plastic wrap, and refrigerate for 1 hour.

4. Preheat the oven to 350°F. Line 2 cookie sheets with parchment paper.

5. Shape the dough into 1 ½ -inch balls. Place the balls on the cookie sheets 1½ inches apart and press to flatten. Bake for 15 to 20 minutes, until golden. Transfer to a wire rack to cool.

6. Use the Rosewater Icing to attach the whole pistachios and candied rose petals, if using, to the tops of the cookies.

Left: Pistachio Cookies.

Almond Paste

1 cup water

½ cup granulated sugar

¼ cup corn syrup

1¼ cups ground almonds

1¼ cups confectioners' sugar

Cookies

1½ cups all-purpose flour

½ teaspoon salt

3 large eggs, separated

¾ cup granulated sugar

¾ cup Almond Paste (recipe above)

1 cup (2 sticks) butter, softened

1 teaspoon almond extract

15 drops yellow food coloring

15 drops red food coloring

15 drops green food coloring

¼ cup Dutch-process cocoa powder

1 cup apricot or raspberry preserves

8 ounces bittersweet chocolate, chopped

⅔ cup chocolate sprinkles

Seven-Layer Cookies

Type of cookie: Bar

24 cookies

On my visits back home to New York, when the tray of Italian cookies comes out after dinner, the seven-layer cookies are the ones I snatch. I love them so much, I had to learn how to make them at home. They're easier than they look: You essentially make a big layer cake and then cut it into cookie bars. This recipe is made with homemade almond paste, just in case you can't find it in the store. Fill the cookies with either apricot preserves or raspberry preserves.

1. Preheat the oven to 350°F. Butter four 8-inch square baking pans and line the bottoms with parchment paper, leaving an overhang on two ends of the pan. This will make it easier for you to remove the layers intact later. Butter the paper.

2. Make the almond paste: Put the water, granulated sugar, and corn syrup in a saucepan over medium heat and stir until the sugar is dissolved; set aside.

3. Put the almonds and confectioners' sugar in a food processor or blender and pulse to combine. Gradually add the sugar syrup and pulse until combined; set aside.

4. Make the cookies: Combine the flour and salt in a medium bowl and set aside.

5. Beat the egg whites with an electric mixer until stiff peaks form. Gradually add ¼ cup of the sugar and beat until stiff and glossy.

6. Beat in the almond paste and the remaining sugar.

7. Add the butter, egg yolks, and almond extract. Beat to combine.

8. Fold in the flour mixture.

9. Divide the batter among 4 bowls. Stir the yellow food

coloring into one batch, red food coloring into another, green food coloring into another, and cocoa powder into the last.

10. Pour each batter into a baking pan. Bake 8 to 10 minutes, until set. Transfer the layers, with the parchment paper, to racks to cool.

11. Stack the layers, spreading ⅓ cup preserves between layers.

12. Wrap tightly with plastic wrap, pressing the layers together, and refrigerate for 4 hours.

13. Heat the chocolate in a double boiler over simmering water, stirring constantly until melted. Spread the chocolate in a thin layer on top of the stacked cookie layers, and top with sprinkles. Refrigerate for 1 hour, or until the chocolate hardens.

14. While the layers are cold, cut them into 2-inch strips, and then cut the strips into 1¼-inch cookies.

TEA PARTY COOKIES

Tea parties are favorites of little girls but are tons of fun for adults, too. I adapted the practice of having tea with my friends years ago at the loft building where I lived in downtown Los Angeles. We would all work really hard all day, and then at 4 P.M. we'd take a break and converge for home-baked cookies, tea, and conversation. Nowadays I schedule business meetings over high tea at trendy hotels around town and learn about all of the tasty treats traditionally served at tea. In this section you'll find delicate tea cookies flavored with herbs, and cookies that are ideal for savoring with tea. For a more formal tea party you can serve madeleines, marzipan fruit cookies, lemon meringues, and lemon champagne buttercream cookies that have a striking presentation.

Chocolate-Dipped Madeleines.

Chocolate-Dipped Madeleines

Type of cookie: Molded

24 madeleines

2 large eggs

½ cup sugar

Grated zest of 1 lemon

½ teaspoon vanilla extract

½ cup (1 stick) butter, melted and
cooled

1 cup sifted cake flour

Chocolate Glaze (page 277)

½ cup chopped white chocolate

1 tablespoon butter

Madeleines are tender French tea cakes that are made in a special shell-shaped pan. They were the ultimate tea cake in Victorian times and were later made famous by Proust, whose narrator in *Remembrance of Things Past* experiences an involuntary memory triggered by a few tea-soaked crumbs of a madeleine. Here I dip them in chocolate and then pipe French-inspired patterns over them in white chocolate. Refer to the patterns on page 44 or create your own. If you don't have a madeleine mold, bake them in small muffin pans.

1. Preheat the oven to 375°F. Butter 2 madeleine molds. Line a baking sheet with waxed paper.

2. Beat the eggs, sugar, lemon zest, and vanilla with an electric mixer for 2 to 3 minutes, until light and fluffy.

3. Add the butter and flour and beat until the mixture thickens.

4. Spoon 1-teaspoon mounds of the batter into the molds; *do not spread.*

5. Bake for 12 to 15 minutes, until the cakes are golden. Remove from the pans and transfer to racks to cool.

6. Dip the madeleines in the Chocolate Glaze, and set aside on waxed paper to harden. Heat the white chocolate and butter in a double boiler over simmering water, stirring constantly until melted. Transfer to a pastry bag with a fine tip, and pipe patterns over the chocolate glaze. Set aside until hardened.

Variations

Green Tea Madeleines: Matcha powder is a green tea powder added to flavor baked goods in Japan. It can be found in Asian groceries. Add 1½ teaspoons matcha powder to the batter. Omit the chocolate glaze and white chocolate. Drizzle cooled madeleines with honey.

Chocolate Madeleines: Reduce the flour to ¾ cups. Add ⅓ cup cocoa powder to the dry ingredients.

Marzipan Fruit Cookies

Type of cookie: Rolled cutout

24 cookies

Marzipan is an amazingly powerful old-fashioned candy that has been reinterpreted throughout the ages. Here is a colorful collection of marzipan fruits on top of tartlike cookies filled with almond buttercream. Make your own marzipan from scratch or purchase at cake decorating supply stores.

1. Line 2 cookie sheets with parchment paper.

2. Roll the dough out to ¼ inch thick on a floured cutting board. Cut into shapes using a tart pan or cookie cutters. Poke holes in the surface with a fork to prevent bubbles from forming as the cookies bake. Place on the cookie sheets 2 inches apart, cover, and refrigerate for 20 minutes.

3. Preheat the oven to 350°F.

4. Bake for 14 to 18 minutes, until golden. Transfer to a rack to cool.

5. Make the marzipan: Combine the almonds, confectioners' sugar, and superfine sugar in a bowl and mix well.

6. Add the lemon juice, almond extract, and egg. Mix well; then gather together with your fingers to form a ball.

7. Knead the marzipan until smooth on a surface lightly dusted with confectioners' sugar. Color the marzipan with food coloring as desired and form into marzipan fruits (see below).

8. Put the buttercream in a piping bag with a star tip and pipe it in a spiral in the center of each cookie. Set the marzipan fruits on top.

Cookies and Toppings

Chinese Sesame and Almond
  Cookie dough (page 232)
Almond Buttercream Frosting
  (page 275)

Marzipan

2¼ cups almonds, finely ground
1 cup confectioners' sugar
1 cup superfine sugar
1 teaspoon lemon juice
½ teaspoon almond extract
1 large egg
Food coloring

Marzipan Fruits

BANANAS

1. Roll yellow marzipan into a tiny ball.

2. Then roll it into a banana shape, pressing to taper one edge, and bending it slightly.

3. Square off the thick end by pinching it with your fingers. Let it dry for 1 hour.

4. Paint it with green and brown food coloring depending on how ripe you would like it to look.

STRAWBERRIES

1. Roll red marzipan into a tiny ball, and green marzipan into a smaller ball. Taper one side of the red ball to make it look like a strawberry.

2. Roll the strawberry over a fine grater to texture the surface.

3. Shape the green ball into a four-pointed star to look like a hull. Flatten and attach it to the top of the strawberry.

ORANGES

1. Roll orange marzipan into a tiny ball.

2. Roll the ball over a fine grater or use a toothpick to texture the surface.

3. Press a clove into the orange to make an indented star-shaped pattern.

LEMONS AND LIMES

1. Roll yellow or green marzipan into a tiny ball.

2. Taper both ends of the ball to make it resemble a lemon or lime.

3. Roll the ball over a fine grater to texture the surface or make dents with a toothpick.

4. Use a toothpick to create indentations in the tapered ends.

CHERRIES

1. Roll red marzipan into a tiny ball.

2. Make a groove in the side of the cherry.

3. Roll brown marzipan and form into a stem.

BLACKBERRIES AND RASPBERRIES

1. Form red or purple marzipan into an oblong berry shape.

2. Create the berry pattern with an embossing tool or toothpick.

Herb and Spice Cookies

Type of cookie: Icebox
24 cookies

Herb-scented and spiced icebox cookies are simple and sophisticated, and a great accompaniment to a cup of tea. Prepare the dough and divide it into two batches so you can add the herbs or spices of your choice to each batch. You can also mix and match. These are plain, but you can also top them with Lemon Icing (page 276) and Sugared Flowers (page 277) if you'd like a fancier cookie.

1. Make the basic dough: Combine the flour, baking powder, and salt in a food processor or blender.

2. Add the butter, and pulse until the mixture resembles coarse meal. Add the egg and sugar, and pulse until the dough gathers into a ball.

3. Divide the dough into 2 batches. Knead the herbs and spices of your choice into each.

Dough
1⅔ cups all-purpose flour
1 teaspoon baking powder
⅛ teaspoon salt
½ cup (1 stick) butter, cubed
1 large egg
¾ cup sugar

For ½ Batch Fennel Cookies
½ teaspoon ground fennel
1 teaspoon fennel seeds

For ½ Batch Rosemary Cookies
1 teaspoon fresh rosemary, finely chopped

For ½ Batch Mint Cookies

1 teaspoon minced fresh mint leaves

1 teaspoon fresh mint flowers

For ½ Batch Anise Cookies

1 teaspoon anise seeds

For ½ Batch Lavender Cookies

1 teaspoon fresh lavender, finely chopped

For ½ Batch Cardamom Cookies

1 teaspoon ground cardamom

For ½ Batch Caraway Cookies

1 teaspoon caraway seeds

For ½ Batch Marigold Cookies

¼ cup fresh marigold petals

For ½ Batch Pepper Cookies

½ teaspoon ground black pepper

¼ teaspoon ground white pepper

4. Form the dough into 2 logs about 2 inches in diameter. Wrap in plastic wrap and freeze for 2 hours.

5. Preheat the oven to 350°F. Line 2 cookie sheets with parchment paper.

6. Slice the logs into ½-inch cookies. Place on the cookie sheets 1 inch apart. Bake for 8 to 10 minutes, until golden. Let cool on the pans for 5 minutes. Transfer to a rack to cool completely.

Right: Herb and Spice Cookies (with tea).

1½ cups all-purpose flour

¼ teaspoon salt

2 tablespoons finely ground
   chai-spiced tea

1 cup (2 sticks) butter, softened

½ cup confectioners' sugar

1 large egg

1 tablespoon grated lemon zest

1 large egg white, lightly beaten

Masala Chai Tea Cookies

Type of cookie: Rolled cutout

30 cookies

Flavored with chai tea and lemon, these are really tasty cookies for a tea party. Chai, from India, is not a particular tea but a black tea blended with various spices, most prominently black pepper, cardamom, and cinnamon. Vary the tea to change the flavor. Grind the tea leaves in a spice grinder.

1. Combine the flour, salt, and ground tea in a bowl; set aside.

2. Beat the butter and confectioners' sugar until blended. Beat in the egg and lemon zest.

3. Gradually add the flour mixture until well blended. Wrap in plastic wrap and refrigerate for 30 minutes.

4. Preheat the oven to 325°F. Butter 2 cookie sheets.

5. Roll the dough out to ¼ inch thick, and cut with cookie cutters. Place on the cookie sheets 1½ inches apart. Brush with the egg white.

6. Bake for 10 to 12 minutes, until golden. Transfer to a rack to cool.

Variations

Earl Grey Tea-Cake Cookies: Replace the chai-spiced tea with finely ground Earl Grey tea. Replace the lemon zest with orange zest.

Green Tea-Cake Cookies: Matcha powder is a green tea powder added to flavor baked goods in Japan. It can be found in Asian groceries Replace the chai-spiced tea with 1½ tablespoons matcha powder.

Meringues

4 large egg whites

1 cup superfine sugar

1 teaspoon lemon juice

Filling

1 cup granulated sugar

3 tablespoons cornstarch

⅛ teaspoon salt

3 large egg yolks, lightly beaten

1 cup water

5 tablespoons lemon juice

1½ tablespoons grated lemon zest

1½ tablespoons butter, melted

Lemon-Filled Meringues

Type of cookie: Piped

20 cookies

Meringues are made of just two ingredients and a flavoring. With no butter, flour, or leavener, their soft, melt-in-your-mouth texture is produced by nothing more than beaten egg whites and sugar. These, however, have lemon filling hidden on the inside.

1. Preheat the oven to 250°F. Line 2 cookie sheets with parchment paper. Fit a piping bag with a large plain tip.

2. Make the meringues: Beat the egg whites in a medium bowl until stiff.

3. Add 1 tablespoon of the superfine sugar, and beat until stiff and shiny. Gradually add the remaining sugar and the lemon juice.

4. Spoon the mixture into the piping bag. With half of the batter, pipe 1½-inch round mounds on the cookie sheets. With the other half, pipe spiral towers that gradually get smaller and form a point at the top.

5. Bake for 50 minutes to 1 hour, until dry. Let cool on the pans.

6. Make the filling: Combine the sugar, cornstarch, and salt in a medium saucepan. Add the egg yolks, water, and lemon juice. Stir over low heat until thick. Remove from the heat and add the lemon zest and butter. Let cool.

7. Make a small hole in the center of the flat side of a meringue mound. Using a pastry bag, fill the holes with lemon cream. Attach a tower to hide the filling.

Variations

Chocolate Meringues: Before beating, add 3 tablespoons cocoa powder to the meringue mixture. Replace the lemon juice with vanilla. Replace the filling with 4 ounces melted semisweet chocolate.

Peppermint Meringues: Replace the lemon juice with peppermint extract. Fill with mint cream (page 71).

Polenta Cookies with Chocolate Mascarpone Cream

Type of cookie: Piped

18 cookies

Polenta is like cornmeal, but its coarse grain adds a richer texture. These cookies can be served plain with a cup of coffee or tea, or as a sandwich, with a filling of mascarpone cream.

1. Preheat the oven to 325°F. Line 2 cookie sheets with parchment paper. Fit a pastry bag with a ½-inch plain tip.

2. Make the cookies: Beat the butter and sugar until light and fluffy. Add the salt, lemon juice, vanilla, and lemon zest. Add the whole egg and egg yolk and mix until blended.

3. Gradually add the flour and polenta until just mixed. Put the dough in the pastry bag. Press out strips 3½ inches long on the cookie sheets 1½ inches apart. Bake for 20 to 25 minutes, until golden. Transfer to a rack to cool.

4. Make the filling: Heat the chocolate in a double boiler over simmering water, stirring constantly until melted. Let cool.

5. Combine the mascarpone, sugar, and cocoa powder in a small bowl. Stir into the melted chocolate.

6. Spread a thin layer of filling on half of the cookies, and top with the remaining cookies. Refrigerate until ready to serve.

Cookies

1 cup (2 sticks) butter, softened
¾ cup sugar
¼ teaspoon salt
1 teaspoon lemon juice
½ teaspoon vanilla extract
Grated zest of 2 lemons
1 large egg
1 large egg yolk
1¾ cups all-purpose flour
⅔ cup cornmeal polenta

Filling

2 ounces bittersweet chocolate
1 cup mascarpone
1 tablespoon granulated sugar
1 tablespoon cocoa powder

Variation

Rosemary Polenta Cookies: Add 1 tablespoon finely chopped rosemary along with the polenta to the cookie dough. Serve without the filling.

Lemon Champagne Buttercream Cookies

Type of cookie: Drop

18 cookies

Long after the food is gone, memories from the time spent with friends remain. I have a very good memory when it comes to details about what I made or ate on specific occasions. These cookies were one of the first recipes I ever created and the first buttercream flowers that I ever piped, for a tea party more then twenty years ago. They may look fancy, but they are simple to make, and a perfect recipe for a beginning baker and decorator.

Cookies

1½ cups all-purpose flour
¼ teaspoon salt
⅔ cup butter, softened
1¼ cups granulated sugar
2 tablespoons lemon juice

Lemon Icing (page 276),
  made thin enough for dipping

Champagne Buttercream Icing

¼ cup vegetable shortening
¾ cup (1½ sticks) butter, softened
3 tablespoons champagne, or more
  if needed
4½ cups confectioners' sugar
Food coloring

1. Line 2 cookie sheets with parchment paper. Prepare a cooling rack with parchment underneath.

2. Combine the flour and salt in a bowl and set aside.

3. Beat the butter and sugar until creamy. Stir in the lemon juice.

4. Gradually add the flour mixture, stirring until incorporated. Shape the dough into balls about 1½ inches in diameter. Place the balls on the cookie sheets 2 inches apart, flattening the bottoms. Cover and refrigerate for 30 minutes.

5. Preheat the oven to 300°F.

6. Bake for 20 to 25 minutes, until lightly browned. Transfer to a rack to cool.

7. Dip the cookies in the Lemon Icing and place them on the rack, allowing the icing to drip to the parchment below. Let sit for 30 minutes to dry.

8. Make the champagne buttercream icing: Beat the shortening and butter until smooth. Beat in the champagne. Slowly add the confectioners' sugar. If necessary, add additional champagne to make the frosting piping consistency.

9. Divide the buttercream among different bowls and add food coloring to each as desired.

10. Decorate the cookies as desired.

To Make a Rose
Using a flat tip, first pipe a dot as the base. Starting at the center, add petals that stand straight up, making a circle around the center in overlapping segments as you go. To make different shaped roses, vary the size of the segments, making them small in the center and larger toward the perimeter.

To Make a Pansy
Using a flat tip, first pipe a dot as the base. Use a flat tip and make the petals flush with the surface of the base. Add dots to the center.

To Make Leaves for the Rose and Pansy

Using green icing and a flat tip, radiate the frosting from the flower. The leaves can surround the entire flower or you can add just a few.

Variation

Hazelnut Buttercream Cookies: Replace the lemon juice in the cookie dough with 2 teaspoons vanilla extract. Add 1 cup ground hazelnuts to the dry ingredients. Replace the lemon juice in the icing with warm water and add 1 teaspoon vanilla extract. Add ¼ cup ground hazelnuts to the buttercream.

SUMMER PARTY COOKIES

The cookies of summertime are just as good as summer itself. Watermelon cookies and ginger peach cookies are ideal ways to pack summer flavor for a picnic party at the beach, and hula girl cookies make the ultimate tiki party. I am a happy camper, and since my birthday falls in the summer I celebrate with my favorite treat—s'mores out in the woods. Sole mates, cookies, sorbet and ice cream that are made into pies, sorbet-filled cookie cones, and chocolate minty pops are all cookie desserts that are perfect for a late-night summertime barbeques.

Hula Girl and Hibiscus Flower Cookies

Type of cookie: Rolled cutout

12 cookies

> I love everything Hawaiian. I was proposed to in Hawaii, much of our sugar comes from there (and how would we make cookies without that?), and I am constantly blown away by the beauty of the islands. And I love the tropical-Polynesian-kitsch-Americana aspects of the place too. When I am not there I pretend I am by having tiki parties, and they always feature cookies like these. If you want to offer a selection of even more Hawaiian cookies, consider adding Pineapple Cookies (page 127) and White Chocolate Macadamia Cream Cookies (page 66) to the mix.

Cookies

1½ cups all-purpose flour

2 teaspoons baking powder

⅛ teaspoon salt

½ cup (1 stick) butter, softened

1 cup granulated sugar

1 teaspoon vanilla extract

2 large eggs

Food coloring

Topping:

Royal Icing (page 274)

Green sugar

Hula Girl and Hibiscus Flower Cookies.

1. Combine the flour, baking powder, and salt in a medium bowl; set aside.

2. Beat the butter and sugar until creamy. Stir in the vanilla.

3. Add the eggs and beat until just blended.

4. Add the flour mixture and stir to make a soft dough. Divide the dough into batches; leave some plain, and color small batches with food coloring. I used yellow, orange, blue, red, and green. Wrap in plastic wrap and refrigerate for 30 minutes, or until firm.

5. Preheat the oven to 350°F. Line 2 cookie sheets with parchment paper.

6. Roll the doughs out to ¼ inch thick on a floured work surface. Use a utility knife to cut out the hula girls and flowers. Place the shapes on the cookie sheets 1½ inches apart. Bake for 12 to 14 minutes, until golden around the edges. Let cool on the pans for 10 minutes, or until the cookies are firm. Transfer to a rack to cool.

7. Divide the royal icing into small batches, and color it green, skin tone, orange, yellow, black, and red. With a piping bag, first draw the hair, then the skirt. Sprinkle the skirt with green sugar and let dry completely to prevent bleeding.

8. Fill in the face, skin, feet, and flowers. Pipe green lines to create the grass skirt.

Cookies

1 cup dried pineapple, chopped
3 cups all-purpose flour
2¼ cups (4½ sticks) butter, softened
1 cup confectioners' sugar
Grated zest of 1 orange
Royal Icing (page 274)
Food coloring

Pineapple Filling (optional)

3 pineapples, peeled, cored, and cut into chunks
1 cup granulated sugar
½ teaspoon ground cinnamon
¼ teaspoon ground cloves
⅓ cup light corn syrup

Pineapple Cookies

Type of cookie: Rolled cutout sandwich
24 unfilled cookies or 12 sandwiches

Pineapples, the symbol of hospitality, make these shortbread cookies extra-flavorful and festive for a tiki party or luau. The pineapple filling in the sandwich cookies adds another hit of pineapple flavor.

1. Make the cookies: Put the pineapple and flour in a food processor and pulse until finely chopped; set aside.

2. Beat the butter, confectioners' sugar, and orange zest until fluffy.

3. Add the flour mixture and stir until blended. Form into 2 balls and wrap in plastic wrap. Refrigerate for 1 hour.

4. Preheat oven to 325°F. Line 2 cookie sheets with parchment paper.

5. Roll one ball of dough out to ¼ inch thick on a lightly floured surface.

6. Cut out pineapple shapes (an oval with spiky leaves coming out the top) with pineapple cookie cutters or a utility knife, and prick the cookies in a few places with a fork. Place the shapes on the cookie sheets 1½ inches apart. Bake for 17 to 20 minutes, until just lightly browned. Let cool on the pans for 5 minutes. Transfer to a rack to cool completely.

7. Divide the royal icing in 3 batches and color yellow, light brown and green. With a medium writing tip, pipe an oval outline with the yellow icing and fill with yellow icing. With a medium writing tip pipe a green outline on the spiky leaves and fill with green icing. Let dry. With a small writing tip, pipe a gridded crosshatched pineapple pattern over the yellow icing. Outline the leaves with remaining light brown icing. Let dry.

8. Make the filling, if desired: Pulse the pineapple for 10 to 20 seconds in a food processor. Drain off ¾ of the juice.

9. Put the pineapple, sugar, cinnamon, and cloves in a saucepan. Cook over low heat, stirring frequently, until thick, about 5 minutes.

10. Add the corn syrup and cook until the filling thickens further and is glossy, about 7 minutes. Remove from the heat and refrigerate for 3 hours to cool.

11. Assemble the cookies into sandwiches by spreading half of the cookies with the filling and topping them with the remaining cookies.

Graham Crackers and S'mores

Type of cookie: Cutout, sandwich

24 graham crackers, 12 s'mores

S'mores are even better than you might remember, especially when made with these homemade graham crackers. Graham flour is a type of wheat flour with a coarse grain. You can use all whole-wheat flour, but the crackers will have a slightly different

Graham Crackers

1½ cups whole-wheat flour
1¼ cups graham flour
½ teaspoon salt
½ teaspoon baking soda
½ teaspoon ground cinnamon
¾ cup (1½ sticks) butter, cubed
⅓ cup granulated sugar
¼ cup brown sugar
¼ cup honey
1 teaspoon vanilla extract
1 large egg

S'mores

6 milk chocolate bars, 1.5 ounce
    each
2 cups minimarshmallows
1½ cups milk chocolate chips

texture. Make the toasted marshmallows for s'mores in the oven set to broil or toast the marshmallows in a fireplace or over an open fire.

1. Make the graham crackers: Combine the flours, salt, baking soda and cinnamon in a medium bowl; set aside.

2. Beat the butter and sugars with an electric mixer until fluffy. Add the honey, vanilla, and egg. Beat until combined.

3. Gradually add the flour mixture and stir until it is incorporated. Wrap the dough in plastic wrap and refrigerate for 45 minutes.

4. Preheat the oven to 350°F. Butter 2 cookie sheets.

5. Roll the dough out to a rectangle ¼ inch thick on a floured work surface.

6. Measure and mark 3-inch squares. Cut with a pastry cutter. Place the squares on the cookie sheets 2 inches apart. Prick patterned dots with a fork and stamp "Happy Camper" with an alphabet rubber stamps into half of the crackers.

7. Bake for 10 to 12 minutes, until lightly browned. Let cool on the pans for 5 minutes. Transfer to a wire rack to cool further.

8. Make the s'mores: Preheat the oven on broil.

9. Arrange half of the graham crackers on a cookie sheet. Top each with ½ chocolate bar.

10. Arrange 2 to 3 tablespoons marshmallows on each cracker. Place the cookie sheet on the top rack and broil until lightly toasted. Keep a careful watch not to burn the cookies and marshmallow. This will take between 20 seconds and 2 minutes depending on your oven. Remove immediately. Top with remaining crackers and press together.

11. Heat the chocolate chips in a double boiler over simmering water, stirring until melted. Dip the s'mores in the chocolate and place on a rack to harden.

Variation

Peanut Butter Graham Crackers and S'mores: Reduce the butter in the crackers to 10 tablespoons and add 2 tablespoons peanut butter along with the butter to the dough. Before placing the chocolate bar on the crackers, spread them with peanut butter. Spread peanut butter on the bottom of the top cracker, too.

Below: S'mores.

Ginger Cookie Cones with Sorbet

Type of cookie: Hand shaped

12 cones

These rather fancy homemade ginger cookie cones filled with sorbet make a nice light summer party treat. I avoid the precision of wrapping a perfect cone by sealing the tip of the cone and plugging the bottom with icing or peanut butter. These cookie cones also taste really good filled with ice cream, gelato, or buttercream frosting

1. Preheat the oven to 350°F. Butter 2 cookie sheets. Butter a rolling pin. Prepare a pastry bag with a large tip.

2. Combine the flour, salt, and ginger in a medium bowl; set aside.

3. Beat the butter and sugar until fluffy. Beat in the egg whites and vanilla.

4. Scoop the dough into the pastry bag and pipe ovals on the cookie sheets about 2½ inches long and 3 inches apart.

5. Bake for 6 to 8 minutes, until golden around the edges. Drape the hot cookies over the rolling pin one at a time, first forming a round, then removing it immediately to shape it further into a cone by overlapping the edges and pinching the tip to seal. Let cool, and bake more batches as needed.

6. Fill the bottom of each cone with ½ teaspoon White Buttercream Frosting. Scoop in the sorbet.

Variation

Chocolate Cookie Cones: Omit the ginger. Add ⅓ cup cocoa powder to the dry ingredients. Fill the cones with Almond Buttercream Frosting (page 275).

Watermelon Cookies

Type of cookie: Icebox

48 cookies

Real watermelon flavor is hard to capture in cookies; the best way to get the flavor is to use watermelon drink mix or crushed watermelon-flavored hard candies. These cookies are very candylike. I like to slice mine into rounds, but half rounds and wedges also work.

1. Dissolve the drink mix in the milk.

2. Combine the flour, baking powder, and salt in a medium bowl; set aside.

3. Beat the butter and sugar until fluffy. Beat in the egg, vanilla, and the milk mixture.

3 tablespoons powdered watermelon-flavored drink mix, or ½ cup
crushed watermelon hard candies
2 tablespoons warm milk
1½ cups all-purpose flour
1 teaspoon baking powder
⅛ teaspoon salt
½ cup (1 stick) butter, softened
¾ cup sugar
1 large egg
1 teaspoon vanilla extract
3 drops red food coloring
3 drops green food coloring
¼ cup chocolate chips, chopped
2 large egg whites, lightly beaten

4. Gradually add the flour mixture, stirring until blended. Divide the dough into 2 batches, one larger than the other. Mix the red food coloring into the larger batch and the green food coloring into the smaller batch. Mix the chocolate chips into the red batch.

5. Form the red dough into a 12-inch log. Brush with the egg whites. Roll the green dough out into a rectangle 12 inches long by the circumference of the log. Wrap the green dough around the red dough. Press the seal together. Wrap in plastic wrap and refrigerate for 1 hour.

6. Preheat the oven to 325°F. Line 2 cookie sheets with parchment paper.

7. Slice the log into ¼-inch rounds. Place the rounds on the cookie sheet 1½ inches apart and bake for 8 to 10 minutes, until firm. Let cool on the pans for 5 minutes. Transfer to a rack to cool further.

Mint Chip Ice Cream Pops

Type of cookie: Icebox cookie pop
24 cookies, 12 pops

Brownie Cookie dough (page
78), made with 1 teaspoon mint
extract
1 (1.75-quart) box mint chip ice
cream

These super-cool melt-in-your-mouth cookie pops are deliciously simple to make. I like making all ice cream sandwich pops bite size so they are all eaten up before the ice cream has a chance to melt. Freezing the pops after the stick is inserted is very important: It ensures that the ice cream gets a good grip on the stick. If you want to explore the world of ice pops further, look for my book *Pops! Icy Treats for Everyone* and visit icypops.com.

1. Roll the dough into 2 long, rounded—but sort of irregular-shaped—logs about 1½ inches across, wrap in plastic wrap, and freeze for 1 hour.

2. Preheat the oven to 325°F. Line 2 cookie sheets with parchment paper.

3. Slice the logs with a sharp knife into ¼-inch-thick

cookies. Place on the cookie sheets 1½ inches apart, and bake for 7 to 10 minutes. Transfer to a rack to cool.

4. Place half of the cookies on a work surface facedown, and top with a scoop of ice cream. Cover with the remaining cookies placed faceup. Gently press the sandwich together. Insert a short stick into the ice cream, and freeze for 1 hour to harden.

Mandarin Cookie dough (page 172)

Orange Glaze
¼ cup (½ stick) butter, softened
2 cups confectioners' sugar
1½ tablespoons grated orange zest
¼ cup freshly squeezed orange juice

Filling
1 pint Orange sherbet
1 pint Vanilla ice cream

Creamsicle Cookie Pops

Type of cookie: Icebox cookie pops
24 cookies, 12 pops

The name of these cookies, based on the ice cream favorite, says it all.

1. Preheat the oven to 300°F. Butter 2-inch minimuffin cups.

2. Press the dough into the bottoms of the muffin cups to ¼ inch thick. Bake for 5 to 7 minutes, until the edges are golden. Flip the cookies out onto a rack to cool.

3. Make the orange glaze: Beat the butter and confectioners' sugar until fluffy. Mix in the orange zest and juice, stirring until the mixture reaches the desired spreading consistency, adding more orange juice or sugar if necessary. Spread on the cookies and let dry.

4. Place half of the cookies on a work surface facedown, and top each with a small scoop of ice cream and a small scoop of sherbet. Cover with remaining cookies faceup. Gently press the sandwiches together. Insert a short ice cream stick in the ice cream, and freeze for 1 hour to harden.

Variation

Orange Rum Cinnamon Cookies: Add 1 teaspoon ground cinnamon to the dry ingredients, 2 tablespoons rum to the wet ingredients. Use rum raisin ice cream instead of vanilla.

Cookies

2¾ cups all-purpose flour
1 teaspoon baking soda
½ teaspoon salt
1 cup (2 sticks) butter, softened
¼ cup granulated sugar
½ cup light brown sugar
1 large egg
¼ cup peach nectar
½ cup peach preserves
1 teaspoon grated fresh ginger
¾ cup dried peaches, chopped
¼ cup candied ginger, chopped

Peach Glaze

¼ cup peach nectar
1½ cups granulated sugar

Topping

2 tablespoons candied ginger,
   chopped

Ginger Peach Cookies

Type of cookie: Drop

36 cookies

In these extra-tasty cookies, pieces of candied ginger soften while baking and impart a spicy sharpness. Sweetened with peach preserves and nectar, they are perfect to pack for a summertime picnic party.

1. Preheat the oven to 300°F. Line 2 cookie sheets with parchment paper.

2. Combine the flour, baking soda, and salt in a bowl; set aside.

3. Beat the butter and sugars until fluffy. Beat in the egg, peach nectar, preserves, and fresh ginger.

4. Gradually add the flour mixture, stirring until well blended. Stir in the dried peaches and candied ginger. Drop rounded-teaspoon mounds of dough on the cookie sheets 2 inches apart. Bake for 18 to 22 minutes, until golden. Let cool on the pans for 5 minutes. Transfer to a rack to cool further.

5. Make the peach glaze: Combine the peach nectar and sugar in a small saucepan over medium heat, stirring until the sugar is dissolved, about 10 minutes. Brush on the tops of the cookies.

6. Top with candied ginger.

Cookie Pie

2½ cups all-purpose flour
1 teaspoon baking powder
½ teaspoon baking soda
½ teaspoon salt
1½ cups (3 sticks) butter, softened
1 cup granulated sugar
1 cup brown sugar
2 teaspoons vanilla extract
1½ cup semisweet chocolate chips
1 cup chopped walnuts
4 large eggs

Topping

1 pint cookie dough ice cream
¼ cup walnut halves
¼ cup chocolate chips

Chocolate Chip Cookie Pie

Type of cookie: Pie

8-inch pie

No matter how you slice it, chocolate chip cookie dough is the best. It is even tasty raw in ice cream. I don't really know why, but one day when I was making chocolate chip cookie dough for a summer party, I changed my mind and instead of making cookies I baked the dough in a pie pan, then filled it with ice cream. Needless to say, it was a big hit with my friends. The variation, in which the cookie dough is baked in a piecrust, is delicious too.

1. Preheat the oven to 325°F. Generously butter and flour an 8-inch pie pan.

2. Combine the flour, baking powder, baking soda, and salt in a bowl; set aside.

3. Beat the butter, sugars, and vanilla until fluffy. Add the chocolate chips and walnuts.

4. Beat the eggs until foamy.

5. Add the eggs, alternating with the flour mixture, to the butter mixture, stirring until incorporated.

6. Press the dough into the bottom and up the sides of the pie pan. Bake for 45 to 50 minutes, until firm. Transfer to a rack to cool for 20 minutes.

7. Top with ice cream, walnuts, and chocolate chips.

Variation

Crusted Cookie Dough Pie: Make your favorite shortbread crust recipe or buy a premade unbaked piecrust. Press the dough into the crust and bake as in the recipe.

Crust

Chocolate Cookies (page 208)
¼ cup (½ stick) butter, melted

Cookies and Cream Ice Cream

1½ cups milk
¾ cup sugar
3 cups heavy cream
2 teaspoons vanilla extract
1¼ cups cookie chunks (from
   Chocolate Cookie recipe,
   page 208)
Whipped cream

Cookies and Cream Ice Cream Pie

Type of cookie: Pie

9-inch pie

Here's the story. You can make this pie with a store-bought chocolate cookie crust and cookies and cream ice cream. It will be quick and it will taste good. Or you can buy your favorite chocolate sandwich cookies and make your own crust and add them to vanilla ice cream. Or you can make your own cookies, your own crust, and your own ice cream (for bragging rights or just because you need some alone time in the kitchen). This pie will taste fantastic however you choose to make it.

1. Preheat the oven to 350°F. Butter and flour a shallow 9-inch pie pan.

2. Make the crust: Break up enough of the cookies to make 1¼ cups chunks; set them aside for the ice cream. Crush the remaining cookies, and stir in the butter. Press into the bottom and sides of the pie pan, and bake for 8 to 10 minutes. Transfer to a rack to cool.

3. Make the cookies and cream ice cream: Beat the milk and sugar with a mixer until the sugar dissolves. Stir in the cream and vanilla.

4. Pour into an ice cream maker, and churn for 15 to 20 minutes, or according to the manufacturer's instructions. Add the reserved cookies, and churn for 5 minutes.

5. Spoon the prepared ice cream into the piecrust, cover with plastic wrap, and freeze for 2 to 3 hours, until set.

6. Top the pie with whipped cream and serve.

COCKTAIL PARTY COOKIES

Any excuse is a good excuse to have a cocktail party. Preparing these cookies spiked with sweet liquor tops the list. Here the seductive power of alcohol is embedded in playful rum ball kabobs, piña colada cookies, and gelatin shot cookies. For a more grown-up after-dinner dessert, try the mulled wine cookies, brandy snaps, and margarita bars. Of course, all of these also make great cookies for everyday indulgences.

Right: Rum, Mint, and Bourbon Ball Kabobs.

Cookies

2¼ cups (½ recipe) finely ground
  Shortbread Butter Cookies (page
  271), or more as necessary
¾ cup confectioners' sugar
1 cup pistachios, toasted and
  ground
1 cup peanuts, toasted and ground
¼ cup light corn syrup
⅓ cup rum or bourbon
¼ cup Dutch-process cocoa
  powder

Toppings

⅛ cup confectioners' sugar
¼ cup shredded sweetened coconut
⅛ cup cocoa powder
⅛ cup sesame seeds
¼ cup chopped pistachios
¼ cup chopped peanuts

Rum, Mint, and Bourbon Ball Kabobs

Type of cookie: No-bake

48 rum balls, 12 kabobs

Traditionally rum balls are served around the holidays, so I created these cookies as a reminder of the seasonal flavors for cocktail parties any time of year. For an infinite number of flavors, vary the nuts and the toppings. Most dense cookies will work well for this recipe. I usually use the shortbread butter cookie dough in either plain or the chocolate versions (page 256). Or if you prefer not to turn on the oven purchase the cookies at a bakery.

1. Combine the ground cookies, confectioners' sugar, pistachios, and peanuts.

2. Stir in the corn syrup and rum, and mix well. Add more corn syrup or cookies as necessary to make a mixture that you can form into a ball.

3. Divide the mixture in half; add the cocoa powder to one half and form two balls.

4. Wrap in plastic wrap and chill for 30 minutes. Shape into 1-inch balls.

5. Roll the balls in one topping per ball or mix and match, pressing them into the surface. Place on bamboo skewers to serve.

Cornmeal Cookie dough (page
  224), made with lemon juice
  and zest instead of orange juice
  and zest
¾ cup green olives with pimentos,
  chopped
¾ cup black olives, chopped

Cornmeal Olive Cookies

Type of cookie: Rolled cutout

24 cookies

Olives baked into sweet cornmeal cookies make for a tasty accompaniment to a martini. For a cocktail party they also make good appetizers spread with soft cheeses such as Brie or goat cheese and drizzled with honey.

1. Prepare the Cornmeal Cookie recipe with lemon juice and zest instead of orange juice and zest. Divide the dough in half.

2. Add the green olives to one batch and the black olives to the remaining batch. Flatten the dough into disks, wrap in plastic wrap, and refrigerate for 1 hour.

3. Preheat the oven to 350°F. Line 2 cookie sheets with parchment paper.

4. Roll the dough out to ⅛- to ¼-inch thick on a work surface dusted with cornmeal. Cut with cookie cutters and punch a hole in the center of each with a small cutter or straw. Place the shapes on the cookie sheets 1½ inches apart, and bake for 12 to 15 minutes, until golden. Transfer to a rack and let cool for 10 minutes.

5. Place each cookie on a cocktail skewer with an olive. Either rest the cookies on the rim of the cocktail glass or skewer the olive to support the cookies, and serve.

Variations

Sun-Dried Tomato Cookies: Replace the chopped olives with ½ cup sun-dried tomatoes and ¼ teaspoon white pepper. Mix 1 cup ricotta with ½ cup sugar. Spread on cooled cookies.

Jalapeño Pepper Cookies: Replace the chopped olives with 2 small chopped jalapeño peppers. Top with Cream Cheese Icing (page 275).

Chile Cookies: Add 1 teaspoon crushed dried chilies to the dry ingredients. Top with your favorite melted chocolate.

Cookies

2 cups red wine

1 teaspoon anise seeds, crushed

¼ teaspoon ground cinnamon

1 cup sugar

1 cup vegetable oil

1 cup vegetable shortening

3 tablespoons baking powder

1 tablespoon anise extract

6 cups all-purpose flour

Wine Glaze

1 cup confectioners' sugar, or more
  if necessary

⅛ teaspoon ground cinnamon

5 tablespoons red wine, or more if
  necessary

½ teaspoon anise extract

Mulled Wine Cookies

Type of cookie: Hand shaped

36 cookies

These cookies are based on the Spanish cookies called *rosquillos de vino*. The flavor varies drastically depending on the wine you use. For a wine cookie tasting, try merlot, shiraz, cabernet, pinot noir, and Chianti. For a pure wine flavor, omit the anise and cinnamon.

1. Preheat the oven to 325°F. Line 2 cookie sheets with parchment paper.

2. Put the red wine, anise seeds, and cinnamon in a saucepan, and cook over medium-high heat until reduced to 1 cup.

3. Combine wine reduction with the sugar, oil, shortening, and baking powder in a large bowl. Add the anise extract and mix well. Gradually add the flour, stirring until incorporated; the dough will be dry.

4. On a floured work surface, roll a handful of dough into a rope ⅓ inch thick. Cut into 4-inch lengths. Form each length into a ring by making a loop and pinching both ends. Transfer to the cookie sheets, placing the rings 2 inches apart. Bake for 14 to 16 minutes, until golden. Transfer to a rack, and let cool for 10 minutes.

5. Make the wine glaze: Combine the confectioners' sugar, cinnamon, red wine, and anise extract, adding more sugar or wine until the mixture is of thin icing consistency. Dip the cookies in glaze and let dry on a cookie sheet.

Variation

Champagne Cookies: Replace the red wine in both the cookies and the glaze with champagne.

Cookies

4 large egg whites

1⅓ cups granulated sugar

3 tablespoons rum

3 cups shredded sweetened coconut

1 cup macadamia nuts, ground

½ cup dried pineapple, finely chopped

Topping

24 pineapple wedges

24 maraschino cherries

Piña Colada Macaroons

Type of cookie: Molded drop

24 cookies

A chewy pineapple macadamia and coconut macaroon with a touch of rum, topped with a drink garnish, will transport you straight to the beaches of the tropics. To make the cookies tall enough to hold the cocktail stick, I made them in small square silicone molds. Leave them in the molds until they have cooled and hardened or they may break apart. For a different shape, they can be made as thumbprint cookies on cookie sheets with pineapple filling (page 127) in the center and drizzled with rum glaze (page 277).

1. Preheat the oven to 350°F. Spray 1½-inch square silicone molds with cooking spray.

2. Beat the egg whites until they hold soft peaks. Gradually add the sugar, beating until the peaks are stiff and glossy.

3. Stir in the rum, coconut, macadamia nuts, and pineapple.

4. Fill the molds three-quarters full with the dough. Bake for 14 to 18 minutes, until light golden. Let cool for 15 minutes in the molds; then peel back the molds to pop the macaroons out.

5. Skewer 1 pineapple wedge and 1 cherry on each of 24 cocktail spears, and stick into the macaroons.

Jelly Shot Cookies

Type of cookie: Icebox

30 cookies

Friends flip over these psychedelic treats in which frat party-inspired gelatin shots sit on top of alcohol-infused butter cookies; in the variation, gelatin is used in the cookie itself. I used my

Jelly Shots

2 cups water

1 (6-ounce) packet flavored gela-
    tin (see Note)

1 (6-ounce) packet unflavored
    gelatin

13 ounces cold 30- to 50-proof
    alcohol and 3 ounces cold
    water, or 10 ounces cold 80- to
    100-proof alcohol and 6 ounces
    cold water, or 6 ounces cold
    150- to 200-proof alcohol and
    10 ounces cold water

Cookies

Rolled Cutout Butter Cookie
    dough (page 272), made with
    an extra ¼ cup all-purpose flour
Orange, yellow, green, and blue
    food coloring
2 tablespoons alcohol to match the
    gelatin

favorite pyramid candy mold to mold the gelatin and added unflavored gelatin to make it extra-firm. Check the proof of your alcohol and add the cold water in the proportion listed at left so that the gelatin sets properly.

1. Spray 1½-inch pyramid silicone molds with cooking spray.

2. Make the jelly shots: Bring the water to a boil. Remove from the heat, and stir in the gelatins until dissolved. Stir in the alcohol and cold water and pour into the molds. Refrigerate for 2 to 3 hours, until firm.

3. Make the cookies: Divide the dough into 5 batches, and add 8 drops food coloring to each of 4 of the batches; leave 1 batch plain.

4. Form a ball from the dough, adding a little of each color at a time. Divide the ball in half; then roll gently into 2 logs 2 inches in diameter. Wrap in plastic wrap and freeze for 2 hours.

5. Preheat the oven to 325°F. Line 2 cookie sheets with parchment paper.

6. With a sharp knife, slice the logs into ¼-inch rounds. Place on the cookie sheets 1½ inches apart. Bake for 10 to 12 minutes, until firm. Transfer to a rack to cool.

7. When the cookies are cool and the jelly shots are firm, release the shots from the mold by flipping it over onto a plate. If they do not release, carefully help them free with a knife. Place one on top of each cookie. Chill until ready to serve.

Variation

Gelatin Cookie Shot: After you divide the cookie dough and are adding the food coloring, knead ½ packet (3 ounces) flavored gelatin into each batch of dough. The cookie will have a candylike mixed-fruit-punch taste.

Cherry and raspberry gelatins go well with brandy, vodka, and rum. Lime and lemon gelatins go well with coconut rum, tequila, and triple sec. Orange gelatin goes well with amaretto, vodka, and cognac.

Margarita Cheesecake Cocktail Bites

Type of cookie: Bar

16 bars

These cocktail bites are just the right selection to spoil your guests at a dessert cocktail party. Margarita cheesecake bars are made with a graham cracker crust, and in the related cocktail treats, Coffee Liqueur and Cream Cheesecake Bites and Strawberry Daiquiri Custard Bars, the coffee liqueur cheesecake has a chocolate crust and the strawberry daiquiri custard bars have a shortbread crust. Each is garnished like a cocktail.

1. Preheat the oven to 300°F. Butter and flour an 8-inch square baking pan.

2. Make the crust: Combine the graham crackers, butter, honey, and tequila, stirring until all the graham crackers are moistened. Press the mixture into the bottom of the baking pan; set aside.

3. Make the filling: Beat the cream cheese and sugar until smooth. Add the eggs one at a time, beating well after each addition. Fold in the lime and lemon juice, tequila, and lime zest.

4. Pour the filling onto the crust, and bake for 20 to 24 minutes, until firm. Let cool in the pan in the oven with the door slightly ajar for 40 minutes. Remove from the oven and transfer to a rack to cool completely. Refrigerate for 3 to 4 hours before serving.

5. Cut with a sharp knife into 2-inch squares.

6. For the topping, combine the sour cream and lime juice

Graham Cracker Crust

1½ cups crushed graham crackers

5 tablespoons butter, melted

1 teaspoon honey

2 tablespoons tequila

Filling

8 ounces cream cheese

⅔ cup sugar

3 large eggs

2 tablespoons lime juice

2 tablespoons lemon juice

2 tablespoons tequila

½ teaspoon grated lime zest

Topping

½ cup sour cream

Juice of 1 lime

2 limes, cut into wedges

and pool it in the center of each square. Top the cream with a lime wedge.

Coffee Liqueur and Cream Cheesecake Bites

Type of cookie: Bar

16 bars

The soothing flavors of coffee, cream, and chocolate cookies in these bars is straight from the buzzing dessert cocktail party wonderland.

1. Preheat the oven to 300°F. Butter and flour an 8-inch square baking pan.

2. Make the crust: Combine the cookies, butter, coffee liqueur, and ground coffee beans, stirring until all the cookies are moistened. Press the mixture into the bottom of the baking pan; set aside.

3. Make the filling: Beat the cream cheese and sugar until smooth. Add the eggs one at a time, beating well after each addition. Fold in the espresso.

4. Pour the filling onto the crust, and bake for 20 to 24 minutes, until firm. Let cool in the pan in the oven with the door slightly ajar for 40 minutes. Remove from the oven and transfer to a rack to cool completely. Refrigerate for 3 to 4 hours before serving.

5. Cut with a sharp knife into 2-inch squares.

6. For the topping, heat the chocolate chips in a double boiler over simmering water, stirring until melted, and dip the coffee beans in the chocolate. Set on parchment paper to harden.

7. Combine the whipped cream and coffee liqueur, and pool it in the center of each square. Top with the chocolate-covered espresso beans.

Chocolate Crust

1½ cups chocolate cookies, crushed

5 tablespoons butter, melted

3 tablespoons coffee liqueur

1 teaspoon ground coffee beans

Filling

8 ounces cream cheese

⅔ cup sugar

3 large eggs

2 tablespoons brewed espresso

Topping

¼ cup semisweet chocolate chips

⅛ cup coffee beans

½ cup whipped cream

3 tablespoons coffee liqueur

Left: Margarita Cheesecake Cocktail Bites, Coffee Liqueur and Cream Cheesecake Bites, Strawberry Daiquiri Custard Bars.

Shortbread Crust

1 cup all-purpose flour

⅓ cup confectioners' sugar

½ cup (1 stick) butter, softened

2 tablespoons sour cream

½ teaspoon vanilla extract

Filling

½ cup granulated sugar

2 tablespoons all-purpose flour

¼ teaspoon salt

½ cup milk

3 large egg yolks

3 tablespoons lime juice

Grated zest of 2 limes

3 tablespoons rum

1 cup fresh strawberries, sliced

Strawberry Syrup

¼ cup granulated sugar

2 tablespoons lime juice

2 tablespoons light rum

2 teaspoons strawberry schnapps

Topping

½ cup strawberries, sliced

Strawberry Daiquiri Custard Bars

Type of cookie: Bar

16 bars

This combination of strawberry, rum, and custard makes a cock-tail cookie bar with a sweet-tart taste. Garnish with a slice of strawberry.

1. Preheat the oven to 350°F. Butter and flour an 8-inch square baking pan.

2. Make the shortbread crust: Combine the flour, confectioners' sugar, and butter in a food processor or blender. Pulse until the dough resembles coarse meal.

3. Add the sour cream and vanilla, and pulse until the dough holds together.

4. Roll the dough out to ½ thick and 8 inches square on a floured work surface.

5. Place in the pan, and bake for 17 to 20 minutes, until golden. Transfer pan to a rack to cool.

6. Make the filling: Combine the granulated sugar, flour, and salt in a small saucepan. Whisk in the milk, egg yolks, lime juice, and zest. Cook over low heat for 5 to 7 minutes, until the mixture thickens.

7. Remove from the heat and stir in the rum and strawberries. Let sit for 30 minutes to cool completely.

8. Make the strawberry syrup: Combine the granulated sugar and lime juice in a saucepan over low heat, stirring to dissolve the sugar. Remove from the heat and stir in the rum and schnapps. Brush the syrup over the crust.

9. Spread the filling over the crust. Bake for 20 to 30 minutes, until set. Transfer to a rack to cool. Refrigerate for 1 hour.

10. Cut into 2-inch squares and top with strawberries.

Variations

Cherry Daiquiri Bars: Replace the strawberries with fresh pitted cherries.
Pineapple Daiquiri: Replace the strawberries with chopped fresh pineapple.

Cookies

½ cup (1 stick) butter

¾ cup brown sugar

⅓ cup light corn syrup

1 tablespoon lemon juice

1½ tablespoons brandy

1 cup all-purpose flour

½ teaspoon ground ginger

½ teaspoon freshly grated nutmeg

Brandy Whipped Cream

1½ cups heavy cream

1 tablespoon granulated sugar

1 tablespoon brandy

Brandy Snaps

Type of cookie: Drop, hand shaped

30 cookies

Brandy snaps are delicate cookies that are formed after they are removed from the oven. It is best to prepare the cookies one sheet at a time, since you will need some time to shape them while they are warm. These rolls are filled with brandy whipped cream, but you can also form them into small cups and fill with the cream.

1. Preheat the oven to 375°F. Line a cookie sheet with parchment paper. Prepare a pastry bag with a medium tip.

2. Make the cookies: Put the butter, brown sugar, corn syrup, lemon juice, and brandy in a large saucepan. Cook over medium heat, stirring until the butter has melted and the sugar is dissolved. Remove from the heat. Stir in the flour, ginger, and nutmeg.

3. Drop 1-teaspoon mounds of the dough on the cookie sheet 2 inches apart. Bake for 8 to 10 minutes, until lightly browned. Let cool on the pan for 20 seconds; then remove from the pan with a spatula and wrap the cookies around a ½-inch wooden dowel or wooden spoon handle. If the cookies become too firm to roll, return them to the oven for a minute to soften. When set, remove the rolls from the dowel and place on a plate.

4. Make the brandy whipped cream: Whip the cream and sugar until stiff peaks form. Stir in the brandy. Put the whipped cream in the pastry bag and pipe into the cookies.

Variations

Brandy Cups: Butter the backside of minimuffin pans. Drape the cookies over the cups to shape. Remove and fill with brandy cream.

White Chocolate-Dipped Brandy Snaps: After you have formed and cooled the cookies, dip one end in 1 cup melted white chocolate. While the chocolate is still wet, roll the cookies in ⅓ cup ground pistachios. Fill with the brandy whipped cream.

Coffee Liqueur Crinkle Cookies

Type of cookie: Drop

24 cookies

1¼ cups all-purpose flour
1 tablespoon baking powder
½ teaspoon salt
12 ounces bittersweet chocolate
4 tablespoons (½ stick) butter, softened
2 large eggs
½ cup coffee liqueur
2 tablespoons granulated sugar
½ cup walnuts
1 cup confectioners' sugar

The texture of crinkle cookies is always fun. The balls of dough are rolled in sugar before they are baked. As the dough bakes, cracks appear on the surface. These cookies are flavored with coffee liqueur and are a delightful addition to your cocktail-party offerings.

1. Combine the flour, baking powder, and salt in a medium bowl; set aside.

2. Heat the chocolate and butter in a double boiler over simmering water, stirring until melted; let cool.

3. Beat the eggs, coffee liqueur, and granulated sugar until smooth. Stir in the walnuts.

4. Add the flour mixture and the chocolate to the egg mixture. Wrap in plastic wrap and refrigerate for 2 to 3 hours, until firm.

5. Preheat the oven to 350°F. Butter 2 cookie sheets.

6. Put the confectioners' sugar on a plate. Shape the dough into 1-inch balls and roll them in the confectioners' sugar. Place the balls on the cookie sheets 2 inches apart. Bake for 10 to 12 minutes, until firm. Let cool on the pans for 5 minutes. Transfer to a rack to cool completely.

Variation

Irish Cream Crinkle Cookies: Replace the coffee liqueur with Irish cream liqueur.

MORE PARTY COOKIES

If you're looking for more excuses to throw a party with cookies—and who isn't?—here are some of my favorites.

Family Tree

Type of cookie: Rolled cutout

1 large cookie

Shortbread Butter Cookie dough (page 271)
Royal Icing (page 274)
Green, yellow, and red food coloring
Black nonpareils

For most families it is rare to get everyone together in one place, and at a family reunion the dessert is the last thing all the guests will leave with. You want to create something that will stick in their memories for years to come, and this interactive family tree certainly fits the bill. The tree is about 10 inches tall and 6 inches wide, big enough for 20 people to have a little taste by breaking off their own leaf. You can double the recipe to create a bigger cookie, but before you do, make sure it will fit in your oven. If you make it bigger, you will need to cover it with foil halfway though baking to keep it from browning too quickly at the edges. Another option for a larger family tree is to make it in several pieces.

1. Line a cookie sheet with parchment paper. Adjust the shape on page 152 to accommodate your family tree.

2. Flatten the dough into a disk, wrap in plastic wrap, and refrigerate for 30 minutes. Roll out the dough to ½ inch thick on a floured work surface, making sure that the thickness is even. Cover and freeze for 1 hour.

3. Using a utility knife and the template, cut out the tree. Use the scraps for other cookies, or make more leaves to attach to the branches. Carefully transfer the tree to the cookie sheet. Cover and refrigerate for 30 minutes.

4. Preheat the oven to 325°F.

5. Bake for 17 to 22 minutes, keeping an eye on the cookie and covering any edges that brown too quickly with aluminum foil. Let the cookie cool on the pan for 2 hours (or overnight) before transferring it to a board or serving platter.

Above: Family Tree.

6. Color the royal icing with food coloring: Prepare two greens, one dark and one light, and lesser amounts of the other colors. First create an outline in dark green for the grass and flower stems; then fill with dark green icing.

7. Next start at the top of the tree and create an outline for the leaves and the trunk, working your way to the grass. Fill in with icing, section by section, as you work your way down. Make sure the grass is dry before you make both colors meet to prevent bleeding.

8. When both the greens are dry, fill in the bird (drop in a nonpareil eye) and the flowers. When the flowers are dry, add the centers. You can also add names to the trunk, grass, and flowers if you'd like.

Variation

Have your relatives send you fun photos of themselves, and make photo transfers for cookies. Prepare them in the style of a family tree, attaching the photos to the leaves with royal icing.

Housewarming Invites

Type of cookie: Rolled cutout

16 cookies

The way to make sure people get the invitation and directions to your housewarming party is to send all the information on a cookie. (Remind them to save the cookie with the map for the day of the event!) I created these maps by combining, simplifying, and redrawing maps of my area that I found online. If you are so motivated, you can also re-create your house by taking a picture of it and making that into a photo transfer. Here I opted to go for the more iconic house shape and left the surprise of what my house is like for when the guests arrived. You could also make a gingerbread version of your house for the guests to enjoy when they arrive.

1. Preheat the oven to 325°F. Line 2 cookie sheets with parchment paper.

---

*Shortbread Butter Cookie dough
    (page 271)*
*Frosting transfers ¼ inch smaller
    than the cookie size*
Royal Icing (page 274)
Food coloring

---

2. Roll the dough out on a floured work surface to ⅜ inch thick. Cut out cookies a bit smaller than your invitation mailing box; they will expand slightly while baking. Poke holes in the surface with a fork to ensure that they bake flat and even, with no air bubbles.

3. Place the shapes on the cookie sheets 1½ inches apart. Bake for 15 to 18 minutes, until light golden. Let cool on the pans for 30 minutes. Transfer to a rack to cool further.

4. Cut out the map photo transfer, and freeze it for 20 minutes, or until firm. Spread a light coat of plain royal icing on each cookie. While the icing is still wet, peel the transfer off the backing paper and set it on top of the icing. Press down slightly to remove air bubbles.

5. Cover the house with white icing. Let dry completely. Color the remaining royal icing with food coloring., pipe on icing to decorate further. Pipe a line around the map with colored icing to make the border.

Sugared Nuts

1¼ cups granulated sugar

¾ cup water

3 cups salted mixed nuts

2 teaspoons vanilla extract

Beer Cookies

2 cups all-purpose flour

½ teaspoon baking soda

½ teaspoon ground cinnamon

¼ teaspoon ground cloves

½ cup (1 stick) butter, softened

½ cup brown sugar

1¼ cups dark beer

Opposite: Beer and Mixed Nut Cookies, Potato Chip Cookies, and Butter Rum Popcorn Cookies.

Beer and Mixed-Nut Cookies

Type of cookie: Drop

30 cookies

Is there such a thing as a manly cookie? Probably not, although these cookies made with beer and candied nuts are a far cry from dainty tea-party cookies. These are perfect to make for your fantasy football, Super Bowl, World Series, or NBA finals party. And yes, we ladies will like them too.

1. Butter 3 cookie sheets.

2. Make the sugared nuts: Combine the granulated sugar and the water in a saucepan over medium heat, stirring until sugar is dissolved.

3. Add the nuts and vanilla and cook, stirring occasionally, until the water is evaporated.

4. Spread the nuts on one of the cookie sheets and let sit until hardened.

5. Preheat the oven to 350°F.

6. Make the beer cookies: Combine the flour, baking soda, cinnamon, and cloves in a bowl; set aside.

7. Beat the butter and brown sugar until blended. Stir in the flour mixture, alternating with the beer, stirring until smooth. Stir in the sugared nuts.

8. Drop 1-tablespoon mounds of dough on the cookie sheets 2 inches apart. Bake for 10 to 12 minutes, until lightly browned. Transfer to racks to cool completely.

Variations

Root Beer Cookies: Omit the sugared nuts. In the cookie dough, replace the beer with root beer. Add ½ cup chopped root beer candy to the dough after the wet and dry ingredients are combined.

Cashew Beer Cookies: Replace the mixed nuts with cashews.

1 cup (2 sticks) butter, softened

½ cup sugar

1 teaspoon vanilla extract

2 cups all-purpose flour

2 cups coarsely crushed potato chips

Potato Chip Cookies

Type of cookie: Drop

36 cookies

TV and game parties are a time to indulge friends in the ultimate snack junk food, cookies packed with potato chips. Sound a bit strange? They are, but believe me, the saltiness of the chips complements the sweet, buttery cookies in a way that is completely addictive.

1. Preheat the oven to 325°F. Line 2 cookie sheets with parchment paper.

2. Beat the butter and sugar until fluffy. Beat in the vanilla, flour, and 1 cup of the potato chips; mix well.

3. Shape the dough into 1-inch balls, and roll them in the remaining chips. Place on the cookie sheets 2½ inches apart, and press a bit to flatten.

4. Bake for 12 to 15 minutes, until lightly browned. Let cool on the pans for 5 minutes. Transfer to a rack to cool further.

Variations

Chocolate Pretzel Cookies: Replace the potato chips with crushed pretzels and add ¾ cup chocolate chips to the dough after the wet and dry ingredients are combined.

Peanut Butter Cheesy Cracker Cookies: Replace the potato chips with crushed cheese crackers. Add ¾ cup peanut butter chips to the dough after the wet and dry ingredients are combined.

Spicy Tortilla Chip Cookies: Replace the potato chips with spicy tortilla chips and add ⅛ teaspoon chopped jalapeño peppers to the dough after the wet and dry ingredients are combined.

Butter Rum Popcorn Cookies

Type of cookie: No bake

2½ quarts popped popcorn
1 cup almonds
½ cup light corn syrup
⅓ cup water
1 cup sugar
½ teaspoon salt
¼ cup (½ stick) butter, cut into
    pieces
2 tablespoons rum

Every movie theater in America should expand its popcorn offerings, and candied popcorn cookies should be the first addition. While still warm, the butter, rum, and almond mixture can be shaped into round cookies or prepared in clusters. I made these with a gourmet popcorn that comes in red, blue, and yellow kernels. These are the perfect treat for an Academy Awards party or a casual night at home with a movie.

1. Line 2 baking sheets with waxed paper.

2. Put the popcorn and almonds in a large heatproof bowl; set aside.

3. Combine the corn syrup, water, sugar, and salt in a medium saucepan over medium heat. Stir constantly until the sugar dissolves and the mixture reaches the hard-ball stage (255°F). Remove from the heat.

4. Add the butter and stir until melted. Add the rum.

5. Pour the syrup over the popcorn and almonds, stirring until coated.

6. Spread the mixture on the baking sheets and let cool for 2 to 3 minutes. Shape into 3-inch rounds. Let sit for 20 minutes to harden slightly before serving.

Variations

Cherry Popcorn Cookies: Replace the almonds with ½ cup chopped dried cherries. Replace the rum with 1 tablespoon vanilla extract. Add 3 drops red food coloring to the wet ingredients.

Peanut Popcorn Cookies: Replace the almonds with peanuts and the rum with 1 tablespoon vanilla extract.

Chapter 4

Occasions Cookies

BIRTHDAY COOKIES

I love birthdays! Especially when they're not mine. On friends' and family members' birthdays I get to create and bake the treats. I like to think of clever ideas for gifting cookies—a box of Birthday Wishes cookies, or an extra-large cookie to suit the specialness of the occasion. And since many people consider pets members of the family, I have included some birthday treats for them, too.

Birthday Wishes

Type of cookie: Rolled cutout

24 cookies

Shortbread Butter Cookie dough (page 271)
Royal Icing (page 274)
Red, black, yellow, blue, purple, and green food coloring

Next time you can't think of a birthday gift, give your friend a box of birthday wish cookies. There are no candles to blow out, but the cookies each symbolize the most common things people wish for when blowing out the candles on a cake: love, money, luck, peace, and a balanced life. Choose the box first; then make the cookies to fit it. My box was just the right size for 2-inch round cookies.

1. Roll the dough out to ¼ inch thick on a floured cutting board. Cover and chill for 30 minutes to harden.

2. Preheat the oven to 350°F. Line 2 cookie sheets with parchment paper.

3. Cut the dough with cookie cutters. Place the shapes on the cookie sheets 1½ inches apart. Bake for 10 to 12 minutes, until light golden. Let cool on the pans for 10 minutes. Transfer to a rack to cool further.

4. Color the royal icing with food coloring.

5. To make the heart: Pipe a black outline first. Let dry completely. Fill with red icing. Let dry completely. Pipe a yellow border ¼ inch in from the edge of the cookie and fill with yellow icing.

6. To make the money symbol: Pipe a green border ¼ inch in from the edge of the cookie and fill entirely with green icing. Let dry completely. Pipe a money symbol.

7. To make the peace sign: Pipe a green border ¼ inch in from the edge of the cookie; then pipe a blue or black peace sign. Let dry completely; then fill with purple icing.

8. To make the clover: Pipe a green clover outline, and fill it with green icing. Let dry completely. Pipe a white border ¼ inch in from the edge of the cookie, and fill with white icing.

9. To make the yin-yang symbol: Pipe a black border ¼ inch in from the edge of the cookie. Pipe the black side of the symbol. Let dry completely. Fill in the white side. Let dry completely. Pipe the white dot on the black side and the black dot on the white side.

Black Forest Brownie Ice Cream Cake

Type of cookie: Cake

9-inch round cake

To show you how versatile some of these cookie recipes are, I created this very adult ice cream birthday cake. I chose the German Black Forest cake, one of the most recognized cakes in the world, and revamped it as an ice cream cake. The crust is essentially a brownie soaked in kirsch liqueur, and the cookie crunch is made from chocolate cookies. The cake is good any

Brownie Bites batter (page 185),
with ¾ cup chocolate chunks
mixed in
¼ cup kirsch liqueur
1½ cups halved and pitted cherries
Black cherry ice cream, softened
¾ cup chocolate chunks
1 ½ cups coarsely crushed
Chocolate Cookies (page 208)
Whipped Cream (page 275)
8 cherries with stems

time of year but especially when cherries are at their freshest, at the end of August, conveniently around the time of my birthday.

1. Preheat the oven to 350°F. Butter and flour a 9-inch springform pan.

2. Make the crust: Spread the batter ½ inch thick in the springform pan. (If there is batter remaining, put it in mini–cupcake pans for a few extra brownie bites.) Bake for 15 to 18 minutes, until a knife inserted in the center comes out clean. Brush on the kirsch. Let cool for 1 hour.

3. Clean any batter or flour off the sides of the cake pan with a wet towel. Arrange the cherry halves around the sides of the pan with the cut sides facing out. Scatter some cherry halves over the top of the brownie.

4. Set aside ¼ cup of the crushed cookies for topping.

5. Press the softened ice cream, alternating with the

chocolate chunks and 1¼ cups crushed cookies, into the pan, filling it almost to the top. Cover and freeze for 2 to 3 hours, until firm.

6. Remove the sides of the pan, and transfer the cake to a serving platter. I usually keep the bottom of the pan under the cake to support it, but you can carefully remove it if you'd like.

7. Top the cake with the remaining crushed cookies. Pipe whipped cream in 8 places around the perimeter. Top each mound of whipped cream with a stemmed cherry.

Happy B-Day Cookie Cake

Type of cookie: Cake
9-inch round cake

The love my husband, Brian, has for the chocolate chip cookie inspired me to re-create it in cake form for his birthday. Shamelessly rich and irresistibly tasty, this cake is gussied up for the big occasion with chocolate glaze and vanilla and chocolate buttercream.

1. Preheat the oven to 350°F. Butter and flour a 9-inch springform pan.

2. Make the cookie cake: Combine the flour, baking powder, baking soda, and salt in a medium bowl; set aside.

3. Beat the eggs and sugars until light and fluffy. Beat in the sour cream, butter, and vanilla.

4. Add the flour mixture, stirring until combined. Stir in the chocolate chips and walnuts.

5. Spread the batter in the pan and bake for 25 to 30 minutes, until the cake springs back when lightly touched. Let cool in the pan for 10 minutes. Remove the sides of the pan and transfer to a rack to cool completely.

Cookie Cake

2 cups all-purpose flour
1½ teaspoons baking powder
½ teaspoon baking soda
⅛ teaspoon salt
3 large eggs
½ cup light brown sugar
½ cup granulated sugar
¾ cup sour cream
6 tablespoons butter, melted and cooled
2 teaspoons vanilla extract
1¼ cups semisweet chocolate chips
¾ cup walnuts, chopped

Topping

Chocolate Glaze (page 277)
½ cup chocolate chips
½ cup walnut halves
1 cup Chocolate Buttercream (page 274)
1 cup White Buttercream (page 274)

6. Spoon the glaze over the center of the cake so that it covers everything but a ¾-inch border around the edge. Top with the chocolate chips and walnuts.

7. Using a star tip, pipe "Happy B-Day" on the cake with chocolate buttercream. Pipe chocolate flowers around the rim, leaving space between them for vanilla flowers.

8. Using vanilla buttercream and a small plain tip, pipe "Happy B-Day" over the chocolate letters. Add vanilla dots to the centers of the chocolate flowers.

9. Using a star tip, pipe vanilla flowers around the cake in the spaces between the chocolate flowers.

10. Finally, using a plain tip and chocolate buttercream, pipe chocolate dots in the centers of the vanilla flowers.

Variations

Peanut Butter Cookie Cake: Substitute peanut butter chips for the chocolate chips. Replace the walnuts with peanuts.

White Chocolate Macadamia Cookie Cake: Substitute white chocolate chips for the chocolate chips. Replace the walnuts with macadamia nuts. Use all vanilla buttercream.

Butterscotch Cookie Cake: Substitute butterscotch chips for the chocolate chips. Omit the walnuts. Use all vanilla buttercream.

Toffee Pecan Cookie Cake: Replace half of the chocolate chips with toffee crunch. Replace the walnuts with pecans.

Shortbread Butter Cookie dough
(page 271)
⅛-inch dragées or other small,
round candies
Royal Icing (page 274)
Food coloring
2-inch acrylic boxes, found in
crafts, container, and box stores

Party Favors

Type of cookie: Rolled cutout

24 cookies

I collected birthday party favors when I was a kid. I couldn't wait to receive the bag of party favors filled with silly plastic games and treats given out at the end of every party I went to. I displayed them all on my shelf in my room, and I wrote the name of the friend who'd given them to me on the back of each one. Every time I looked at my collection it reminded me that someday I was

Above: Party Favors.

going to be an artist and make toys like this too. I didn't realize then that I'd also be inspired to make them as cookies!

1. Roll the dough out to ¼ inch thick on a floured cutting board. Cover and chill for 30 minutes to harden.

2. Cut the dough with a pizza cutter or knife into 1 ¾-inch squares. Punch holes in the cookies for the animal eyes and the flower centers with a ¼" diameter straw. Cut smiley mouths with a utility knife.

3. Bake for 10 to 12 minutes, until light golden. Let cool on the pans for 10 minutes. Transfer to a rack to cool further.

4. When the cookies have cooled slightly, make sure they fit inside the boxes. If not, trim with a utility knife to fit. They are easier to trim when they are still a little warm. Check the holes. If the dough has expanded too much and the dragées do not fit, open up each hole a bit by rotating a knife in the hole.

5. Color the royal icing. Pipe all of the outlines with a small writing tip. Let dry.

6. Fill in with other colors—for example, the white of the elephant's face, the blue of the owl—and let dry. Then top with details— such as the beak, feathers and wings on the birds and owls or the candy mouth of the frog. Let dry.

7. Place a cookie in a box with as many dragées as there are holes in the cookie. Place the lid on the box and play the game.

2 cups all-purpose flour
2 cups shredded cheddar cheese
2 cloves garlic, chopped
½ cup vegetable oil
6 tablespoons water (more or less
    as needed)

Above: Cheddar and Herb Doggie Cookies.

2 teaspoons active dry yeast
½ cup warm water
1½ cups chicken broth
3 tablespoons honey
2 large eggs
3 tablespoons rosemary
3½ cups whole-wheat flour

Cheddar Dog Bone Cookies

Type of cookie: Rolled cutout

20 small dog bones

On their birthdays, dogs deserve to be kings or queens for the day too. Here are two of my favorite dog bone recipes; one is made with cheese and the other with herbs. (Most dogs like rosemary, but sage, thyme, and parsley are also popular flavors.) They are all very tasty; you may be tempted to snatch a few up for yourself.

1. Combine the flour, 1½ cups of the cheese, the garlic, and oil in a food processor or blender.

2. Gradually add the water until the mixture comes together in a ball. Wrap in plastic wrap and refrigerate for 30 minutes.

3. Preheat the oven to 400°F. Ready 2 ungreased cookie sheets.

4. Roll the dough out to ½ inch thick, and cut out the bones with a dog-bone cookie cutter or template (see page 278). Place the shapes on the cookie sheets 1½ inches apart. Bake for 8 minutes, until light brown. Sprinkle with the remaining cheese, and bake for 5 to 7 minutes longer. Transfer to a rack to cool.

Honey Herb Dog Bone Cookies

Type of cookie: Rolled cutout

12 large dog bones or crowns

1. Combine the yeast and water. Set aside, allowing the yeast to activate and become foamy, 7 to 10 minutes.

2. Combine the broth, honey, and eggs, and mix until blended. Stir in the rosemary and the yeast mixture.

3. Gradually add the flour, stirring until the dough becomes stiff. Knead the dough on a floured work surface until smooth. Roll the dough out ¼ inch thick. Cover and let sit for 30 minutes in a cool, dry place.

4. Preheat the oven to 350°F. Ready 2 ungreased cookie sheets.

5. Cut into dog bone and crown shapes. Place the shapes on the cookie sheets 2 inches apart. Bake for 20 minutes. Flip them over and bake for 20 minutes longer. Transfer to a rack to cool.

WEDDING COOKIES

Weddings plus cookies is a marriage made in heaven. Everyone wants their wedding to stand out, and there are so many ways to personalize the day with rich, luxurious cookies. Cookies provide a wonderful counterpart to the wedding cake centerpiece and are a playful way to enrich your dessert options at the big event. Stacked cookies, masterpieces of visual art, can also star at a wedding shower, engagement party, or anniversary celebration.

Wedding Cake Cookies

Type of cookie: Cutout

1 stack of 10 cookies

Here shortbread cookies are stacked 10 layers high to make a tiered wedding cake. The cookies are iced with a transparent coat of royal icing, and the sides are adorned with dots, flowers, and stripes. The cookies are not attached to one another, so guests can remove them one at a time. The lucky ones who wait for last get the biggest cookies, but the first to the scene gets the marzipan rose. Or you can follow tradition and save the top cookie for your first anniversary. (It takes up a lot less freezer space than a cake!)

1. Roll the dough out to ⅜ inch thick on a floured cutting board. Cover and refrigerate for 30 minutes to harden.

2. Preheat the oven to 350°F. Line 2 cookie sheets with parchment paper. Set up a cooling rack with parchment underneath.

3. Cut the dough with cookie cutters in graduated sizes.

Shortbread Butter Cookie dough (page 271)
Royal Icing (page 274), thinned to a glaze consistency
Yellow and green food coloring
⅛ cup Marzipan (page 115)

For each cookie stack

1 marzipan rose
1 (1¼-inch) cookie
3 (2¼-inch) cookies
3 (2¾-inch) cookies
3 (3¾-inch) cookies

Right: Wedding Cake Cookies.

Place the shapes on the cookie sheets 1½ inches apart. Bake for 12 to 14 minutes, until light golden. Let cool for 10 minutes on the pans. Transfer to a rack to cool further.

4. Dip each cookie face down in the icing; then place it right side up on the rack. Smooth out the areas where your fingers were and let the excess icing drip onto the parchment. If too much icing drips off, add more sugar to the glaze and dip the cookie again. Glaze all of the cookies. Let dry completely.

5. Thicken the icing a bit by adding a few tablespoons of sugar. Reserve ¼ cup white icing, and color the rest

yellow. With a small writing tip, draw a line around the center of the edge of 4 cookies, one of each size.

6. With the same tip, draw dots ¼ inch apart on one of each of the cookies in each of the 3 sizes left. Draw a line around the top rim of each of the 3 cookies.

7. Change the tip to a flower tip, and pipe flowers on the remaining cookies, one next to the other. When the flowers have dried, pipe the reserved white icing in the center of each flower. Let dry.

8. Divide the marzipan into ¾ of the marzipan for one large ball and ¼ of the marzipan for one small ball. Color the large ball yellow and the small ball green.

9. Form a small yellow ball of marzipan into a cone shape. You will use this core to support the rose petals. Roll yellow marzipan into tiny balls. Flatten the balls into petal shapes slightly thicker at one end. Wrap one petal around the cone and press it in. Use your fingers to curl the ends of the petal out. Overlap a second petal with the first petal. Repeat with additional petals.

10. Make the leaves out of flattened green marzipan. Make vein indentations in the leaves with a knife.

11. Attach the leaves to the rose and the rose to the small cookie with royal icing.

12. Stack the cookies with the large striped cookie on the bottom, the large flowered cookie in the middle, and the large dot cookie with the border on the top. Repeat these patterns with the graduated cookie sizes. Top with the small rose-topped cookie.

2 cups all-purpose flour

¼ teaspoon salt

1 cup (2 sticks) butter, softened

1 cup confectioners' sugar

1 cup pecans, ground

1 teaspoon vanilla extract

Mexican Wedding Cookies

Type of cookie: Hand shaped

36 cookies

Served at weddings in Mexico and the southwestern United States, these cookies are very similar to Russian tea cakes. Nicely packaged, they make great wedding favors.

1. Preheat the oven to 350°F. Butter 2 cookie sheets.

2. Combine the flour and salt in a medium bowl; set aside.

3. Cream the butter and ½ cup of the confectioners' sugar with an electric mixer until fluffy.

4. Add the flour mixture to the butter mixture, stirring until blended. Stir in the pecans and vanilla.

5. Shape the dough into 1½-inch balls. Place the balls on the cookie sheets 2 inches apart and bake for 12 to 15 minutes, until light brown. Let cool for 5 minutes on the pans.

6. Put the remaining ½ cup confectioners' sugar on a small plate. Roll the cookies in the sugar while still warm. When ready to serve, freshen the cookies with more sugar.

Variations

Russian Tea Cakes: Replace the pecans with ground walnuts.

Almond Mexican Wedding Cookies: Replace the vanilla with almond extract and the pecans with ground almonds.

Cinnamon Anise Mexican Wedding Cookies: Add 1 teaspoon ground cinnamon and 1 teaspoon anise seeds to the dry ingredients.

Tie the Knot Pretzel Cookies

Type of cookie: Hand shaped

8 large cookies

2¼ cups all-purpose flour

⅛ teaspoon salt

½ teaspoon baking powder

2 ounces unsweetened chocolate

1 cup (2 sticks) butter, softened

½ cup sugar

½ teaspoon vanilla extract

1 large egg

1 large egg white, lightly beaten

2 tablespoons nonpareils

Chocolate pretzel cookies are symbolic of the partnership made on the day a couple ties the knot. Serve them next to the wedding cake or box them as wedding invitations, favors, or an anniversary gift.

1. Combine the flour, salt, and baking powder in a medium bowl; set aside.

2. Heat the chocolate in a double boiler over simmering water, stirring until melted. Let cool.

3. Beat the butter and sugar until light and fluffy. Beat in the vanilla, whole egg, and melted chocolate.

4. Gradually add the flour mixture, stirring until smooth. Flatten the dough into a disk, wrap in plastic wrap, and refrigerate for 1 hour.

5. Preheat the oven to 350°F. Line 2 cookie sheets with parchment paper.

6. Roll the dough into 8 ropes, each about 10 inches long. Take the ends of each rope and form a loop, crossing the ends. Secure firmly on the top and place on the cookie sheets 2 inches apart.

7. Brush the cookies with the egg white, and sprinkle with nonpareils. Bake for 15 to 18 minutes, until firm. Let cool on the pans for 5 minutes. Transfer to a rack to cool.

BABY COOKIES

Everyone I know is having babies, and there are many events that revolve around new arrivals, baby showers, christenings, and introduction parties. Not only are cookies a tasty addition to the event, but they can also be used as invitations or given out as favors or thank-you gifts. It is also a nice gesture to bake and send a gift box of homemade cookies or bring a tray of cookies on a visit to see a new baby. And when the baby gets old enough, he or she can enjoy the fruity toddler cookies too.

"Party at My Crib" Baby Invite

Type of cookies: Rolled cutout

6 large cookies

Shortbread Butter Cookie dough (page 271)
Frosting photo transfer ¼ inch smaller than the cookie size
Royal Icing (page 274)
Food coloring
Nonpareils
4 x 5-inch boxes
Tissue paper, hemp, and ribbon

Passing out cigars and hanging blue or pink banners proclaiming "It's a boy!" or "It's a girl!" are so *yesterday* when it comes to baby-related celebrations. Today, baby showers are for both parents, and colors are gender neutral. These invites, made with photo transfers, are classy and appeal to modern sensibilities. I use a shortbread dough as the base because it's relatively strong and held up to multiple mailings as I was testing it, but if you're handing out the cookies in person, another rolled cutout cookie dough will work as well. To mail invitations, put the 4 x 5-inch box into another slightly larger box with cornstarch packing peanuts around it for extra protection. When designing the photo transfer, remember to leave plenty of room around the edge of the cookie for the icing border.

1. Preheat the oven to 350°F. Line 2 cookie sheets with parchment paper.

2. Roll the dough out to ⅜ inch thick. Cut cookies about ⅜ inch smaller than the invitation box; the cookies will expand slightly as they bake. Poke holes in the surface of the cookies with a fork to ensure a flat, even surface.

Right: "Party at My Crib" Baby Invite.

3. Place the shapes on the cookie sheets 1½ inches apart. Bake for 15 to 18 minutes, until light golden. Let cool on the pans for 30 minutes. Transfer to a rack to cool further.

4. If the cookies have expanded too much to fit in the boxes, trim them to size with a knife; the cookies will crumble less if they are chilled in the freezer or left out to harden overnight first.

5. Cut out the photo transfers and freeze them for 20 minutes, until firm. One at a time, spread a light coat of royal icing on the cookies. While the icing is still wet, peel the transfers off of the backing paper and set them on top of the icing. Press down gently to remove air bubbles.

6. Color the remaining royal icing with food coloring. Pipe flowers around the cookies' borders. Place a nonpareil in the center of each flower. Let dry.

7. Set each cookie on tissue paper in a box lined with wax paper and tie the box with hemp and ribbon.

Shortbread Butter Cookie dough
(page 271)
Royal Icing (page 274)
Food coloring
Black sugar and white candy
stars

Baby Toys

Type of cookies: Rolled cutout

6 large cookies

When a friend is expecting, a group of us get together and do something crafty for her, like customizing a set of blocks or baking baby cookies. When we made these, each of us picked our favorite toddler toy and designed a cookie to make as a gift. This cookie dough needs to be chilled well before baking to prevent it from spreading.

1. Roll the dough out to ¼ inch thick on a floured cutting board. Cover and refrigerate for 1 hour.

2. Preheat the oven to 350°F. Line 2 cookie sheets with parchment paper.

3. Cut out the cookies using a utility knife and templates (page 278). Place the shapes on the cookie sheets 1½ inches apart. Bake for 12 to 14 minutes, until firm and lightly browned. Let cool on the pans.

4. Divide the royal icing into 10 small bowls. Leave one bowl of icing white and color the others with pink, light brown, dark brown, yellow, orange, light green, bright green, blue, and black food coloring. Put the icing in piping bags, and pipe the outlines of the designs first. Let dry for 20 minutes.

5. Fill the outlines with royal icing. Sprinkle cookies with black sugar (as for the monkey) or top with star candies (as for the jack-in-the-box). Let dry; then top with small details and patterns (such as the faces or the jack's crosshatching). Let dry completely.

TODDLER COOKIES

These extra-healthful, fruity, bite-size cookies are perfect for a play date with a group of toddlers, who are the perfect age to explore the wonderful world of baked treats. When served with yogurt—a baby favorite—the cookies make a complete protein. These cookies can also be made into full-size treats for adults.

Banana Nut Cookies

Type of cookie: Drop molded

36 cookies

The darker and riper the banana, the better it is for baking. These moist and fluffy cookies have a rich banana flavor that deepens as the cookies sit. Make them without nuts, if you wish, for tiny toddlers, and with nuts for those who have mastered chewing.

1. Preheat the oven to 375°F. Ready 1½-inch silicone molds or line 2 cookie sheets with parchment paper.

2. Combine the flour, baking powder, baking soda, and salt in a medium bowl; set aside.

3. Beat the butter and sugars until fluffy. Add the eggs, bananas, and vanilla and beat well.

4. Gradually add the flour mixture and stir until blended. Stir in the nuts.

5. Drop heaping teaspoons of the dough into the molds or on the cookie sheets 2 inches apart. Bake for 8 to 10 minutes, until golden. Transfer to a rack to cool.

6. Use a mini–cookie cutter to cut shapes from the banana slices. Toss them with the lemon juice; then attach them to the cookies with the yogurt.

Cookies

2¼ cups all-purpose flour
½ teaspoon baking powder
½ teaspoon baking soda
1 teaspoon salt
1 cup (2 sticks) butter, softened
½ cup granulated sugar
½ cup brown sugar
2 large eggs
1 cup mashed ripe bananas
2 teaspoons vanilla extract
1 cup chopped walnuts

Topping

1 banana, cut into ¼-inch rounds
2 tablespoons lemon juice
3 tablespoons plain yogurt

Variation

Chocolate Banana Nut: Reduce the flour to 2 cups. Add ⅓ cup cocoa powder to the dry ingredients. Add 1 cup chocolate chips along with the nuts.

Right: Hidden Cherry Cookies, Mandarin Orange Cookies, Banana Nut Cookies.

1½ cups all-purpose flower
⅛ teaspoon salt
½ cup (1 stick) butter, softened
¼ cup confectioners' sugar
1 teaspoon vanilla extract
1 teaspoon cherry juice
36 cherries, pitted

Hidden Cherry Cookies

Type of cookie: Drop molded

36 cookies

Cherries are the fun that is baked right into the center of these cookies. At first they appear to be little cherry flowers, but when toddlers bite into them they squeal with surprise and excitement as they find the hidden cherry. If you don't have a flower-shaped mold, simply cover any piece of fruit with dough and form it into a ball about 1 inch in diameter; bake on a cookie sheet.

1. Preheat the oven to 350°F. Butter and flour 2 small flower-shaped molds or cookie sheets.

2. Combine the flour and salt in a small bowl; set aside.

3. Beat the butter and confectioners' sugar until smooth. Stir in the vanilla and cherry juice.

4. Gradually add the flour mixture, stirring until the dough can be gathered into a ball.

5. Wrap the dough around the cherries, forming balls about 1 inch in diameter. Press the balls into the molds. Alternatively, place the balls directly on the cookie sheets.

6. Bake for 8 to 10 minutes, until light golden. Let cool for 5 minutes in the molds or on the pans. Transfer to racks to cool further.

Variations

Cherry Cookies with Cherry Icing: Combine 1 cup confectioners' sugar with 3 tablespoons cherry juice, stirring until the icing reaches a drizzling consistency. Drizzle the icing over the cookies.

Hidden Strawberry Cookie: Replace the cherries with halved strawberries and the cherry juice with strawberry juice.

Hidden Dried Apricot Cookie: Replace the cherries with dried apricots and the cherry juice with apricot nectar. Slice dried apricots in half if necessary.

2½ cups all-purpose flour

1 teaspoon baking powder

½ teaspoon salt

1 cup (2 sticks) butter, softened

1 cup granulated sugar

1 large egg

½ cup orange marmalade

Grated zest of 1 orange

3 tablespoons orange juice

½ cup mandarin orange segments

Topping

½ cup mandarin orange segments

¼ cup plain yogurt

Mandarin Orange Cookies

Type of cookie: Drop molded

36 cookies

Bite-size mandarin orange segments are so cute, they are the perfect topping for kids' cookies. If the cookies are going to be eaten right after baking, attach the oranges to the cookie with yogurt; if they will be served to the little princes and princesses later, use Royal Icing (page 274).

1. Preheat the oven to 300°F. Butter 2-inch minimuffin cups.

2. Combine the flour, baking powder, and salt in a medium bowl; set aside.

3. Beat the butter and sugar until light and fluffy. Beat in the egg.

4. Stir in the marmalade, orange zest and juice, and mandarin oranges.

5. Gradually add the flour mixture until blended.

6. Drop rounded teaspoons of the dough into the molds. Bake for 4 to 6 minutes, until the edges are golden. Flip out onto a rack to cool.

7. Attach the mandarin orange segments to the tops of the cookies with yogurt or icing.

Variation

Chocolate Chip Orange Cookies: Add ¾ cup chocolate chips to the cookie dough after the wet and dry ingredients are mixed or icing.

KIDS' COOKIES

The word that sums up these cookies: *fun!* Baking for or with kids is probably one of the more nostalgic activities for me, prompting memories of the excitement of learning to bake myself. The following cookies are easy to make with kids, perfect for slumber parties, bake sales, and baking play dates. But remember: These cookie treats are not just for kids; they're for all of us who refuse to grow up.

Pizzelle Malt Ice Cream Sandwiches

Type of cookie: Pressed

24 cookies, 12 sandwiches

I was one of those few kids who were allowed to eat waffles and ice cream for breakfast. If I had known then about crisp and delicate pizzelles, which are essentially waffles, these ice cream sandwiches would have been my favorite. The sandwiches in the picture are made with one chocolate cookie and one plain cookie. Malted milk powder gives a distinctive taste to the cookies that's reminiscent of a milkshake—and what kid doesn't like milkshakes? They can also be shaped into waffle ice cream cones by following the cookie cones technique on page 131.

2 cups all-purpose flour
½ cup cocoa powder
1 tablespoon malt powder
1½ teaspoons baking powder
3 large eggs, at room temperature
1 cup sugar
½ cup (1 stick) butter, melted and cooled
½ cup milk
1 teaspoon vanilla extract

1. Preheat a pizzelle maker.

2. Combine the flour, cocoa powder, malt powder, and baking powder in a medium bowl; set aside.

3. Beat the eggs and sugar until blended. Beat in the butter, milk, and vanilla.

4. Gradually add the flour mixture, and stir until smooth.

5. Drop a heaping tablespoon of the batter on the pizzelle iron slightly off center (a little closer to the back). As you close the lid, the machine will push the batter forward. Lower the lid and cook for about 30 to 45 seconds. Remove with a fork and transfer to a wire rack to cool. Assemble pizzelles into sandwiches.

Variations

Plain Pizzelles: Omit the cocoa powder. Use 2 teaspoons vanilla extract.

Anise Pizzelles: Omit the cocoa powder. Replace the vanilla with anise extract.

Chocolate Orange Pizzelles: Replace the vanilla with orange juice. Add 1 tablespoon grated orange zest with the juice.

Hazelnut Pizzelles: Decrease the flour to 1¾ cups. Add ⅓ cup ground hazelnuts to the dry ingredients.

Chocolate Cookie dough
(page 208)

Cookie Dough Centers

4½ cups all-purpose flour
2 teaspoons baking soda
½ teaspoon salt
2 cups (4 sticks) butter, softened
1½ cups granulated sugar
1½ cups brown sugar
4 large eggs
1 teaspoon vanilla extract

Toppings

¾ cup chocolate chips
½ cup walnuts
½ cup raisins
½ cup peanuts
1 cup shredded sweetened coconut
1 cup large marshmallows
1 cup minimarshmallows
½ cup chocolate malt balls

Everything Pizza Cookie

Type of cookie: Extra-large

2 cookies

This enormous "pizza" cookie has a chocolate crust and cookie dough center and is topped with the works. It is fantastic for a kids' slumber party. Some of the toppings are added before it is baked, and the rest are added afterward. Make sure the center dough is fully baked before toasting the marshmallows—they will toast quickly. This is a double batch, so you can to make two pizzas with different toppings.

1. Refrigerate the chocolate cookie dough until needed.

2. Make the cookie dough centers: Combine the flour, baking soda, and salt in a large bowl; set aside.

3. Beat the butter and sugars until fluffy. Beat in the eggs and vanilla until creamy.

4. Gradually add the flour mixture, stirring until blended.

5. Preheat the oven to 350°F. Butter 2 (14-inch) round pizza pans

6. Spread the mixture in the pans with a spatula, leaving a ¾-inch border around the edges.

7. Roll the chocolate dough into a rope about ½ inch in diameter, and wrap it around the edge of each pan to form a border. Pinch the dough together where the two ends meet.

8. Top the cookies with chocolate chips, walnuts, raisins, peanuts, and half of the coconut. Bake for 18 to 22 minutes, until golden. Check with a knife to see if the cookie is firm. Add the marshmallows, and bake for 3 to 5 more minutes, until the marshmallows are browned (be careful not to let them burn). Let cool on the pans.

9. Top with the remaining coconut and the malt balls. To serve, cut into wedges with a pizza cutter.

Chocolate Chip Cookie dough
    (page 208)
1 cup all-purpose flour
½ teaspoon baking soda
½ teaspoon salt
½ cup (1 stick) butter, softened
6 tablespoons granulated sugar
6 tablespoons brown sugar
½ teaspoon vanilla extract
1 large egg, at room temperature
1 cup chocolate chips

Topping

1 cup chocolate chips, chopped
Vanilla Cream Frosting
    (page 276)

*Below: Gingerbread Cupcakes, Chocolate
Chip Cookie Cupcakes, Cookies and Cream
Cupcakes.*

Chocolate Chip Cookie Cupcakes

Type of cookie: Drop, cupcakes

18 cupcakes

Kids making cookies and cupcakes could not be more proud, and here the two are combined into one. The bottom of each cupcake has a chocolate chip cookie crust, and, well, you can see what is on the top—a mini–chocolate chip cookie.

1. Preheat the oven to 375°F. Butter 2 cookie sheets. Line cupcake pans with liners.

2. Make 18 mini–chocolate chip cookies from ¾-inch balls of dough; set aside.

3. Place 1 rounded teaspoon cookie dough in the bottom of each cupcake liner. Bake for 7 minutes; they should be underbaked. Let cool in the pans.

4. Combine the flour, baking soda, and salt in a small bowl; set aside.

5. Combine the butter, sugars, and vanilla. Beat with an electric mixer on medium speed until creamy. Beat in the egg.

6. Gradually add the flour mixture, stirring until smooth; then stir in the chocolate chips.

7. Fill the cupcake liners three-quarters full over the partially baked cookies. Bake for 15 to 20 minutes, until a toothpick inserted in the center comes out clean. Let cool in the pans.

8. For the topping, stir the chocolate chips into the frosting. Spread on top of the cupcakes. Top with the minicookies.

Cookies and Cream Cupcakes

Type of cookie: Cookie cupcakes

18 cupcakes

Two flavors that always work well together—cookies and cream—team up again in a cookie cupcake. Cookie cupcakes combine the great flavors and textures of cookies and the cakey moisture of cupcakes.

2 cups all-purpose flour

¾ cup Dutch-process cocoa powder

1 tablespoon baking powder

½ teaspoon salt

½ cup (1 stick) butter, softened

1⅔ cups granulated sugar

1 cup milk

2 teaspoons vanilla extract

3 large egg whites

2½ cups crushed Chocolate Cookies (page 208)

Vanilla Cream Frosting (page 276)

1. Preheat the oven to 350°F. Line cupcake pans with liners.

2. Combine the flour, cocoa powder, baking powder, and salt in a medium bowl; set aside.

3. Combine the butter, sugar, milk, and vanilla with an electric mixer, blending until smooth. Stir in the flour mixture.

4. Add the egg whites and beat for about 2 minutes.

5. Mix in 1½ cups of the crushed cookies, reserving the rest for topping.

6. Fill the cupcake liners three-quarters full. Bake for about 20 minutes, until a toothpick inserted in the center of a cupcake comes out clean. Let cool in the pans.

7. Spread the frosting on top of the cupcakes and roll the tops of the frosted cupcakes in the remaining cookie crumbs.

Cupcakes

2½ cups all-purpose flour

1½ teaspoons baking soda

1 teaspoon ground cinnamon

1¼ teaspoons ground ginger

½ teaspoon ground cloves

½ cup (1 stick) butter, softened

¼ cup dark brown sugar

¼ cup granulated sugar

1 large egg

⅔ cup light molasses

2 teaspoons grated lemon zest

1 cup sour cream

1 cup crushed Vegan Ginger
  Cookies (page 85)

Cream Cheese Spice Frosting

1 (8-ounce) package cream cheese,
  softened

6 tablespoons butter, softened

3 cups confectioners' sugar

1 teaspoon vanilla extract

½ teaspoon ground cinnamon

½ teaspoon ground ginger

Topping

Candied ginger

1½ cups crushed Vegan Ginger
  Cookies (page 85)

Gingerbread Cupcakes

Type of cookie: Cookie cupcakes

18 cupcakes

This is a far cry from those plain cake-mix cupcakes you had as a kid. Now that the world has gone cupcake crazy, there is no turning back, and kids and adults alike have cravings for exotic flavor combinations. The cookies here provide the crunch of the topping.

1. Preheat the oven to 375°F. Line regular cupcake pans with liners.

2. Make the cupcakes: Combine the flour, baking soda, cinnamon, ginger, and cloves in a medium bowl; set aside.

3. Beat the butter and sugars together until fluffy. Add the egg, molasses, and lemon zest. Beat well.

4. Add the flour mixture alternately with the sour cream until blended. Stir in the crushed cookies.

5. Fill the cupcake liners one-half to three-quarters full. Bake for 15 to 20 minutes, until a toothpick inserted in the center of a cupcake comes out clean. Let cool in the pans.

6. Make the cream cheese spice frosting: Beat the cream cheese and butter until smooth.

7. Slowly sift in the confectioners' sugar and continue beating. Mix until all lumps are gone. Add the vanilla, cinnamon, and ginger, and beat until blended. Frost the cupcakes.

8. Top with candied ginger and crushed cookies.

Scraps of Chocolate and Shortbread Butter Cookie doughs
(page 271)
1 cup Assorted candies, malt balls,
chocolates, and chocolate raisins
Royal Icing (page 274)
Food coloring

Zen Stones

Type of cookie: Drop

30 cookies if made from a full batch of dough

These cookies are a good introduction for kids to baking and decorating. They are super-easy to make, even for a little kid. I usually make these from the scraps left over from a batch of cutout cookies, but they're so much fun, you might want to make a fresh batch of dough and cut it into strips just for these. If you have different flavors of dough, so much the better: Mix the flavors together into balls (with candy hidden in the middle); then bake. To decorate, pipe icing to outline the shapes formed by the different doughs—kind of like coloring, but it doesn't matter if you fill it in; they'll still look good. I named these cookies Zen Stones because they look like the rocks I had in my rock collection when I was a kid that I believed had superpowers.

1. Preheat the oven to 350°F. Line 2 cookie sheets with parchment paper.

2. Gather the scraps to form 1-inch balls, hiding the candy in the center. Place the balls on the cookie sheets 1½ inch apart. Bake for 12 to 15 minutes, until firm. Transfer to a rack to cool.

3. Color the icing (here I made it black), and put it in a pastry bag with a small tip. Pipe lines where the two doughs meet.

TEEN COOKIES

Throughout the teen years there are many milestones to celebrate. Bar and bat mitzvahs, confirmations, *quinceañeras*, debutante parties, sweet sixteens, and graduations—all are good excuses to mix up some special cookies. These recipes are also simple to prepare, so they're just right for baking at teen parties. Aspiring cookie decorators can try the fondant cookies.

Brownie Bites

Type of cookie: Molded

24 brownies

These petite brownie bites are packed with ultrarich chocolate, making them the perfect choice for a group of teens having a girly slumber party or a movie night. The brownies sink in the middle as they bake, and the chocolate icing fills the cracks and grooves. Offer a selection of different toppings so all the guests can create their own favorite combinations.

1. Preheat the oven to 350°F. Butter 2 minicupcake pans.

2. Make the brownies: Heat the chocolate and butter in a double boiler over simmering water, stirring until melted. Remove from the heat and stir in the vanilla. Set aside to cool.

3. Combine the flour and baking powder in a medium bowl; set aside.

4. Beat the sugars and eggs until blended.

5. Add the flour mixture, alternating with

Brownies

2 ounces semisweet chocolate, cut into pieces

¾ cup (1½ sticks) butter

2 teaspoons vanilla extract

¾ cup all-purpose flour

¾ teaspoon baking powder

¾ cup granulated sugar

½ cup dark brown sugar

3 large eggs

Topping

Chocolate Icing (page 277)

White chocolate chips

Toffee

Walnuts and pecans

Dried cranberries and other fruits

the chocolate mixture, stirring until well mixed. Put tablespoons of the batter in the cupcake pans. Bake for 15 to 18 minutes, until a toothpick inserted in the center comes out clean. Let cool in the pans.

6. Spread the icing on the brownie bites. Top with assorted candy, nuts, and dried fruits.

Sugar-and-Spice Cinnamon Butterflies

Type of cookie: Rolled cutout

12 cookies

Sugar and spice and everything nice, these dimensional butterflies are as tween and teen girly as can be. So how did I get the cookies to bake on an angle? I sacrificed a cookie sheet to the cause and bent it, then baked them on an angle. They cooled on the sheet and set into the form. Do I expect you to do that too? You can, but there are a couple of other ways you can achieve the dimensional effect. The first is to build a cardboard form at the desired angle (glue supports on the back to hold the angle and wrap in aluminum foil) and drape the cookies on it immediately after they are taken out of the oven. The second is to bake the butterflies in two symmetrical parts, once cooled set them on the cardboard form and attach them with royal icing at the seam.

1. Combine the flour, spices, and salt in a medium bowl; set aside.

2. Beat the butter and sugar until light and fluffy. Beat in the egg and vanilla.

3. Add the flour mixture and stir until blended. Divide into two batches, flatten into disks, and refrigerate for 1 hour.

4. Preheat the oven to 350°F. Bend a thin cookie sheet by pressing it over the edge of a table, using a hammer if necessary. Line the cookie sheet with parchment paper.

5. Roll the dough out on a floured work surface to ¼ inch thick, and cut out the butterflies with a utility knife.

Butterfly Cookies

2 cups all-purpose flour

2½ teaspoons ground cinnamon

¼ teaspoon ground allspice

¼ teaspoon freshly grated nutmeg

¼ teaspoon ground ginger

½ teaspoon salt

½ cup (1 stick) butter, softened

1 cup granulated sugar

1 large egg

1 tablespoon vanilla extract

Topping

Royal Icing (page 274)

Pink, orange, purple, and yellow food coloring

Colored sugar

Candy dots in assorted sizes, candy balls, candy hearts

Place on the bent cookie sheet, and bake for 12 to 14 minutes, until firm. Let cool on the cookie sheet. Transfer to a plate.

6. Leave ⅓ of the icing white and color the rest with orange, yellow, pink and purple food coloring. Cover some of the cookies entirely with royal icing, and leave some plain. Add some candies to make patterns (such as the line of hearts down the center of the middle cookie and the pink dots on the front and blue dots on the back of the other cookies. Sprinkle some of the cookies with colored sugar, like the purple butterfly on the far left). Let the icing dry.

7. Pipe the plain cookies with lines, dots, and other butterfly patterns. Add some sugar to the outlines. Once all the icing has dried, pipe more butterfly details and attach candies and sugars.

Girls on the Verge Cookies

Type of cookie: Rolled cutout

12 cookies

These dreamy, glamorous, and tasty cookies are fun to make, and very impressive looking but really not that hard for an aspiring cookie decorator. You can use this book's recipe for fondant or purchase some at a cake supply store. Keep in mind when rolling out the fondant that thicker fondant (about ⅛-inch) is best for embossing and decorations and thinner fondant (about 1/16-inch) is better for wrapping cookies.

1. Divide the fondant into two batches. Knead one of the food colorings into each.

2. Divide the royal icing in half. Leave one bowl and use to attach the pieces of fondant to the cookies. Make the other bowl thicker for piping by adding ¼ to ½ cup confectioners' sugar.

To Make Embossed Cookies

1. Dust a work surface with confectioners' sugar. Roll the fondant out to ⅛ inch thick. Dust a rubber stamp with a little confectioner's sugar and gently press it into the fondant, without pressing all the way through.

2. Cut out a circle of fondant surrounding the stamped area large enough to encase the whole cookie. Attach to the cookie with royal icing. Trim the edges if necessary.

To Make Braid and Flower Cookies

1. Dust a work surface with confectioners' sugar. Roll the fondant out to 1/16 inch thick. Cut the fondant in a circle large enough to wrap around the top and sides of the cookie. Attach to the cookie with royal icing. Trim the edges if necessary.

2. Dust a work surface with confectioners' sugar. Roll one

piece of green and one piece of blue fondant into ropes each ⅛-inch wide and length of the circumference.

3. Pinch one end of the strips together. Twist the strips into a rope. When the twist is complete, wrap it around the top edge of the cookie and pinch the ends together. Attach to the cookie with royal icing.

4. Cut graduated sized flowers out of fondant with cookie cutters. Attach with royal icing.

To Make Basket-Weave Cookies

1. Dust a work surface with confectioners' sugar. Roll some of the fondant out to ¹⁄₁₆-inch thick and some to ⅛-inch thick.

2. Cut the ¹⁄₁₆-inch-thick fondant into a circle large enough to wrap around the top and sides of the cookie. Attach to the cookie with royal icing. Trim the edges if necessary.

3. Cut the ⅛-inch-thick fondant into 8 strips about the same length as the diameter of the cookie you are decorating. Lay out the parallel strips with ⅛ inch between each strip. Cut more identical-size strips from the other fondant color. Weave the new strips perpendicular to, and in and out of, the first set of strips.

4. Trim the basket weave into a circle with a cookie cutter the size of the cookie. Attach to the cookie with royal icing.

5. Pipe stars around the border of the basket weave.

To Make Bow Cookies

1. Dust a work surface with confectioners' sugar. Roll half of the fondant out to ¹⁄₁₆ -inch thick. Cut into a circle large enough to top the cookie. Attach to the cookie with royal icing. Trim the edges if necessary.

2. Cut two more strips 1½-inch to create ribbon ends. Notch the ends by cutting triangles out of them. Pinch the other ends to the back of the bow. Attach to the cookie with royal icing.

3. Roll the second batch of fondant to ⅛-inch. Cut two strips 3-inch length and form two loops for the bow. Pinch the loops together to attach in the center. Cut another 2″ strip to wrap around and cover the intersection of the loops.

4. Pipe a royal icing border around the edge of the fondant.

To Make Striped and Dotted Cookies

1. Dust a work surface with confectioners' sugar. Roll the fondant out to ¹⁄₁₆- inch thick. Cut into a square large enough to wrap around the top and sides of the cookie. Attach to the cookie with royal icing. Trim the edges if necessary.

2. Cut out fondant dots with a straw. Attach to the cookies in an offset grid with royal icing.

3. Cut out fondant ⅛-inch stripes with a utility knife. Attach to the cookies with royal icing leaving ¹⁄₁₆-inch space in between the stripes.

To Make Flower Cookies

1. Dust a work surface with confectioners' sugar. Roll the fondant out to ¹⁄₁₆- inch thick. Cut into a circle large enough to sit on the top of the cookie. Attach to the

cookie with royal icing. Trim the edges if necessary. Pipe a royal icing border around the edge of the fondant.

2. Cut out graduated sized flowers with cookie cutters and a dot for the center with a straw. Attach with royal icing.

Grad Cookies

Type of cookie: Rolled cutout

18 cookies

Shortbread Butter Cookie dough
  (page 271)
Royal Icing (page 274)
Black food coloring
Photo transfers

I am a big fan of vintage ads. It is fun to see how life milestones are interpreted in different eras. Some are beautifully illustrated, and others are just hysterical. My collection dates all the way back to the late 1800s, and I have the ads organized by theme—graduation, baby, birthday, wedding, and so on. This assortment of cookies with graduation ads from different eras is made with photo transfers. The border is piped to make the cookies formal.

1. Refrigerate the dough for 1 hour; then roll it out to ¼ inch thick. Cut out shapes ½ inch larger than your photo transfer images. This will leave a ¼-inch border all the way around the cookies. Cover and refrigerate for 30 minutes.

2. Preheat the oven to 325°F. Line 2 cookie sheets with parchment paper.

3. Place the shapes on the cookie sheets 2 inches apart. Bake for 10 to 14 minutes, until light golden. Let cool on the pans for 30 minutes. Transfer to a rack to cool further.

4. Cut out the photo transfers and freeze for 20 minutes, or until firm. Divide the icing into two bowls. Leave one white and color the other black. Spread a light coat of white royal icing on each cookie. While the icing is still wet, peel the transfers off of the backing paper and set it on top of the icing. Press down gently to remove air bubbles.

5. Pipe a scalloped border around the transfer using a small patterned tip. Let dry.

Chapter 5

Holiday Cookies

NEW YEAR'S EVE COOKIES

Come New Year's Eve, everyone in America has eaten enough fruitcake, peppermint, and gingerbread to last them the next dozen months, and it's time for a big change. Some resolve to diet, but others know their limits and don't even try. For those of you who like to live life to the fullest, here is a collection of cookies for the last night of the year—worthy of a celebration.

Bow-Tie Cookies

Type of cookie: Fried

24 cookies

> 1½ cups all-purpose flour
>
> 2 tablespoons baking powder
>
> ¼ teaspoon salt
>
> 5 large egg yolks
>
> 2 tablespoons granulated sugar
>
> 2 tablespoons sour cream
>
> 2 teaspoons rum
>
> 1 cup vegetable oil
>
> ½ cup confectioners' sugar

Inspired by the formal nature of the occasion, celebrate the last night of the year with black-and-whites, bow-tie cookies, and champagne.

1. Combine the flour, baking powder, and salt in a medium bowl; set aside.

2. Beat the egg yolks and granulated sugar until thick; then beat in the sour cream and rum until blended.

3. Add the flour mixture and stir until smooth. Gather the dough into a ball and press it into a flat disk, wrap in plastic wrap, and refrigerate for 30 minutes.

Left: Bow Tie Cookies, Black and White Anisette Cookies.

4. Roll the dough out to ⅛ inch thick. Cut ¾ inch -wide strips with a knife. To make serrated edges cut the strips into 2½-inch lengths with a pastry cutter.

5. Wrap half of the strips around the centers of the other half of the strips, and press together to make bow shapes.

6. Heat the oil to 350°F. Fry the cookies a few at a time for 1 to 2 minutes, turning them to brown evenly on each side. Use a slotted spoon to transfer them to paper towels to drain. Dust with confectioners' sugar.

Black-and-White Anisette Cookies

Type of cookie: Drop

12 cookies

These cookies say "New York" and "Times Square" to me. As a native New Yorker, I grew up seeing these cookies in every Italian and Jewish bakery. Also known as half moons, they are cakey and light in texture. I use anisette to give them a slight black licorice taste.

1. Preheat the oven to 350°F. Butter 2 cookie sheets.

2. Make the cookies: Combine the flours, baking powder, and salt in a large bowl; set aside.

3. Beat the granulated sugar and butter until fluffy. Add the eggs, milk, anisette, and vanilla and mix until smooth.

4. Add the flour mixture in batches, stirring until each batch is thoroughly incorporated. Drop 2-tablespoon mounds of the dough on the cookie sheets 2 inches apart. Bake for 15 to 18 minutes, until the edges are golden. Transfer to a rack to cool.

5. Make the icing: Put the confectioners' sugar in a bowl. Gradually stir in water, mixing to make a spreadable icing.

6. Transfer half of the icing to a double boiler, and add the chocolate. Heat over simmering water, stirring until the

Cookies

2½ cups cake flour
2½ cups all-purpose flour
1 teaspoon baking powder
½ teaspoon salt
1¾ cups granulated sugar
1 cup (2 sticks) butter, softened
4 large eggs
1 cup milk
2 tablespoons anisette
1 teaspoon vanilla extract

Icing

4 cups confectioners' sugar
⅓ to ½ cup water
2 ounces bittersweet chocolate,
  chopped

chocolate is melted and the frosting is smooth. Remove from the heat.

7. With an icing spatula, coat half of each cookie with white icing and the other half with chocolate icing. Let sit for 30 minutes to harden.

Fortune Cookies

Type of cookie: Hand shaped

12 cookies

Although we think of fortune cookies as Chinese, they are a modern California invention. I like to prepare them for New Year's Eve and make up fortunes for the coming year. Hand forming these cookies while they're warm is a bit tricky. Bake them in small batches and work quickly, returning the cookies to the oven if necessary to soften them if they harden before you've formed them.

1. Preheat the oven to 225°F. Draw 5-inch circles on parchment paper and use it to line a cookie sheet. Ready a wide bowl.

2. Combine the flour, confectioners' sugar, and salt in a small bowl; set aside.

3. Beat the egg whites for about 30 seconds, until blended. Stir in the butter, cream, and vanilla.

4. Gradually add the flour mixture, stirring until well mixed.

5. Spoon ½ to 1 tablespoon of the batter into the center of each circle. With the back of a spoon, spread the batter to fill the circles. Bake for 17 to 20 minutes, until cookies begin to color but are not golden. Remove from the oven.

6. Working quickly, with a spatula lift a cookie from the cookie sheet. Place a fortune in the center and fold the circle in half, pinching the edge together to

---

1 cup plus 2 tablespoons all-purpose flour

1 cup confectioners' sugar

⅛ teaspoon salt

4 large egg whites

5 tablespoons butter, melted and cooled

3 tablespoons heavy cream

1 teaspoon vanilla extract

12 fortunes printed with printer or hand written on assorted pastel paper

Royal Icing (page 274)

¼ cup assorted colored sugars

form a semicircle. Bend the semicircle in the center over the edge of the prepared wide bowl. Set on a plate to harden. Repeat with the remaining cookies.

7. Dip the closed ends of the cookies into the icing. Sprinkle with colored sugars.

Fortunes

My friend Mark and I came up with this list based on common phrases. You can use them as a starting point to create your own.

- You are the greatest thing since sliced bread
- Happiness is just around the corner
- Good wine needs no bush
- Dot your i's and cross your t's
- When life gives you lemons, make lemonade
- Fight fire with fire
- You will live to be older than God
- Order takeout
- It takes two to shake the money tree
- A watched pot never boils
- Necessity is the mother of invention
- A friend is a gift
- Taste forbidden fruit
- Creativity springs up like mushrooms
- Make quick, rash decisions
- The walls have ears
- Act as nutty as a fruitcake
- Follow your pie-in-the-sky ideas
- Have yourself a field day
- He who laughs last didn't get the joke
- You can prosper in the field of door-to-door salesmanship
- Sanity is overrated
- Why do today what you can put off until tomorrow
- A visitor is coming your way
- To shine is better than to reflect
- You take the cake
- Recruit a sidekick

Champagne–White Chocolate Meringues

Type of cookie: Piped

18 cookies

6 large egg whites

¼ teaspoon salt

2 cups superfine sugar

½ cup champagne

2 ounces white chocolate, melted and cooled

With a touch of champagne, these melt-in-your-mouth white chocolate meringues are a tasty way to toast the New Year. These are piped with a large star tip and at 3 inches are pretty big and impressive, but they can also be made into 1 inch smaller bites. Just cut down the baking time to 50 to 60 minutes.

1. Preheat the oven to 250°F. Line 2 cookie sheets with parchment paper.

2. Beat the egg whites and salt until soft peaks form. Gradually add the superfine sugar and champagne, beating until stiff, glossy peaks form.

3. Fold in the chocolate.

4. Fit a pastry bag with a 1-inch star tip, and fill halfway with the meringue mixture. Pipe 2-inch rosettes on the cookie sheets 2 inches apart. Bake for 70 to 80 minutes, until the meringues are dry. Turn off the oven and leave the pans in the oven for 1 hour to allow the cookies to dry out.

5. Transfer the parchment and cookies to racks to cool. Peel off the paper when ready to serve.

Thumbprints with Mocha Icing

Type of cookie: Drop

20 cookies

On New Year's Eve, the party usually doesn't get into full swing until just before midnight, way past my normal bedtime. In order to stay up extra late, I created these cream cheese thumbprint cookies with hidden chocolate-covered espresso beans and mocha icing. In my opinion, cream cheese, chocolate, and coffee is the greatest flavor combination ever discovered, and together in these cookies they taste unbelievable.

Cream Cheese Cookies

1 ¾ cups all-purpose flour
1 teaspoon baking powder
¼ teaspoon salt
½ cup butter, softened
⅓ cup cream cheese, softened
½ cup granulated sugar
1 large egg
½ teaspoon vanilla extract
2 tablespoons brewed espresso

Mocha Filling

¾ cup (1½ sticks) butter, softened
2½ cups confectioners' sugar or
  more if needed
2 tablespoons coffee liqueur
⅛ teaspoon salt
2 large egg yolks
1 tablespoon vanilla extract
2 tablespoons cocoa powder
¾ cup semisweet chocolate, melted
  and cooled
20 espresso beans

Top right: Thumbprints with Mocha Icing.

1. Preheat the oven to 325°F. Line 2 cookie sheets with parchment paper.

2. Make the cream cheese cookies: Combine the flour, baking powder, and salt in a medium bowl; set aside.

3. Beat the butter, cream cheese, and granulated sugar until blended. Add the egg, vanilla, and espresso, and beat until blended.

4. Gradually add the flour mixture, stirring until blended.

5. Form the dough into 1½-inch balls. Flatten them slightly; then press down into the center with your thumb, leaving an indentation. Place the balls on the cookie sheets 2 inches apart. Bake for 10 to 12 minutes, until golden.

6. Make the filling: Cream the butter and confectioners' sugar until smooth.

7. Beat in the liqueur, salt, egg yolks, vanilla, cocoa powder, and chocolate. Add more sugar if necessary to reach desired piping consistency. Fit a piping bag with a large tip, and fill the bag with the filling.

8. Place an espresso bean in the indentation in each cookie and with a star tip pipe the filling on top.

VALENTINE'S DAY COOKIES

I recently realized I miss that time in grammar school when I prepared Valentine's Day cards for everyone in my class, even the bullies . Once I gave them the card, they seemed a lot nicer. As an adult I upped the ante from a small paper card with cheesy illustrations to these special Valentine's cookies. Whether your friends and family receive the down-home red velvet cookies or the fancier saffron gifts and extra-special tattoo cookies, everyone appreciates the gesture.

Saffron Heart Necklaces

Type of cookie: Rolled cutout

24 cookies

½ teaspoon saffron threads
1½ teaspoons hot water
1¾ cups all-purpose flour
2 tablespoons cornstarch
½ teaspoon baking soda
½ teaspoon cream of tartar
⅛ teaspoon salt
½ cup (1 stick) butter, softened
½ cup sugar
1 large egg
1 tablespoon honey
1 drop orange food coloring
Royal Icing (page 274)

Valentine's Day is a good excuse to break out the saffron, the most expensive spice in the world. Sweetened with honey for your sweeties, these heart necklaces strung on a ribbon and packaged in little white fabric bags are thoughtful gifts to give out as valentines.

1. Soak the saffron threads in the hot water for 30 minutes.

2. Combine the flour, cornstarch, baking soda, cream of tartar, and salt in a medium bowl; set aside.

3. Beat the butter and sugar until creamy. Add the egg, honey, food coloring, and saffron mixture, and beat until smooth. Gradually add the flour mixture, stirring until combined.

4. Form the dough into 2 flat disks, wrap in plastic wrap, and refrigerate for 30 minutes.

5. Preheat the oven to 300°F. Line 2 cookie sheets with parchment paper.

6. Roll the dough out on a floured work surface to ¼ inch thick. Cut out with a heart-shaped cookie cutter. Cut smaller hearts or holes in the center. Place on the cookie sheets 1½ inches apart. Bake for 12 to 15 minutes, until golden. Transfer to racks to cool.

7. Pipe delicate details with royal icing.

Chocolate Cookie dough
    (page 271)
Royal Icing (page 274)
White, red, green, black, yellow,
    and red food coloring

Valentine's Tattoos

Type of cookie: Rolled cutout

12 cookies

Who said Valentine's Day needs to be all sweet and cutesy? Roses and hearts can have a sweet toughness about them, as they do in these love tattoos. Made with a rich chocolate cookie (what is Valentine's Day without chocolate?), these designs are inspired by Sailor Jerry, (1911–73), a tattoo artist from Hawaii.

1. Roll the dough out to ¼ inch thick on a floured cutting board. Cover and refrigerate for 1 hour.

2. Preheat the oven to 350°F. Line 2 cookie sheets with parchment paper.

3. Using a utility knife and the photo at left, cut out the cookies. Place the shapes on the cookie sheets 1½ inches apart. Bake for 10 to 12 minutes, until firm. Let cool on the pans for 10 minutes. Transfer to a rack to cool completely.

4. Divide the royal icing into 3 small batches for white, yellow, and green and 2 slightly larger batches for red and black. Color each batch with one food coloring. With a small writing tip, pipe all of the black outlines for hearts, banners, leaves, flowers, and birds; let dry. Fill the outlines with colors and let dry. Write text over the banners and add the final details.

Red Velvet Cookies with Cream Cheese Filling

Type of cookie: Cake mix, drop

20 cookies, 10 sandwiches

Instead of purchasing a red velvet box of candy for Valentine's Day, make some red velvet cookies. Red velvet, a popular cake flavor in the American South, has become a national favorite for cupcakes, and it works just as well for cookies. These cookies are made with cake mix, so they are super easy for kids to make for parents and friends.

Red Velvet Cookies

1 box red velvet cake mix

⅓ cup cocoa power

2 large eggs

⅓ cup oil

10 drops red food coloring

¾ cup chocolate chips

Toppings

Cream Cheese Filling (page 275)

2 ounces semisweet chocolate,
    melted and cooled

½ cup pecans, chopped

½ cup shredded sweetened coconut

1. Preheat the oven to 350°F. Line 2 cookie sheets with parchment paper.

2. Make the red velvet cookies: Combine the dry cake mix, cocoa powder, eggs, oil, and food coloring in a bowl. Mix until well blended. Stir in the chocolate chips.

3. Shape the dough into 1½-inch balls. Place the balls on the cookie sheets 2 inches apart. Bake for 10 to 12 minutes, until firm. Transfer to a rack to cool.

4. Divide the frosting into 2 batches. Stir the chocolate into one batch.

5. Spread the plain cream cheese filling on one quarter of the cookies and the chocolate frosting on another quarter of the cookies. Top with the remaining cookies to make sandwiches. Roll the edges of some of the sandwiches in pecans and the edges of others in coconut and leave some plain.

EASTER COOKIES

Easter is the most important Christian religious holiday in many countries but in many places in America it is as much about the new beginnings associated with spring as it is about religion. Baskets of eggs, flowers, bunnies, and their favorite food, carrots, are the symbols of the season. Candy is the treat.

3 cups Shortbread Butter Cookie
  dough (page 271)
¼ cup cocoa powder
Blue, orange, and green food
  coloring
Royal Icing (page 274)
Green sugar
1 cup jelly beans
¼ cup malt balls
¼ cup candied almonds
1 tablespoon mini–candy flowers

Butter Cookie Easter Baskets

Type of cookie: Molded

12 baskets

On Easter Sunday these cookies are real kid pleasers. And oh, the extras—jelly beans, malt balls, and candied almonds—are just the right size to fill up the entire basket. I made these in tartlet pans, but small cupcake pans work just as well. The baskets are easiest to assemble and complete one at a time so that the royal icing remains wet and doubles as glue for the handle and the candies.

1. Preheat the oven to 300°F. Butter minitartlet pans and place on a rimmed baking sheet. Line a second baking sheet with parchment paper.

2. Divide the dough into 4 batches. Add the cocoa to one batch, blue food coloring to another, and orange to another. Leave the last plain. Reserve ¼ batch of each color for basket handles.

3. To make the basket, use your fingers to press the doughs one color at a time into the tartlet pans so the top edges sit ¼ inch from the rim. Bake for 9 to 12 minutes, until firm. Let cool in the pans for 10 minutes. Turn the cookies out onto a rack to cool further.

4. For the handle, roll 3 colors of dough into ¼-inch-thick ropes 4 inches long. Braid the ropes together, alternating the colors. Place on a cookie sheet and bend into a U shape, making sure it is sized to fit ⅜ inch from

the edge of the basket on both sides. Line up the ends of the tips of the U so they are even and will sit flat on the top of the basket when inverted. Bake for 5 to 7 minutes, until firm. Let cool on the pans.

5. Color the icing with green food coloring. Add half of the icing to a pastry bag with a small tip. With a spoon, pool the icing in the baskets; then pipe textured grass by piping icing back and forth around the top edge of the basket. While the icing is still wet, attach the handles. Keep them upright with toothpicks on each side to hold them in place while the icing dries. Attach the candies to the pooled green icing, and sprinkle with green sugar. Attach miniflowers to the candies with icing.

Orange Butter Cookies

1½ cups all-purpose flour

¼ teaspoon salt

⅔ cup butter, cubed

⅓ cup granulated sugar

1 tablespoon grated orange zest

2 tablespoons orange juice

2 large egg yolks

Toppings

Royal Icing (page 274)

Blue, green, black, and yellow food coloring

Dragées or other candies

Colored sugars

Orange Bunny and Flower Cookies

Type of cookie: Rolled cutout

12 large cookies

Filling Easter baskets with homemade bunny and flower cookies is so much more thoughtful than purchasing premade ones at the supermarket. These butter cookies are orange flavored, but you can use lemon or lime juice and zest instead of orange.

1. Make the orange butter cookies: Combine the flour and salt in a food processor or blender. Add the butter, and pulse until the mixture resembles coarse meal.

2. Add the granulated sugar, orange zest, orange juice, and egg yolks. Pulse until the dough gathers into a ball.

3. Wrap in plastic wrap and refrigerate for 30 minutes.

4. Preheat the oven to 325°F. Butter 2 cookie sheets.

5. Roll the dough out to ¼ inch thick on a floured work surface. Cut out bunnies and flowers in assorted sizes and dots. Place the cookies on the cookie sheets 1½ inches apart. Bake for 8 to 10 minutes, until golden. Transfer to a rack to cool.

6. Divide the icing into 5 batches, one large and 4 smaller batches. Color 4 batches of icing with one each of the food colorings, leaving the large batch plain white. Pipe an outline on each of the bunnies with white icing and fill. Attach candies and sprinkle with colored sugar. Let dry. Pipe faces and details on the bunnies.

Below: Orange Bunny and Flower Cookies.

7. Pipe outlines and patterns on the flowers, and cover details with dragées and sugar. Then attach the cookies to each other to make dimensional flowers.

Variation

Marshmallow Bunnies: Omit the royal icing and top the cookies with Marshmallow Frosting (page 276).

Sunflower Carrot Cookies ♥

Type of cookie: Drop

30 cookies

3¾ cups all-purpose flour
1 tablespoon baking powder
1½ teaspoons ground cinnamon
½ teaspoon ground allspice
¼ teaspoon salt
1 cup (2 sticks) butter, softened
1 cup light brown sugar
3 large eggs
½ cup honey
1 teaspoon vanilla extract
2 cups shredded carrots
½ cup chopped walnuts
¼ cup sunflower seeds

Floppy, our rabbit when I was growing up (he had one ear that was bent), liked sunflower seeds with his carrots. I think he was on to something, so I included them in these healthy cookies.

1. Preheat the oven to 350°F. Line 2 cookie sheets with parchment paper.

2. Combine the flour, baking powder, cinnamon, allspice, and salt in a large bowl; set aside.

3. Beat the butter and brown sugar until fluffy. Add the eggs, honey, and vanilla and beat well.

4. Gradually add the flour mixture, and beat until combined. Stir in the carrots, walnuts, and sunflower seeds.

5. Drop rounded-teaspoon mounds of the dough on the cookie sheets 2 inches apart. Bake for 10 to 12 minutes, until lightly browned. Let cool on the pans for 3 minutes. Transfer to a rack to cool completely.

Variation

Carrot Raisin Cookies: Omit the walnuts and add ¾ cup golden raisins. Top with Lemon Icing (page 276).

Above: Sunflower Carrot Cookies.

1 cup (2 sticks) butter, softened

½ cup confectioners' sugar plus more for dusting

2¼ cups all-purpose flour

½ teaspoon ground ginger

1 teaspoon grated lemon zest

4 large eggs

1¾ cups granulated sugar

⅔ cup freshly squeezed lemon juice, about 5 lemons

½ teaspoon baking powder

Lemon Bars

Type of cookie: Bar

12 bars

The tartness of lemons tastes, to me, like the Springness of Easter. I added some ginger to the crust to give it a bit of bite. These bars are quick and easy to make and would be a refreshing alternative to lemonade for the kids' next capital venture.

1. Preheat the oven to 350°F. Butter and flour a 9 x 13-inch baking pan.

2. Beat the butter and confectioners' sugar until fluffy.

3. Stir in 2 cups of the flour, the ginger, and the lemon zest.

4. Press the dough into the bottom of the pan and bake for 20 to 25 minutes, until golden. Set aside.

5. Combine the eggs, granulated sugar, and lemon juice in a medium bowl and stir until blended. Stir in the remaining ¼ cup flour and the baking powder.

6. Pour over the baked crust and bake for 20 to 25 minutes, until firm. Let cool for 10 minutes.

7. Dust with confectioners' sugar and cut into squares.

Variations

Lime Coconut Squares: Replace the lemon zest with lime zest and lemon juice with lime juice. Add ½ cup shredded sweetened coconut along with the flour to the crust and sprinkle ¼ cup over the crust before adding the custard.

Orange Almond Squares: Replace the lemon zest with orange zest and lemon juice with orange juice. Add ½ cup ground almonds along with the flour to the crust. After the bars are baked, top with candied almonds.

Above: Lemon Bars.

MOTHER'S DAY AND FATHER'S DAY COOKIES

Baking cookies for Mom and Dad is gratifying both for the baker and for the receiver. Cookies are some of the simplest desserts to put together, and the perfect introduction to baking for kids. These simple cookie recipes were designed with lots of wow factor, so they're ideal for kids to make and grown-ups to enjoy.

Shortbread Butter Cookie dough
   (page 271)
Photo transfers
Royal Icing (page 274)

Old Family Photo Cookies

Type of cookie: Rolled cutout

12 cookies

Surprise your parents with cookies made with old family photos. Pictures of special moments or funny times spent growing up are good choices.

1. Refrigerate the dough for 1 hour.

2. Line 2 cookie sheets with parchment paper.

3. Roll the dough out on a floured work surface to ¼ inch thick. Cut the cookies ½ inch bigger than your photo transfer images. This will leave a ¼-inch border all the way around. Place the shapes on the cookie sheets 2 inches apart, cover with plastic wrap, and refrigerate for 30 minutes.

4. Preheat the oven to 350°F.

5. Bake the cookies for 10 to 14 minutes, until light golden. Let cool on the pans for 30 minutes. Transfer to a rack to cool further.

6. Cut out the photo transfers and freeze for 20 minutes, or until firm. Spread a light coat of icing on a cookie. While the icing is still wet, peel the transfer off the backing paper and set it on top of the icing. Press down gently to remove air bubbles.

7. Pipe a border of royal icing around the transfer using a small writing tip. Let dry.

Thank-You Cookies

Type of cookie: Rolled cutout

40 cookies, 5 thank-you sets

On Mother's Day and Father's Day it is really nice to also thank parents, grandparents, and stepparents for all they do. These sweetly packaged chocolate cookies, which spell "thank you," have lots of good karma. There are many ways to make these; here I made simple circles and embossed the letters in the cookie, then piped in some white chocolate to highlight the letters. They can also be cut out into letter shapes, or the letters can be punched out of the center. You can also, of course, make them to thank a friend for a thoughtful gesture or to thank donors at a fund-raiser.

1. Make the chocolate cookies: Combine the flour, cocoa powder, baking soda, cream of tartar, and salt in a medium bowl; set aside.

2. Beat the butter and brown sugar with a mixer in a medium bowl until smooth and creamy. Add the eggs and vanilla and mix well.

3. Gradually add the flour mixture to the butter mixture, mixing on low speed until blended. Divide the dough into 2 flattened disks, wrap in plastic wrap, and refrigerate for 30 minutes.

4. Preheat the oven to 350°F. Line 2 cookie sheets with parchment paper.

5. Roll the dough out on a floured work surface to ⅛ inch thick. Using a 2-inch round cutter, cut 8 cookies for each thank-you set. Cut the leftover dough into extra cookies.

6. With alphabet cookie cutters, emboss the letters that spell "thank you" into the individual cookies. Emboss the remaining cookies with star, heart, or flower cutters. Place the shapes on the cookie sheets 1½ inches apart. Bake for 8 to 10 minutes, until crisp. Transfer to a rack to cool.

Chocolate Cookies

3½ cups all-purpose flour

1 cup cocoa powder

1½ teaspoons baking soda

1½ teaspoons cream of tartar

½ teaspoon salt

1½ cups (3 sticks) butter, softened

3 cups light brown sugar

3 large eggs

1 tablespoon vanilla extract

Topping

1 cup white chocolate

1 tablespoon butter

7. Make the topping: Heat the white chocolate and butter in a double boiler over simmering water, stirring until melted. Put in a pastry bag with a small tip and pipe around the inside of the embossed letters.

8. Package in a long, narrow box with nuts or candy in between the letters.

Coconut Bars

Type of cookie: Cake mix, bar
20 bars

There is something about making a recipe from cake mix that makes the whole process seem easier. Here is one of my favorites. It's so easy little kids can make it—big kids, too.

½ cup (1 stick) butter, melted and cooled
1 box yellow cake mix
3 large eggs
2 cups confectioners' sugar
1 (8-ounce) package cream cheese
½ cup shredded sweetened coconut
¾ cup chocolate chips
½ cup maraschino cherries

1. Preheat the oven to 325°F. Butter an 11½ x 7½-inch pan.

2. Stir together the butter, dry cake mix, and 1 of the eggs until moistened. Press into the pan and set aside.

3. Beat the confectioners' sugar, cream cheese, and remaining eggs with a mixer until smooth.

4. Stir in the coconut, chocolate chips, and cherries.

5. Spread evenly over the cake-mix layer. Bake for 40 to 45 minutes, until golden. Let cool in the pan.

6. Cut into squares.

Variation

Coconut Maple Walnut Bars: Replace the chocolate chips with chopped walnuts. Drizzle the baked bars with maple syrup.

FOURTH OF JULY COOKIES

We have our founding fathers to thank for picking this day in the middle of summer to sign the Declaration of Independence. If they had picked a day in February, we wouldn't have the amazing summertime weather throughout this great land to celebrate the day. And what would the Fourth be without fireworks, barbecues, picnics, and block and beach parties? Betsy Ross did a pretty good job too, in designing the flag: She probably knew that stars and stripes would work brilliantly on festive cookies.

Fourth of July Pinwheels

Type of cookie: Hand shaped

6 pinwheels

Pinwheel cookies on a stick are fun to make with kids for a Fourth of July block party or picnic. I experimented with many cookie doughs to make the perfect pinwheels. The addition of almond butter and a lot of eggs makes this dough stretchy and prevents cracking on the folds. For patriotic colors, add some red or blue food coloring to the dough.

1. Make the cookies: Put the flour, confectioners' sugar, and almond butter in a food processor or blender. Pulse until the mixture resembles coarse meal. Transfer the mixture to a bowl.

2. Stir in 6 of the eggs and 2 yolks, one at a time, and vanilla and mix to make a soft dough. Divide the dough in half. Add red food coloring to one batch and blue to the other. Wrap each batch in plastic wrap and refrigerate for 30 minutes.

3. Roll the doughs out on a floured cutting board to ¼ inch thick and a rough square shape. Cover with plastic wrap and refrigerate for 30 minutes.

4. Preheat the oven to 350°F. Line 2 cookie sheets with parchment paper. Ready 6-inch wooden lollipop sticks, dowels, or ice pop sticks.

Cookies

3¾ cups all-purpose flour
3 cups confectioners' sugar
½ cup almond butter
8 large eggs, 2 of them separated
2 teaspoons sugar
2½ teaspoons vanilla extract
12 drops red food coloring
12 drops blue food coloring

Toppings

Royal Icing (page 274)
Red and blue food coloring
Red sugar
Blue sugar
Cinnamon candies

Right: Fourth of July Pinwheels, Stars and Stripes.

5. Cut the dough into 4½-inch squares with a pastry cutter or fluted square cutter. Cut slits in from the corners, stopping about 1 inch from the center. Press a stick in the center and fold every other corner over it. Beat the 2 remaining egg whites in a small bowl. Brush some of the egg wash over the center of the pinwheels. Press the tips down to seal.

6. Place the pinwheels on the cookie sheets 2 inches apart. Bake for 15 to 18 minutes, until the cookies look firm and the edges are browned a bit. Let cool on the pans for 20 minutes.

7. Divide the royal icing into 3 batches; make one batch red and one blue, and leave one plain white. Spread the colored icings on the flat parts of the pinwheels. While they are still wet, top them with colored sugars. Pipe dots and spirals in the center with colored icing. Attach the cinnamon candies to the dot centers.

8. Pipe white dot and striped patterns on the folded parts of the pinwheels.

Stars and Stripes

Type of cookie: Icebox

18 cookies

I usually make a double batch of pinwheel cookies and use half of the dough to make these patriotic treats, but you can use the Shortbread Butter Cookie dough (page 271) with two different colors. Just make sure you brush egg wash between the layers and press them together firmly, or they will separate.

1. Line a 5 x 7-inch loaf pan with waxed paper.

2. Roll the red dough out on a floured work surface to ⅛ inch thick and about 5 x 7 inches. Press the dough into the bottom of the pan. Brush the layer with egg wash.

3. Repeat with the blue dough. Continue adding layers and egg wash until the stack is about 1¾ inches high. Cover and freeze for 2 hours.

4. Preheat the oven to 375°F. Butter 2 cookie sheets.

5. With a sharp knife, slice the loaf into two 2½-inch blocks, and then slice into ¼-inch cookies. Place on the cookie sheets 1½ inches apart. Bake for 8 to 10 minutes, until golden. Transfer to a rack to cool.

6. Dip one edge of each cookie into the icing. While the icing is still wet, top with candy stars. Let set.

Fourth of July Pinwheels dough (page 210), half colored red and half blue
4 large egg whites, lightly beaten
Royal Icing (page 274)
Candy stars

Cookies

3¾ cups all-purpose flour
2 teaspoons baking powder
⅛ teaspoon salt
1 cup (2 sticks) butter, softened
1⅓ cups sugar
2 large eggs
¼ cup cherry juice
2 teaspoons vanilla extract
½ cup pitted fresh cherries,
   chopped
½ cup fresh blueberries, chopped
10 drops blue food coloring

Toppings

Royal Icing (page 274)
Red, blue, yellow, and black food
   coloring
Rainbow nonpareils

Explosion Cookies

Type of cookies: Rolled cutout

8 cookies

These cherry, blueberry and butter cutout cookies highlight the colors of the holiday and the flavors of summertime. "Bam," "pow," "kaboom," "wham," "zap"—these playfully decorated cookies evoke the sounds of fireworks explosions on the Fourth of July, not to mention retro comic books.

1. Combine the flour, baking powder, and salt; set aside.

2. Cream the butter and sugar until fluffy. Beat in the eggs, then the cherry juice and vanilla.

3. Gradually stir in the flour mixture. Divide the dough into thirds. Stir the cherries into one third and the blueberries and blue food coloring into another, and leave the last plain. Wrap in plastic wrap and refrigerate for 1 hour.

4. Preheat the oven to 350°F. Line 2 cookie sheets with parchment paper.

5. Roll the doughs out on a floured work surface to ¼ inch thick. Using a cookie cutter and a utility knife and the template on page 278, cut out the explosion and several star shapes. Place the shapes on the cookie sheets 1½ inches apart. If the dough is soft, cover and refrigerate for 30 minutes before baking.

6. Bake for 15 to 18 minutes, until golden brown. Let cool on the pans for 10 minutes. Transfer to a rack to cool.

7. Divide the royal icing into 4 batches. Color each of the 4 batches with one of the food colorings. Pipe the outlines first and let dry completely. Fill with icing. While the icing is still wet, attach smaller star cookies to larger stars and top with nonpareils.

HALLOWEEN COOKIES

Halloween is the fastest growing holiday around the world. Based on a pagan Celtic tradition of scaring lost souls out of the graveyard with brightly lit sculpted turnips, the holiday is marked in America by carved pumpkins. The jack-o'-lantern cookies are great cookies for your kids and their friends, and the caramel apple cookies are a must for a Halloween party.

Jack-o'-Lantern Spice Cookies

Type of cookie: Rolled cutout

30 cookies

Mini-jack-o'-lanterns are fun to hand out to all of your Halloween-loving friends. Cinnamon, nutmeg, and cloves infuse the cookies with holiday flavor, and faces give each cookie its own personality. Package them in a cellophane bag and tie the bag with hemp.

1. Combine the flour, baking powder, salt, cinnamon, nutmeg, and cloves in a medium bowl; set aside.

2. Beat the butter, shortening, and sugar until fluffy. Beat in the egg, milk, and vanilla.

3. Add the flour mixture to the butter mixture and beat well. Add orange food coloring.

4. Divide the dough in half, wrap in plastic wrap, and refrigerate for 2 hours.

5. Preheat the oven to 375°F. Line 2 cookie sheets with parchment paper.

6. Roll one batch of dough out on a floured work surface to ¼ inch thick. Cut out jack-o'-lantern shapes 2 inch to 2½ inches with a cookie cutter or utility knife. With a blunt tool or the back of a knife, press the stripes into the cookie. Place the shapes on the cookie sheets 1½ inches apart. Bake for 8 to 10 minutes, until firm. Let cool on the pans for 30 minutes.

Cookies

2 cups all-purpose flour

1½ teaspoons baking powder

¼ teaspoon salt

1 teaspoon ground cinnamon

¼ teaspoon freshly grated nutmeg

¼ teaspoon ground cloves

6 tablespoons butter, softened

⅓ cup vegetable shortening

¾ cup sugar

1 large egg

1 tablespoon milk

1 teaspoon vanilla extract

8 drops orange food coloring

Topping

Royal Icing (page 274)

12 drops Black food coloring

7. Color the royal icing black, and pipe faces on the cookies with a small writing tip. Let dry.

Variations

Pumpkin Jack-o'-Lanterns: Use the Pumpkin Cookies recipe (page 222).

Candy Jack-o'-Lanterns: Prepare larger 3 inch to 3½ inch cookies and cut out the eyes, noses, and mouths. Place the cookies on the cookie sheets and fill the eyes, noses, and mouths with crushed hard candy before baking. Follow the technique described in the Stained-Glass Ornament Cookies recipe (page 240).

Cookies

3 cups all-purpose flour

1 teaspoon baking powder

1 teaspoon ground cinnamon

¼ teaspoon salt

1 cup (2 sticks) butter, softened

½ cup granulated sugar

½ cup light brown sugar

2 large eggs

2 teaspoons vanilla extract

¼ cup apple juice

½ cup apple butter

1½ cups peeled and chopped apples

1 cup caramel candies, chopped

Caramel Apple Cookies

Type of cookie: Rolled cutout

12 cookies

I modeled this cookie after my favorite Halloween treat, and these caramel apple cookies turned out even tastier than the caramel apples themselves. These cookies are packed with apple chunks and chewy caramel, and then topped with more caramel, plus peanuts. They are prepared as a rolled cutout cookie, but you can also make them into drop thumbprints, leaving a place for the caramel in the center.

1. Combine the flour, baking powder, cinnamon, and salt in a medium bowl; set aside.

2. Beat the butter with the sugars until fluffy. Add the eggs and vanilla and beat until smooth. Stir in the apple juice and apple butter.

3. Gradually add the flour mixture, stirring until blended. Stir in the apples and caramel candies. Flatten the dough into a disk, wrap in plastic wrap, and refrigerate for 1 hour.

4. Preheat the oven to 300°F. Butter 2 cookie sheets. Put a piece of parchment paper under a cooling rack.

5. Roll the dough out on a floured work surface to ¼ inch thick. Using a utility knife, cut out apple shapes

Toppings

Royal Icing (page 274)
6 drops green food coloring
¼ cup (½ stick) butter
⅓ cup dark brown sugar
2 tablespoons light corn syrup
1 tablespoon heavy cream
½ cup chopped peanuts

like the ones seen below. Place the shapes on the cookie sheets 2 inches apart. Bake for 18 to 20 minutes, until browned. Transfer to the rack to cool.

6. Color the icing with green food coloring, and pipe the stem and the leaf on the top of the apple. Let dry.

7. To make the caramel topping, heat the butter, brown sugar, and corn syrup in a saucepan over medium heat, stirring until the sugar is dissolved. Increase the heat and boil for 1 minute. Remove from the heat and stir in the cream. Pour over the tops of the cookies and sprinkle with peanuts. Let harden to a gooey state.

Variations

Chocolate Almond Apple Cookies: Omit the caramel topping. Melt 1½ cups chopped chocolate and pour it over the apple cookies. Top with almond slices and minimarshmallows.

Tropical Caramel Apple Cookies: Top the cookies with sweetened shredded coconut, macadamia nuts, and dried pineapple instead of peanuts.

Right: Caramel Apple Cookies.

THANKSGIVING COOKIES

There is no better time to share the ephemeral flavors of fall than on the Thanksgiving dessert table. All of these cookies are based on tried-and-true American Thanksgiving flavors: cornmeal, the traditional American starch, and molasses and maple, the traditional North American sweeteners. Fall is nut season, and pecans, walnuts, and chestnuts abound in these recipes. A great way to celebrate in addition to indulging with family and friends is to bake batches of these cookies and donate them to food charities or shelters or offer them to the homeless.

Sweet Potato Cookies

Type of cookie: Rolled cutout

15 large cookies

2¼ cups all-purpose flour
2 teaspoons baking powder
½ teaspoon salt
1 tablespoon ground cinnamon
1 tablespoon ground ginger
¼ teaspoon black pepper
½ cup (1 stick) butter, softened
½ cup light brown sugar
1 large egg
¾ cup cooked and mashed sweet potato
2 large egg whites, lightly beaten
¼ cup pecan halves

Sweet potatoes are a traditional Thanksgiving treat, and they're also good for you. That orange color is vitamin A; sweet potatoes also contain vitamin C and antioxidants. This sweet potato cookie is based on a classic southern colonial American recipe, which I adapted to make less sweet. Of course, if healthfulness is not such a concern, top the cookies with Marshmallow Frosting (page 276) for a cookie take on a 1950s-style Thanksgiving side dish.

1. Combine the flour, baking powder, salt, cinnamon, ginger, and pepper in a medium bowl; set aside.

2. Cream the butter and brown sugar until light and fluffy. Add the egg and sweet potato, and beat well.

3. Add the flour mixture and blend well. Form the dough into a flat disk, cover with plastic wrap, and refrigerate for 30 minutes.

4. Preheat the oven to 325°F. Butter 2 cookie sheets.

5. Roll the dough out on a floured work surface to ⅜ inch thick. Cut with a 3-inch flower or round cookie cutter. Place the shapes on the cookie sheets 2 inches apart.

6. Brush the cookies with the egg whites, and press a pecan half into the center of each cookie. Bake for 15 to 18 minutes, until lightly browned. Let cool on the pans for 5 minutes. Transfer to a rack to cool.

Low-Fat Applesauce Cookies ♥

Type of cookie: Drop

15 large cookies

I like to make these extra-large soft cookies in the fall, right after a day of apple picking in the countryside. They stay moist for days, so they are a perfect cookie to prepare ahead of time for Thanksgiving. Try different varieties of apples—from the tartest green apples to the sweetest red—to customize the flavors.

Above: Sweet Potato Cookies, Applesauce Cookies.

2¼ cups all-purpose flour

½ teaspoon baking powder

1 teaspoon ground cinnamon

½ teaspoon freshly grated nutmeg

½ teaspoon ground ginger

2 large eggs

2 tablespoons vegetable oil

1 cup unsweetened applesauce

2 tablespoons frozen apple juice concentrate

1 cup chopped apples, sautéed in a little butter until just soft

1. Preheat the oven to 350°F. Line 2 cookie sheets with parchment paper.

2. Combine the flour, baking powder, cinnamon, nutmeg, and ginger in a medium bowl; set aside.

3. Beat the eggs, oil, applesauce, and apple juice concentrate until blended.

4. Gradually add the flour mixture to the egg mixture. Stir in the apples.

5. Drop the dough with an ice cream scoop onto the cookie sheets 2½ inches apart. Bake for 13 to 16 minutes, until lightly browned. Let cool on the pans for 5 minutes. Transfer to a rack to cool.

Variation

Chocolate Raisin Applesauce Cookies: Reduce the flour to 2 cups. Add ⅓ cup unsweetened cocoa powder to the flour and ½ cup raisins along with the apples to the dough.

Chocolate Turkeys

Type of cookie: Cookie construction

12 turkeys

> When most people are celebrating the bounty of the harvest season, I am celebrating the abundance of candy corn. Part cookie, part candy, these turkeys will be gobbled up in a flash. After all, chocolate is the world's best glue when it comes to cookies.

2 cups semisweet chocolate chips, melted

1½ cups candy corn

12 small malt balls

12 large malt balls

1 batch 2½-inch round Chocolate Cookies (page 208)

24 candy eyes, or 12 white candy dots and 12 smaller black candy dots

1. Line 1 cookie sheet with parchment paper.

2. To make the turkey tails, spoon 1½-inch round pools of the chocolate onto the parchment paper. Set 5 of the candy corns on the chocolate with the tips facing the center. Cover the white tips with melted chocolate. Let set.

3. Attach a small malt ball (the turkey's head) to a large malt ball (the turkey's body) with melted chocolate. Let set.

4. Pool 1 tablespoon melted chocolate in the center of each cookie. Attach the large malt ball to the cookie, with the small malt ball slightly tilted toward the front. Attach the circle of chocolate with the candy-corn feathers.

5. To make the beaks, cut the white tips from pieces of candy corn and attach them to the small malt ball with chocolate. Attach the candy eyes, or use 2 candy dots, a larger white dot and a smaller black dot on top. Let set.

Maple Walnut Cookies

Type of cookie: Rolled cutout

36 1-inch cookies

One bite of these maple walnut cookies, and you will know without a doubt what time of year it is. Cut the dough into maple leaf shapes. Ice the tops with royal icing in fall leaf colors. I also like to leave some plain to represent the brown leaves. For all you Canadians: These taste just as good in the middle of summer at a barbeque or parade or while watching fireworks for Canada Day. You might want to make all the leaves red.

1. Combine the flour, salt, and cinnamon in a medium bowl; set aside.

2. Beat the butter and sugars until fluffy. Beat in the egg yolk, maple syrup, vanilla, and walnuts. Gather into 2 flat disks, wrap in plastic wrap, and refrigerate for 30 minutes.

---

3 cups all-purpose flour

¼ teaspoon salt

½ teaspoon ground cinnamon

1 cup (2 sticks) butter, softened

½ cup granulated sugar

¼ cup dark brown sugar

1 large egg yolk

½ cup maple syrup

1 teaspoon vanilla extract

½ cup walnuts, finely chopped

Royal Icing (page 274)

5 drops each red, orange, green, yellow food coloring

Maple Walnut Cookies, Pecan Molasses Spice Cookies, Pumpkin Cream Cookies.

3. Preheat the oven to 350°F. Line 2 cookie sheets with parchment paper.

4. Roll the dough out on a floured work surface to ⅛ inch thick. Cut out maple leaves using 1-inch cookie cutters. Place the shapes on the cookie sheets 1 inch apart. Bake for 5 to 7 minutes, until lightly browned around the edges. Transfer to a rack to cool.

5. Divide the icing into 4 bowls and color with the icing. Leave some cookies plain and dip the faces of the cookies into the icing and let sit for 20 minutes to dry.

Variations

Maple Cranberry Sandwich Cookies: Replace the walnuts with dried cranberries. Spread half of the cookies with cranberry filling (page 224) and put the remaining cookies on top.

Maple Cream Cheese Sandwich Cookies: Add 2 tablespoons maple syrup to Cream Cheese Filling (page 275). Spread half of the cookies with the filling and put the remaining cookies on top.

Pumpkin Cream Cookies ♥

Type of cookie: Rolled cutout

24 cookies

The quintessential fall combination of cream cheese and pumpkin is carried a step further in these cookies with toasted pumpkin seeds, which give them a nice roasted flavor and graphic touch. Pumpkin is loaded with beta-carotene, and the dairy and the seeds in these cookies make up a full protein.

1. Make the cookies: Combine the flour, salt, baking soda, cinnamon, nutmeg, and ginger in a large bowl; set aside.

2. Beat the brown sugar, oil, egg, and vanilla until blended.

3. Stir in the pumpkin and orange zest. Gradually add the flour mixture, stirring until combined.

4. Roll the dough out on a floured cutting board to ⅛ inch thick, cover, and refrigerate for 30 minutes.

5. Preheat the oven to 350°F. Butter 2 cookie sheets.

6. Cut the dough into circles. Using a smaller circle cookie cutter, press a ring in the center of each cookie, being careful not to press all the way through. With the back of a spoon, press the dough in the center down to make an indented space to hold the cream.

7. Place the shapes on the cookie sheets 1½ inches apart. Bake for 12 to 15 minutes, until lightly browned. Transfer to a rack to cool.

Pumpkin Cookies

3½ cups all-purpose flour

½ teaspoon salt

½ teaspoon baking soda

¼ teaspoon ground cinnamon

½ teaspoon freshly grated nutmeg

¼ teaspoon ground ginger

1½ cups light brown sugar

½ cup vegetable oil

1 large egg

1 tablespoon vanilla extract

1 cup pumpkin puree

½ teaspoon grated orange zest

Orange Cream Cheese Filling

6 ounces cream cheese, softened

¼ cup confectioners' sugar

½ teaspoon orange juice

Topping

¼ cup hulled pumpkin seeds (pepitas)

8. Make the cream cheese filling: Beat the cream cheese, confectioners' sugar, and orange juice with a mixer until smooth. Spoon into the indented space in the cookies. Top with pumpkin seeds.

Variations

Pumpkin Raisin Cookies: Add 1½ cups raisins along with the orange zest to the dough. Top with rum glaze (page 277).

Pumpkin Chip Cookies: Add 1½ cups chocolate chips along with the orange zest to the dough. Replace the cream cheese filling with Chocolate Glaze (page 277).

Pumpkin Cranberry Cookies: Add 1½ cups chopped fresh cranberries along with the orange zest to the dough. Replace the cream cheese filling with Cranberry Filling (page 224).

Pecan Molasses Spice Cookies

Type of cookie: Molded drop

36 cookies

These ultimate mini–pecan pie cookies are an adaptation of colonial-era molasses cookies. Upping the ante on the traditional flavors of Thanksgiving, I added a caramelized pecan topping.

1. Preheat the oven to 350°F. Butter 2 minicupcake pans.

2. Make the molasses cookies: Combine the flour, cinnamon, cloves, ginger, salt, and baking soda in a medium bowl; set aside.

3. Beat the butter, sugars, and molasses until smooth. Beat in the eggs.

4. Stir in the flour mixture until combined.

5. Drop heaping-tablespoon mounds of the dough into the cupcake tins. Press the dough against the sides of the tins. Create a well in the center of each cookie with a teaspoon.

Molasses Cookies

2½ cups all-purpose flour

1½ teaspoons ground cinnamon

1 teaspoon ground cloves

1 teaspoon ground ginger

¾ teaspoon salt

¾ teaspoon baking soda

1½ cups (3 sticks) butter, melted and cooled

1 cup granulated sugar

½ cup light brown sugar

¾ cup molasses

2 large eggs

Pecan Topping

¾ cup chopped pecans plus ½ cup pecan halves

3 tablespoons maple syrup

2 tablespoons brown sugar

6. Make the topping: Combine the chopped pecans, maple syrup, and brown sugar. Spoon the mixture into the wells. Top each with a pecan half.

7. Bake for 8 to 10 minutes, until browned. While the cookies are still warm and soft, run a knife around the edges of the cookies to loosen them. Let them cool in the pan. Gently lift the cookies from the pan.

Variation

Old-Fashioned Molasses Cookies: Omit the pecan topping. Drop heaping-tablespoon mounds of the dough on a cookie sheet lined with parchment paper 2 inches apart. Bake for 12 to 15 minutes until browned.

Cornmeal Cookies

¾ cup all-purpose flour
⅔ cup stone-ground cornmeal
¾ cup (1½ sticks) butter, softened
¼ cup granulated sugar
⅛ teaspoon salt
Grated zest of 1 orange
1 teaspoon orange juice
1 large egg
1 large egg yolk

Cranberry Filling

1 tablespoon cornstarch
1½ cups water
1½ cups fresh cranberries

Cranberry Cornmeal Sandwiches

Type of cookie: Rolled cutout, sandwiches
36 cookies, 18 sandwiches

This recipe combines two Thanksgiving favorites, cornmeal and cranberries. I like to prepare these cookies as petite sandwiches with a plain cornmeal cookie and cranberry filling, or with fresh cranberries mixed into the cookie dough. The variation is especially good when teamed with chocolate.

1. Make the cornmeal cookies: Combine the flour and cornmeal in a medium bowl; set aside.

2. Cream the butter, sugar, salt, orange zest, and orange juice until light and fluffy. Beat in the egg and egg yolk.

3. Add the flour mixture and stir to combine. Form the dough into a flat disk, wrap in plastic wrap, and refrigerate for 1 hour.

4. Preheat the oven to 350°F. Line 2 cookie sheets with parchment paper.

5. Roll the dough out on a floured work surface to ¼ inch

thick. Cut out the dough with 2-inch-square cookie cutters. Place the shapes on the cookie sheets 1 inch apart. Bake for 12 to 15 minutes, until crisp and light golden. Transfer to a rack to cool.

6. Make the filling: In a saucepan over low heat, dissolve the cornstarch in the water. Add the cranberries. Cook, stirring until thickened. Add a bit more cornstarch if needed. Spread the filling on half the cookies, and top with the remaining cookies.

Variations

Cranberry Cornmeal Cookies: Add ⅔ cup fresh chopped cranberries to the cookie dough. Prepare as single cookies.

Chocolate Chip Cranberry Cookies: Add ⅔ cup chopped semisweet chocolate to the dough. Prepare as single cookies.

Lemon Cornmeal Cookies: Replace the orange juice and zest with lemon juice and zest. Prepare as single cookies. Top with Lemon Icing (page 276).

Pecan Cornmeal Cookies: Add ¾ cup chopped pecans to the dough after the wet and dry ingredients are combined.

JEWISH HOLIDAY COOKIES

In another life I must have been Jewish, or it might just be that Jews and Italians are so much alike when it comes to baking. There has to be a reason why I have such a strong affinity for these cookies and I can't keep myself from stopping to purchase macaroons, rugelach, or hamantaschen every time I pass a Jewish deli or bakery. Jewish baking has tremendous significance, and each of these cookies is made with ingredients and shapes that are directly tied to the holidays when they are prepared. I have recently gotten into the habit of inviting myself to my Jewish friends' celebrations as an excuse to bring the cookies. They don't mind—they're always invited to my Christmas gatherings, which of course also feature an array of festive cookies.

Rugelach

Type of cookie: Hand shaped, filled
20 cookies

Rugelach are prepared for Rosh Hashanah, the Jewish New Year, or Hanukkah, the festival of lights. Once the cream cheese dough is prepared, practice with rolling, and experiment with different fillings.

1. Combine the granulated sugar and cinnamon in a small bowl; set aside.

2. Cream the butter, confectioners' sugar, and vanilla until fluffy. Add the cream cheese, and blend until smooth.

3. Add the flour and mix until the dough comes together into a ball. Divide the dough into 4 batches, wrap in plastic wrap, and refrigerate for 2 hours.

4. Preheat the oven to 375°F. Line 2 cookie sheets with parchment paper.

5. Roll one batch of the dough out on a lightly floured work surface into a 12 x 16-inch rectangle ⅛ inch thick. Spread with one-quarter each of the jam, dried apricots, walnuts, and sugar mixture. Cut the rectangle

---

1½ cups granulated sugar

1 tablespoon ground cinnamon

1½ cups (3 sticks) butter, softened

¾ cup confectioners' sugar

1 teaspoon vanilla extract

1½ (8-ounce) packages cream cheese

3½ cups all-purpose flour

2 cups apricot jam

1½ cups chopped dried apricots

2 cups walnuts, toasted and chopped

1 large egg, beaten

1 tablespoon water

4 tablespoons coarse sugar

into triangles and roll into the shapes seen in the uppser right of the photo above. Refrigerate for 20 minutes. Repeat to make 3 more logs.

6. Mix the egg with the water. Brush on. Sprinkle with coarse sugar.

7. Bake for 20 to 30 minutes, until light brown. Transfer to a rack to cool.

Variations

Raspberry Pecan Rugelach: Replace the apricot jam with raspberry jam and the walnuts with pecans. Omit the dried apricots.

Chocolate Currant Rugelach: Replace the apricot jam, dried apricots,

and walnuts with 2 cups chocolate chips and 2 cups currants.
Strawberry Pistachio Rugelach: Replace the apricot jam with raspberry jam and the walnuts with pistachios. Omit the dried apricots.

Passover Macaroons

Type of cookie: Drop

20 cookies

For Passover, observant Jews eat unleavened foods to commemorate their ancestors' hasty departure from Egypt. These macaroons are flourless and get their texture from stiffly beaten egg whites, making them the ideal cookie for the holiday.

2 large egg whites
⅛ teaspoon salt
⅓ cup granulated sugar
3 cups shredded sweetened coconut
1 teaspoon vanilla extract

1. Preheat the oven to 300°F. Line 2 cookie sheets with parchment paper.

2. Beat the egg whites and salt until soft peaks form. Add 4 tablespoons of the sugar and beat until glossy and stiff.

3. Fold in the remaining sugar, coconut, and vanilla.

4. Drop 1-tablespoon mounds of the dough from a cookie scoop on the cookie sheets 2 inches apart. Bake for 15 to 18 minutes, until golden. Let cool on the pans.

Variation

Chocolate Macaroons: Add 4 ounces melted and cooled bittersweet chocolate along with the vanilla to the dough.

Hamantaschen

Type of cookie: Hand shaped, filled

36 cookies

These filled cookies with a cream cheese dough are traditionally prepared for the late-winter holiday of Purim, celebrated with seeds and bringing gifts to friends and drinking wine. The shape of the pastries represents the three-pointed hat that Haman, the villain in the Purim story, supposedly wore. Many types of filling are used for hamantaschen—poppy seeds, apricot, and prune are the most popular—but I think chocolate is also really good.

Poppy-Seed Filling

½ cup poppy seeds

¼ cup sugar

¼ cup chopped raisins

¼ cup chopped walnuts

1 cup milk

½ cup honey

1 large egg

Cream Cheese Dough

3 cups all-purpose flour

1½ teaspoons baking powder

⅛ teaspoon salt

½ cup (1 stick) butter, softened

6 ounces cream cheese, softened

1 teaspoon vanilla extract

2 teaspoons lemon juice

Grated zest of 1 lemon

1 cup sugar

2 large eggs

Chocolate Filling

1 cup semisweet chocolate chips,
  melted

¼ cup sugar

1 tablespoon butter, melted

1 tablespoon milk

1 teaspoon vanilla extract

1 large egg

1. Make the poppy-seed filling: Grind the poppy seeds and sugar in a food processor or blender. Add the raisins and walnuts, and pulse a few times to chop.

2. Transfer to a saucepan and stir in the milk and honey over low heat for 5 to 7 minutes, until thickened. Remove from the heat, and let cool. Stir in the egg.

3. Make the cream cheese dough: Combine the flour, baking powder, and salt in a medium bowl; set aside.

4. Cream the butter, cream cheese, vanilla, lemon juice, and lemon zest with an electric mixer until smooth. Beat in the sugar and eggs.

5. Add the flour mixture to the butter mixture. Stir until just incorporated; do not overmix. Form the dough into a flat disk, wrap in plastic wrap, and refrigerate for 30 minutes.

6. Preheat the oven to 350°F. Butter 2 cookie sheets.

7. Roll the dough out on a floured work surface to ⅛ inch thick. Cut the dough with a cookie cutter into 4-inch rounds. Wet the edges with cold water. Add 1 tablespoon of the filling to the center of each circle cookie.

8. Score 3 points of a triangle on the dough. Fold ¾ inch of the edge of the dough over towards the middle in 3 sections, leaving the filling exposed. Pinch the edges where the dough meets.

9. Place the cookies on the cookie sheets 1½ inches apart. Bake for 30 to 35 minutes, until golden. Let cool on the pans for 5 minutes. Transfer to a rack to cool completely.

Variations

Orange Raspberry Hamantaschen: Replace the lemon juice and zest with orange juice and zest. Replace the poppy-seed filling with raspberry jam.

Lime Apricot Hamantaschen: Replace the lemon juice and zest with lime juice and the zest of 2 limes. Replace the poppy-seed filling with apricot jam.

Chocolate Hamantaschen: Reduce the flour to 1¾ cups and add ⅓ cup cocoa powder to the dry ingredients. Replace the poppy-seed filling with chocolate filling.

Combine the chocolate, sugar, butter, milk, and vanilla in a medium bowl. Let cool a bit; then stir in the egg until combined.

Hanukkah Honey Butter Cookies

Type of cookie: Rolled cutout

24 cookies

Honey is a symbol of new beginnings for Jewish people. Usually it is eaten for Rosh Hashanah, the Jewish New Year, or in cakes and cookies to celebrate a new baby. Here I used honey in the dough for Hanukkah cookies. This butter cookie recipe can be used for any of the cutout cookies in this book.

2 cups all-purpose flour
2 tablespoons cornstarch
1 teaspoon dry milk
½ teaspoon baking soda
½ teaspoon cream of tartar
¼ teaspoon salt
½ cup (1 stick) butter, softened
½ cup sugar
1 large egg
1½ tablespoons honey
1 teaspoon vanilla extract
Royal Icing (page 274)
4 drops blue food coloring

1. Combine the flour, cornstarch, dry milk, baking soda, cream of tartar, and salt in a medium bowl; set aside.

2. Beat the butter and sugar until fluffy. Beat in the egg, then the honey and vanilla.

3. Gradually stir in the flour mixture.

4. Form the dough into a flat disk, wrap in plastic wrap, and refrigerate for 30 minutes.

5. Preheat the oven to 300°F. Line 2 cookie sheets with parchment paper.

6. Roll the dough out on a floured work surface to ¼ inch thick. Cut with cookie cutters. Place the shapes on the cookie sheets 1½ inches apart. Bake for 15 to 20 minutes, until golden around the edges. Let cool on the pans for 15 minutes. Transfer to a rack to cool completely.

7. Divide the icing into 2 bowls. Leave one batch white and color the second with blue food coloring. Pipe an

outline on each cookie with the white icing and fill. Let dry. Pipe the blue icing on the cookies in polka dot, stripe and crosshatched patterns to decorate.

Variations

Honey Poppy-Seed Cookies: Add ¼ cup poppy seeds along with the honey to the dough.

Honey Almond Cookies: Add ¼ cup sliced almonds along with the honey to the dough.

Right: Hanukkah Honey Butter Cookies.

CULTURAL HOLIDAY COOKIES

The American palette is a global one, and it makes sense to indulge in as much food culture as we can. Los Angeles is an exciting place to live because it is so culturally diverse: I can find just about any type of bakery from almost every culture imaginable around the world. And if there isn't a bakery, there is a community of people who are more than happy to tell you about their favorite flavors and cookies. Lebkuchen for Oktoberfest, almond and sesame cookies for Chinese New Year, and cookies with dulce de leche for all of the Latin American holidays. Here is just a small sampling of the cookies of the world.

Chinese Sesame and Almond Cookies

Type of cookie: Rolled cutout

24 cookies

1 cup blanched almonds
2½ cups all-purpose flour
2¼ cups confectioners' sugar
⅓ cup almond butter
5 large eggs, 1 of them separated
1 teaspoon granulated sugar
1½ teaspoons almond extract
¼ cup sesame seeds

Chinatown is my favorite neighborhood both in New York, where I grew up, and here in Los Angeles. I love visiting during Chinese New Year, for dragon parades, moon cakes, and almond and sesame cookies.

Americanized Chinese restaurants offer fortune cookies at the end of a meal, but many traditional Chinese restaurants offer Chinese almond cookies. Prepare them for the Chinese New Year, which occurs in late January or early February. If you would like a more authentic taste, replace the all-purpose flour with rice flour. The honey-sesame variation is similar to a cookie from my favorite Chinatown bakery.

1. Put ¾ cup of the almonds, ½ cup of the flour, and the confectioners' sugar in a food processor or blender, and pulse until finely ground.

2. Add the almond butter. Pulse until the mixture resembles coarse meal. Transfer the mixture to a bowl.

3. Add the 4 whole eggs plus 1 egg yolk one at a time, stirring in the remaining flour well between additions.

Left: Chinese Honey Sesame Cookies.

Right: Chinese Sesame and Almond Cookies.

Wrap the dough in plastic wrap and refrigerate for 30 minutes.

4. Preheat the oven to 350°F. Butter 2 cookie sheets.

5. Roll the dough out on a floured work surface to ¼ inch thick. Cut with a 2-inch round cookie cutter. Place the shapes on the cookie sheets 1½ inches apart.

6. Combine the egg white, granulated sugar, and almond extract in a small bowl. Brush the egg wash on the cookies. Sprinkle the cookies lightly with sesame seeds. Press an almond into the center of each cookie.

7. Bake for 15 to 18 minutes, until golden. Let cool on the pans for 5 minutes. Transfer to a rack to cool further.

Variation

Chinese Honey Sesame Cookie: Reduce the blanched almonds to ¾ cup. Roll the dough out to ½ inch thick and cut with cookie cutters. Combine ½ cup sesame seeds and 3 tablespoons honey in a small bowl. Brush the cookie all over with egg wash. Spread the sesame seed mixture over the entire cookie. Bake for 10 to 12 minutes.

Matcha Chocolate Swirl Cookie Pops

Type of cookie: Icebox

12 cookie pops

For those who like to eat cookies on a stick, here is one of my favorites. I gave standard icebox cookies a flavor makeover with chocolate and Japanese green tea. Serve them to celebrate Japan's Boys' Day on May 5 or Girls' Day on March 3.

3½ cups all-purpose flour
1 teaspoon baking powder
½ teaspoon salt
1¼ cups (2½ sticks) butter, softened
1½ cups confectioners' sugar
3 large eggs, separated
1 teaspoon vanilla extract
¾ cup cocoa powder
¼ cup chocolate chips, finely chopped
3 tablespoons matcha powder

1. Combine the flour, baking powder, and salt in a medium bowl; set aside.

2. Beat the butter and confectioners' sugar until fluffy. Beat in the egg yolks and vanilla.

3. Gradually add the flour mixture, stirring until combined.

Above: Matcha Chocolate Swirl Cookie Pops.

4. Divide the dough into 3 batches. Leave one batch plain. Add the cocoa powder and chocolate chips to one batch and the matcha powder to the other batch.

5. Gather each batch into a ball, wrap in plastic wrap, and refrigerate for 1 hour.

6. Roll one batch of dough out on a floured work surface into a large rectangle ½ inch thick. Repeat with the other two batches to make close to the same size rectangles.

7. Place a piece of parchment paper on a work surface and stack the three rectangles on top of each other on the paper, brushing the first two layers with the egg white and leaving the top layer plain.

8. Roll up the dough as tightly as you can. Wrap the log in plastic wrap and freeze for 1 hour.

9. Preheat the oven to 350°F. Line two cookie sheets with parchment paper. Ready 12 lollipop or ice pop sticks.

10. Cut ½-inch rounds with a sharp knife. Place the rounds on the cookie sheets 1½ inches apart and insert a stick in each one. Bake for 15 to 18 minutes, until golden around the edges. Transfer to a rack to cool.

Variation

Mocha Swirl Cookie Pops: Replace the matcha powder with ⅛ cup ground espresso beans.

Almond Butter Cookies Filled with Dulce de Leche

Type of cookie: Hand shaped, filled

Dulce de leche is a sweet-milk caramel that is used in Latin American sweets. It's made by cooking milk and sugar together very slowly over a long period of time until reduced and thick. Here I make it into a paste by using less milk than usual and thickening it with a bit of flour at the end. I hide it inside an almond butter cookie dough

Dulce de Leche Filling

2 vanilla beans

6 cups whole milk

2¼ cups granulated sugar

1 teaspoon sea salt

2 to 3 tablespoons all-purpose
  flour (if necessary)

Almond Butter Cookies

1½ cups all-purpose flour

½ cup cornstarch

½ teaspoon baking powder

¼ teaspoon salt

1¼ cups (2½ sticks) butter,
  softened

⅓ cup granulated sugar

3 large egg yolks

1 teaspoon almond extract

1 teaspoon vanilla extract

Topping

¼ cup confectioners' sugar

and form the cookies into traditional peaked dome shapes. If you want to skip making your own dulce de leche, it is available at Latin groceries; just add a few tablespoons of flour to thicken if necessary. Prepare these treats for Cinco de Mayo, widely celebrated in the United States, or for the Independence Day (September 15) observed in many Latin American countries, including Guatemala, Honduras, El Salvador, Nicaragua, and Costa Rica.

1. Make the dulce de leche filling: Split the vanilla beans and scrape the seeds from the pods into a large saucepan. Add the milk, granulated sugar, and salt. Cook over medium heat, whisking until the mixture comes to a full boil. Reduce the heat to a low simmer and cook, stirring occasionally, for 3 to 3½ hours, until reduced. If needed, stir in 2 to 3 tablespoons flour to thicken to a thin paste. Remove from the heat and let cool.

2. Make the almond butter cookies: Combine the flour, cornstarch, baking powder, and salt in a medium bowl; set aside.

3. Beat the butter and granulated sugar until fluffy. Beat in the egg yolks, almond extract, and vanilla extract. Gradually stir in the flour mixture.

4. Preheat the oven to 325°F. Line 2 cookie sheets with parchment paper.

5. Pull a piece of dough, about 1½ tablespoon, from the bowl. Form a 2-inch flat circle by hand. Spoon 1 tablespoon of the filling on top. Close the dough over the filling to form a soft dome, and pull the top into a peak. Repeat with the remaining dough and filling. Place the cookies on the cookie sheets 1½ inches apart. Bake for 14 to 18 minutes, until golden. Let cool on the pans.

6. Dust with confectioners' sugar.

Cookies

3 cups all-purpose flour

1½ teaspoons baking powder

¾ teaspoon baking soda

1 teaspoon ground allspice

1 teaspoon ground cinnamon

½ teaspoon ground cloves

½ teaspoon freshly grated nutmeg

½ teaspoon ground ginger

⅛ teaspoon salt

¼ cup honey

1 cup dark brown sugar

3 tablespoons butter

1 large egg, beaten

Zest of 1 lemon

2 tablespoons lemon juice

Toppings

8 ounces semisweet chocolate

1 large egg white

1½ cups confectioners' sugar

Decorative candies

Lebkuchen

Type of cookie: Rolled cutout

1 large cookie

Lebkuchen are a traditional German honey-spice cookie. Highly decorated lebkuchen are prepared throughout Germany and sold at Oktoberfest. They are often very large and shaped like hearts or rocking horses and worn as necklaces or packaged in decorative tins as souvenirs. They are also prepared for Christmas and given as gifts.

1. Preheat the oven to 350°F. Line a large cookie sheet with parchment paper. Cut a heart shape about 9 x 11 inches from a piece of paper or cardboard.

2. Combine the flour, baking powder, baking soda, allspice, cinnamon, cloves, nutmeg, ginger, and salt in a large bowl. Make a well in the center. Set aside.

3. Combine the honey, brown sugar, and butter in a saucepan. Cook over medium heat, stirring, until melted. Pour into the well in the flour mixture and stir to combine. Stir in the egg, lemon zest, and lemon juice.

4. Knead the dough on a floured work surface until smooth. Roll the dough out to a 9 x 11-inch rectangle ¼ inch thick and place the heart-shaped template on the dough. Cut out the heart with a knife. Use the remaining scraps of dough to add decorative details to the heart. Place the heart on the cookie sheet and bake for 20 to 25 minutes, until lightly browned. Let cool on the pan for 10 minutes. Carefully transfer the paper and cookie to a rack to cool further.

5. Heat the chocolate in a double boiler over simmering water, stirring until smooth. Spread the chocolate over the cookie and let it set.

6. Beat the egg white and confectioners' sugar in a medium bowl until stiff peaks form. Put the frosting in a pastry

bag and pipe decorative designs on the cookie. Attach the candies to the wet frosting and let dry.

Variation

Lemon and Candied Fruit and Almond Lebkuchen: Makes 8 to 10 cookies. Roll out the dough and cut into 2½ to 3 inch individual-size cookies. Bake for 10 to 12 minutes. Top with Lemon Icing (page 277), candied fruits, and candied almonds.

Day of the Dead Cookies

Type of cookie: Rolled cutout

24 cookies

Skeletons are hot this time of year. They start popping up on front lawns for Halloween and then they come out in full force for the Mexican holiday *El Día de los Muertos* (Day of the Dead) or All Souls' day November 2. It is a celebration of friends and family who have passed away.

With roots that are more than three thousand years old, it follows All Saints' Day on November 1.

Shortbread Butter Cookie dough
(page 271)
Royal Icing (page 274)
Green, yellow, red, brown, orange,
and black food coloring
Coarse white sugar

1. Divide the dough into two flattened disks and wrap each in plastic wrap and refrigerate for 30 minutes.

2. Roll the dough out on a floured work surface to ¼ inch thick. Using a utility knife and the template on page 278, cut out skulls. Place the shapes on the cookie sheets 1½ inches apart. Bake for 12 to 14 minutes, until golden around the edges. Let cool on the pans for 10 minutes. Transfer to a rack to cool completely.

3. Divide the icing into 6 small batches, and one large batch. Leave the large batch plain white, and color small batches with food coloring. Pipe an outline on the cookies and fill with white. Let dry.

4. Pipe faces over the white background with colored icings, and sprinkle with white sugar while wet.

Chapter 6

Christmas Cookies

GINGERBREAD MEN AND DECORATED BUTTER COOKIES

Decorating gingerbread and butter cookies is synonymous with Christmas for me. Every year Brian and I make these cookies, and sometimes we invite friends to a cookie-decorating party. We fill bowls with candies and toppings and set out prepared icing. It is tons of fun to see what people create, and we have contests for the most creative, most ridiculous, funniest, and most beautiful. Most of the cookies are pretty unusual, since we have so many friends who are artists. The secret to a good decorating party is to bake the cookies ahead of time: People are having too much fun to be watching cookies in the oven, and they usually end up burned; just jump straight to the decorating.

*Molasses Gingerbread Cookie
    Dough (page 275)*
Lemon Royal Icing (page 276)
*Blue, yellow, red, green, orange,
    and black food coloring*
*½ teaspoon each Candy dots and
    stars*

Gingerbread Robot Cookies

Type of cookie: Rolled cutout

12 robots

This dough is the perfect cookie-cutter dough for making gingerbread robots. I designed these by looking at Brian's collection of tin toys and at the robots I found in his vintage-toy books. The royal icing is flavored with lemon, a great complement to the gingerbread.

1. Preheat the oven to 400°F. Line 2 cookie sheets with parchment paper.

2. Roll the dough out on a floured work surface to ¼ inch thick. Using a utility knife and the templates on page 278, cut out robots. Place the shapes on the cookie sheets 1½ inches apart. Bake for 12 to 14 minutes, until light brown around the edges. Transfer to a rack to cool.

3. Divide the icing into small bowls and color with 6 to 8 drops of food coloring.

4. Pipe the black outlines first; let dry. Fill the outlines with colors, attach candy dots and stars, and let dry. Finally, top with piped details. Let dry.

Stained-Glass Ornament Cookies

Type of cookie: Rolled cutout

8 two-dimensional ornaments

At holiday time we like to have ornament-making parties, and these are our favorite cookie ornaments. The ones with crushed candy have a stained glass effect. Package them up as gifts or make a whole batch to cover your tree. For the three-dimensional ornaments, create 2 slotted cookies and fasten them together with icing. For the easy version, make the cookies flat. The cookie dough will harden over time if exposed to air, so if you have the time let the cookies sit out to harden before decorating.

1. Preheat the oven to 350°F. Line 2 cookie sheets with parchment paper.

2. Roll the dough out on a floured work surface to ¼ inch thick. Use a utility knife and templates on page 279 to create shapes. Leave the cookies solid or cut patterns and shapes in the centers. Punch a hole in the top of each cookie ¼ to ½ inch from the edge with a straw.

3. Place the shapes on the cookie sheets 1½ inches apart. Bake for 4 to 5 minutes. Put the crushed candy in the

Shortbread Butter Cookie Dough or Orange Butter Cookie Dough (page 271 or 203)
2 cups assorted hard candies, sorted by color and crushed
Lemon Royal Icing (page 274)
Orange, green, red, and yellow food coloring
Colored sugar
Candy dots
Dragées

Above: Stained-Glass Ornament Cookies.

cutout areas and bake for 4 to 5 more minutes, until the edges are golden and the candy is melted. Let cool on the pans until the candy has hardened.

4. Divide the royal icing into 5 batches. Color 4 of the batches with one each of the food colorings; leave the fifth batch white. Pipe decorations on the cookies. To create icing hearts and stars pipe an outline first and fill. While the icing is still wet, dust with colored sugar and attach candy dots and dragées. Thread kitchen string or ribbon through the hole to hang.

Variation

Three-Dimensional Ornament Cookie: After cutting out the shapes, cut a small ¼-inch-wide slot three quarters of the way up from the bottom of one cookie and from the top of an identically shaped cookie. Cut holes with a straw on both sides of the slot at least ¼" from the slot and top edges. Cut shapes elsewhere on the cookie to fill with candy. After the cookies are baked and cooled, clean up and widen the slots with a utility knife if necessary. Using royal icing as glue, slide the cookies together at the slots. Thread 2 strings though the holes to hang.

Fondant Snow Globe Cookies

Type of cookie: Rolled cutout

8 snow globes

Fondant-covered snow globe cookies are a kitschy addition to the holiday cookie display. I love working with cutout shapes and fondant because they don't require the drawing skills you need for piping royal icing. Here I made a host of holiday classics: a snowman, a fifties-style Rudolph, a pine forest, a snowflake, and gingerbread people. This is the recipe I use for homemade fondant; it is very pliable. Premade fondant is available at cake-decorating supply stores.

1. Make the fondant: Put the confectioners' sugar in a large bowl and make a well in the center; set aside.

Fondant

2 pounds confectioners' sugar

¼ cup cold water

1 tablespoon unflavored gelatin

½ cup light corn syrup

½ tablespoons glycerin

1 tablespoon vanilla extract

Sugar Cookies

3 cups all-purpose flour

¾ teaspoon salt

1¼ cups (3½ sticks) butter, softened

1 cup confectioners' sugar

1 teaspoon vanilla extract

Toppings

Food coloring

Royal Icing (page 274)

Colored sugars

Nonpareils

2. Put the water and gelatin in a small saucepan and let sit for 5 minutes to dissolve. Place over low heat and stir in the corn syrup and glycerin. Remove from the heat and stir in the vanilla.

3. Pour the liquid mixture into the well in the confectioners' sugar and stir until just blended. Knead until the mixture becomes stiff. If it is too sticky, add more sugar a little at a time. Form into a ball and let rest in an airtight container overnight at room temperature.

4. Make the sugar cookies: Combine the flour and salt in a medium bowl; set aside.

5. Cream the butter and confectioners' sugar until light. Beat in the vanilla.

6. Gradually stir in the flour mixture. Form the dough into 2 flat disks, wrap in plastic wrap, and refrigerate for 3 to 4 hours.

7. Preheat the oven to 350°F. Line 2 cookie sheets with parchment paper.

8. Roll out one disk of dough (for the snow globe bases) on a floured work surface to ½ inch thick. Roll the other disk of dough (for the snow globes) out to ³⁄₁₆ inch thick. Using a utility knife and the templates on page 279, cut out the shapes for the snow globes and the bases. In the center of each base, cut a ¼-inch groove partway through the cookie. This will hold the snow globe.

9. Place the shapes on the cookie sheets 2 inches apart and bake for 13 to 16 minutes, until the edges are golden. Transfer to a rack to cool completely.

10. The cookies may have risen in baking. Check all of the pieces to see whether they fit together properly. If not, cut and clean up the grooves with a utility knife, and test to make sure the globes fit onto the bases.

Right: Fondant Snow Globe Cookies.

11. Knead small amounts of food coloring into the fondant, a little at a time.

12. Roll the fondant out on a work surface dusted with confectioners' sugar to ⅟₁₆ inch thick. Cut into shaped pieces with cookie cutters and a utility knife. Attach the fondant to the cookies with royal icing. Pipe icing around the edges of the globes and sprinkle with colored sugar and nonpareils.

Spice Wreath Cookies

Type of cookie: Hand shaped

24 cookies

These braided holiday wreath cookies sparkle with seasonal flavors. Have fun decorating them with festive candies.

1. Preheat the oven to 350°F. Line 2 cookie sheets with parchment paper.

2. Cream the butter and sugar until light and fluffy. Beat in the brandy.

3. Stir in the flour, cinnamon, and nutmeg and mix well.

4. Roll the dough out on a floured work surface to ¼ inch thick. Cut into ¾ x 5-inch strips and roll each into a rope. Twist the ropes together two at a time. Join the ends of the ropes together to form circles.

5. Place the circles on the cookie sheets 1½ inches apart. Bake for 12 to 15 minutes, until golden. Transfer to a rack to cool.

6. Make the brandy glaze: Beat the confectioners' sugar and butter until blended. Beat in the brandy. To thin, add 1 teaspoon hot water.

7. Top the cookies with the glaze, coarse sugar, and candies.

GINGERBREAD HOUSES AND CONSTRUCTIONS

As a teenager I wanted to be an architect. I've even studied it, and in my career have worked at architecture firms. In college I realized that the scale of real architecture was just too big for me to be creative, so instead I became an industrial designer and now get my architectural fix with gingerbread houses. But why limit gingerbread constructions to houses? You can make just about anything with the same ingredients and processes. Here are some new designs as well as some mini–classic gingerbread houses.

Midcentury Gingerbread House

Type of cookie: Cookie construction

1 house

Although I live in a house built in 1959, it's not quite my dream midcentury-style house. Designer midcentury houses get snapped up in a second here in Los Angeles for millions. But I can certainly have my dream house in gingerbread. The clerestory windows, slightly angled overlapping white rock-covered roofs, and concrete garden walls are details that scream midcentury. Like a true architect, I made a floor plan and foam core model first and adjusted the dimensions to take the rising of the gingerbread cookies in the oven into account. The cactus and aloe landscaping is made from marzipan. Another nice thing about this midcentury gingerbread house is that the minimalist style means that it is not too complicated to construct. Neutra, Schindler, and Eames, step aside.

1. Preheat the oven to 350°F. Line 2 cookie sheets with parchment paper.

2. Roll the dough out on a floured work surface to ¼ inch thick. Using a utility knife and the templates on page 280, cut out the shapes. Emboss the grid pattern into the fireplace and the checkered pattern in the middle of the garden wall with a blunt tool or the back of a knife. Press the candy flowers into the dough the center of the X's on the garden wall. Place the shapes on the cookie sheets and bake for 12 to 14 minutes, until firm. Transfer to a rack to cool.

3. Divide the icing into one large batch and 3 small batches. Color each of 3 of the batches with one of the food colorings. Leave the large batch plain white. Pipe the black outlines for the windows and door; let dry. Fill in the windows and door with white icing and let dry. Pipe the doorknob.

4. Assemble the fireplace by attaching the front wall to the two side walls with icing. Put additional icing on the inside of the corners to strengthen the seams. Attach the fireplace to the two front walls with icing, again reinforcing the corners to strengthen the seams. Let dry.

5. Attach the house's front wall to the sidewalls with icing. Attach the back wall to the sidewalls with icing. Put additional icing on the inside of the corners to strengthen the seams. Let dry.

6. Attach the right roof and the left roof to the tops of all the upright walls with icing, reinforcing at the corners. Place the center roof around the fireplace, reinforcing the corners. Cover all three roofs with icing. While the icing is still wet, top with white sprinkles.

7. Attach the front garden wall to the two sidewalls with icing. Attach the two short walls to the house with icing. Attach the front of the planter to the side of the planter with icing. Attach the two short planter sides to the house with icing. Reinforce all the seams by adding icing at the inside corners.

8. For the cacti and wreath, color a 2 ½ to 3 inch large ball of marzipan green and a smaller ½ inch ball red. Form the cacti and wreath shapes out of the green marzipan and the cactus flower and wreath out of the red marzipan. Place the cacti in the planter and around the house. Attache the wreath to the door with Royal Icing.

10 cups 2 recipes Molasses
    Gingerbread Cookie Dough
    (page 275)
Royal Icing (page 274)
12-inch square green construction
    paper
⅜- or ½-inch-thick plywood 12
    inches square (for the base)
Spray mount or rubber cement
Glue gun with glue
⅜-inch dowel 14 inches long
2 tablespoons confectioners' sugar
Hemp
Nuts, mints, hard candies, gum-
    drops, dragées

Dimensions for Christmas Tree cookie pieces

1 (1 x 1-inch) piece
3 (1 x 2-inch) pieces
2 (1 x 2½-inch) pieces
3 (1 x 3½-inch) pieces
2 (1 x 4-inch) pieces
3 (1 x 4-½ inch) pieces
3 (1 x 5-inch) pieces
3 (1 x 6-inch) pieces
2 (1 x 6½-inch) pieces
3 (1 x 7-inch) pieces

Christmas Tree

Type of cookie: Cookie construction

1 tree

What is Christmas without a tree? Last year by Christmas Eve I still hadn't gotten around to setting one up, so I spent the evening making a cookie tree. Fir, spruce, pine . . . some Christmas trees are short and squat; others are tall and slender. By varying the number and sizes of pieces in the templates, you can make any shape or size tree you like. The holes near the edges allow you to string candies, nuts, and cookie ornaments or set them on the tips of the branches. Larger holes can be punched before baking with a straw; smaller holes can be drilled with a power drill and a small food-safe drill bit or a sharp tool after baking. Make a few extra pieces so you can play around with the shapes—and in case of breakage.

1. Preheat the oven to 350°F. Line 2 cookie sheets with parchment paper.

2. Roll the dough out on a floured work surface to ⅜ inch thick. Cut the rectangular pieces according to the dimensions at left with a pizza cutter. Punch a hole in the center of each piece with a straw. Cut out the star topper with a 2½-inch star cookie cutter and the ornaments with a 1½-inch star cookie cutter. Punch a hole in the center of each ornament. Place the shapes on the cookie sheets 1½ inches apart. Bake for 10 to 12 minutes, until firm. Transfer to a rack to cool.

3. Drill ⅛-inch holes ½ inch in from the ends of the rectangles (for hanging the ornaments). Drill a ⅜-inch hole in the bottom of the star if you prefer to place it on the dowel instead of gluing it to the front of the dowel.

4. Spread icing on all of the ⅜″ sides of the rectangles with your finger. Let dry. Pipe the outline of the star topping, let dry, and then fill with white icing.

5. Attach the paper to the plywood base with spray mount, and drill a hole halfway through the center of

Above: Christmas Tree.

the plywood with a ¼-inch bit. Use a glue gun to glue the dowel in the hole.

6. To build up the shape of the tree, stack the rectangles on the dowel, starting with the largest and getting smaller toward the top. Rotate the rectangles to create a shape you like, leaving space to hang large and small ornaments.

7. Sprinkle the tree with the confectioners' sugar to look like snow on the tips.

8. Cut the hemp to the desired length for hanging the ornaments. Drill or poke holes in nuts and string hemp through them. String hemp through the holes in the star ornament cookies. Attach hemp to hard candies with icing. Hang the ornaments on the tree. Fill empty spaces by attaching candies to the tips of the branches with icing. Place the star on the tip of the dowel. To eat, break the star off the top and lift one cookie off the dowel at a time.

Fifth-Wheel Trailer

Type of cookie: Cookie construction

1 trailer

Although I am a big backpacker, I also like car camping. I have never actually camped in a fifth-wheel trailer, but whenever there is a cool vintage one parked in the campground, I ask the owner for a tour. Owners of these predecessors to the modern RV are usually ecstatic to spend more than an hour giving me a tour of every square inch of their home away from home. My favorites have pop-up sunroofs. Here is my less-than-half-a-square-foot vintage fifth-wheel trailer living out in the forest on a campsite made of chocolate and graham cracker cookie crumbs. My tour will take just a few minutes.

10 cups (2 recipes) Molasses
  Gingerbread Cookie Dough
  (page 275)
½ cup crushed green hard candies
5 cups Royal Icing (page 274)
Black, green, orange, light brown,
  and dark brown food coloring
Silver leaf
12 x 18 inch large piece of
  cardboard
Crushed Chocolate Cookies
  (page 208)
Crushed Graham Crackers
  (page 129)

Below: Fifth-Wheel Trailer.

1. Preheat the oven to 350°F. Line 2 cookie sheets with parchment paper.

2. Roll the dough out on a floured work surface to ¼ inch thick. Using a utility knife and the templates on page 280, cut trailer pieces and trees. Cut out the sunroof and the windows. Place the shapes on the cookie sheets 1½ inches apart. Spoon the crushed candy into the sunroof and windows. Bake for 8 minutes, adding additional candy if a window has thinned too much or there are gaps. Bake for 5 to 7 minutes longer, until the candy has melted and the cookie is golden. Transfer the parchment and cookies to a rack to cool.

3. Divide the icing into 6 batches. Leave one large batch white and 5 smaller batches of black, green, orange, light brown, dark brown.

4. Decorate the trailer: Pipe the white outline around the windows, sunroof, and door, and the white line down the center of the trailer on both the front and back panels. Let dry. Pipe the light brown stripes on the bottom of the front and back panel and fill in the door.

5. Pipe a green outline on the top half of the trailer on the front, back, and side panels and the sunroof. Fill in with icing; let dry. Fill the spaces in between the brown lines with dark brown icing. Cover the right front panel with brown icing.

6. Decorate the wheels: cut the silver leaf into circles and attach to the circular cookies with icing. Pipe spokes over the wheels with black icing.

7. To assemble the trailer, attach supports to the back panel with icing. Put additional icing on the inside of the corners to strengthen the seams. Attach the front panel to the supports with icing, reinforcing the inside corners and making sure to align the back panel with the front panel.

8. Attach the front bottom panel to the right front and the large panel to the back with icing, again reinforcing the inside corners. Let dry. Attach the slatted pieces to the front and back with icing, following the curves. Reinforce the inside corners.

9. Decorate the trees: Pipe black outlines and let dry. Pipe in the orange and green center branches and trunks and let dry. Fill in the trees with colors and let dry completely. Pipe spiral details on top. Attach the supports to the backs of the trees. Spoon mounds of icing on the cardboard and attach the trees to the cardboard with icing. Let dry.

10. Cover the cardboard with white icing and top with crushed chocolate cookies to make the road, using a butter knife to smooth it. Add the crushed graham crackers as the dirt around the road. Place the trailer on the road.

Mini–Gingerbread Houses

Type of cookie: Cookie construction

3 houses

Creating gingerbread houses doesn't need to be overwhelming. It all comes down to the size of the house and the complexity of the decorations. In fact, if you make minihouses, you can create a bunch of them in an assembly line and package them as gifts.

1. Preheat the oven to 350°F. Line 2 cookie sheets with parchment paper.

2. Roll the dough out on a floured work surface to ¼ inch thick. Using a utility knife and the templates on page 281, cut out the house shapes. Place the shapes on the cookie sheets 1 ½ inches apart and bake for 10 to 12 minutes, until firm. Transfer to a rack to cool.

3. Divide the icing into 3 batches. Color one each of 2 of the batches with red and green food coloring; leaving the third batch plain white. Pipe the fronts and sides of

---

Molasses Gingerbread Cookie Dough (page 275)
Royal Icing (page 274)
Green and red food coloring
White nonpareils, shredded coconut, and cinnamon and snowflake candies
Fondant (page 242)

the houses with doors, windows, patterns and flowers. On two of the roof pieces (for one house) create dot patterns on the roofs and attach snowflake candies.

4. Roll out the fondant to ⅛-inch thickness slightly larger then the front, back and sides of the houses. Press patterns into the fondant with rubber stamps. Attach to the cookies with the icing and trim to the sizes of the cookies.

5. Assemble the houses by attaching the front wall to the sidewalls with icing. Attach the back wall to the sidewalls with icing. Put additional icing on the inside of the corners to strengthen the seams. Let dry.

6. Attach the roofs by putting icing on the tops of all the walls and setting the roof pieces on them. Put icing down the center of the roof pieces. For the roof with the snowflakes fill the seam with candies. Cover the other two roofs with icing, coconut, and nonpareils.

Right: Mini-Gingerbread Houses.

10 cups (2 recipes) Molasses
    Gingerbread Cookie Dough
    (page 275)
Royal Icing (page 274)
Green, red, black, orange, and
    purple food coloring
Purple and orange sugar
Candy flowers and stars
White nonpareils
1 cup plus 2 tablespoons chocolate
    chips
1 tablespoon butter
Dragées

Gingerbread Dollhouse

Type of cookie: Cookie construction

1 dollhouse, 12 mini–gingerbread people

We adults make gingerbread houses for the holidays as display pieces for guests to enjoy on the big day. Kids insist that what's inside the house is what matters. So I created this simple gingerbread dollhouse with an open construction that kids can play with. With two beds and a desk in the bedroom and a fireplace in the living room, the kids can play with mini–gingerbread people and create their own holiday adventures. If it's around long enough before it's eaten, that is.

1. Preheat the oven to 350°F. Line 2 cookie sheets with parchment paper.

2. Roll the dough out on a floured work surface to ⅜ inch thick. Using a utility knife and the templates on page 281, cut out the dollhouse pieces, furniture, and mini–gingerbread people. Cut a hole in half of the gingerbread people with a straw. Place the shapes on the cookie sheets 1½ inches apart and bake for 10 to 12 minutes, until firm. Transfer to a rack to cool.

3. Divide the icing into 6 batches, 2 larger and 4 smaller. Color each of the 4 batches with green, red, black, and orange food colorings; color one large batch purple and leave the sixth batch plain white. Spread green icing on two-thirds of the floor. Attach candy flowers while the icing is still wet. Let dry. Spread white icing on the rest of the floor and let dry.

4. Cover the outside of the smaller sidewalls and the longer roof with purple icing and top with purple sugar and white nonpareils. Pipe the top pediment piece and stairs with a design.

5. To assemble the dollhouse, attach the floor to the sidewalls with icing by laying the pieces on their back edges. Add the center support wall. Attach the roof and

the bottom supports. Put additional icing on the inside of the corners to strengthen the seams. Let dry.

6. Spread the front edge of the roof with white icing to use as glue to attach the pediment. Let dry. Pipe stars along the remaining 3 exposed front edges. Let dry.

7. Decorate the fireplace with red and black icing. let dry. Pipe the white lines in a grid to make bricks on the fireplace. Pipe the flame in the fireplace with orange icing. Spread orange icing on the beds. While the icing is still wet, sprinkle with orange sugar. Assemble the beds and desk with icing, reinforcing the inside corners with additional icing. Let dry.

8. To decorate the plain gingerbread people, pipe faces with icing and pipe some icing in the hole. Put an upside-down chocolate chip in the hole and attach a star with icing.

9. To make the chocolate-covered gingerbread people, heat the 1 cup chocolate chips and the butter in a double boiler over simmering water, stirring until melted. Spread over the cookies and attach dragées for buttons while the chocolate is still wet. Let dry.

10. Carefully turn the house upright. Fill in the seams around the corners of the house with purple icing. Use icing to attach the fireplace in the slot at the back of the house and the steps in the front of the house. Place the furniture and people in the house.

INTERNATIONAL CHRISTMAS COOKIES

Almost every culture in the world that traditionally celebrates Christmas has its own special cookies for the season. There are so many, in fact, that it was very difficult for me to decide which ones to include here. I've selected a range of different types of cookies and techniques that will give you plenty of cultural variety at your next holiday party.

Christmas Shortbread

Type of cookie: Rolled

1 cookie

Scottish shortbread is the ancestor of all butter cookies. They are slightly underbaked, with their defining feature being that they are very light; holes are poked in the top (to allow air to escape and keep the cookie flat), and the edges are a very light golden color. The name comes from the large amount of shortening (butter) used in the dough. Originally shortbread was classified as bread and baked in one large round piece and cut after baking, because cookies were taxed but bread was not. Today, shortbread is formed in all sizes and shapes. This large cookie is made in the traditional method of pinching the edges and dressed up for the holidays with nuts and dried fruit.

1. Line a cookie sheet with parchment paper.

2. Combine the flour and salt in a medium bowl; set aside.

3. Cream the butter and confectioners' sugar until light. Beat in the vanilla.

4. Stir in the flour mixture. Form the dough into a flat disk and refrigerate for 3 to 4 hours.

5. Roll the dough out on a floured work surface to ½ inch thick. Invert a plate over the dough and with a sharp knife cut around the edges to make perfect circle. With a small cookie cutter, cut shapes out of the circle. Gather the cut shapes into a ball. Add food coloring to

Cookies

4 cups all-purpose flour

1 teaspoon salt

2¼ cups (4½ sticks) butter, softened

1½ cups confectioners' sugar

1 teaspoon vanilla extract

Food coloring

Toppings

1 cup assorted dried fruits and nuts, such as apricots, pine nuts, walnuts, almonds, and dried cranberries

⅓ cup colored sugar

the ball, and roll it out to ½ inch thick. Cut the same shapes from the colored dough and use them to fill the shapes cut in the circle. Crimp around the edge of the circle with your fingers and prick holes in the top with a fork. Carefully transfer to the cookie sheet.

6. Arrange nuts and dried fruits in a pattern on the top. Press them into the dough, and refrigerate for 20 minutes.

7. Preheat the oven to 325°F.

8. Sprinkle the shortbread with colored sugar and bake for 35 to 40 minutes, until golden but not browned. Let cool on the pan for 5 minutes. Transfer to a rack to cool completely. Cut with a sharp knife into wedges.

Variations

Chocolate Shortbread: Reduce the flour to 3¼ cups. Add 1 cup cocoa powder to the dry ingredients.

Candied Caraway Shortbread: Add 1 tablespoon caraway seeds to the dry ingredients. Omit the toppings and top with candied fruit and citrus peel.

Shortbread Cookies: Roll out the dough to ¼-inch thick and cut into 1½ x 3-inch strips with a pastry cutter. Place on the cookie sheet 1-inch apart and bake for 18 to 22 minutes.

Springerle

Type of cookie: Stamped

36 cookies

4½ cups cake flour
1 teaspoon baking powder
4 large eggs
½ teaspoon anise extract
3½ cups confectioners' sugar
1½ tablespoons grated lemon zest
2 tablespoons anise seeds, crushed
Food coloring

I found these fantastic patterned molds and rolling pins at a flea market and soon learned that they are used to prepare these very pretty detailed German Christmas cookies. Springerle have been prepared for centuries, first for winter harvest festivals and later for Christmas. They are normally a crisp, dry cookie that has a slight anise flavor. It is very important to dry out the tops overnight and bake at low heat so the pattern made by the mold will hold. They can also be detailed and painted with food coloring.

1. Butter 2 cookie sheets.

2. Combine the flour and baking powder in large bowl; set aside.

3. Beat the eggs with an electric mixer until light. Add the anise extract. Gradually stir in the confectioners' sugar and lemon zest.

4. Add the flour mixture and stir to make a stiff dough. Cover the bowl and refrigerate for 30 minutes.

5. Roll the dough out on a floured surface to about ⅜ inch thick. Flour a springerle rolling pin or springerle mold. Lightly roll over the dough or press with the mold. Cut the cookies apart with a sharp knife.

6. Sprinkle the cookie sheets with the anise seeds. Place the cookies on the cookie sheets 1½ inches apart. Remove the seeds from the spaces between the cookies. Let sit, uncovered, in a cool dry spot (not in the refrigerator) overnight to dry out the tops.

7. Preheat the oven to 250°F.

8. Bake for 20 to 25 minutes, until golden brown. Transfer to a rack to cool completely. Paint with food coloring and a small food-safe paintbrush.

Variations

Chocolate Springerle: Reduce the flour to 4 cups. Add ¾ cup cocoa powder to the dry ingredients.

Ginger Springerle: Add 2 tablespoons ground ginger to the dry ingredients.

6 tablespoons butter

10 tablespoons heavy cream

1 cup superfine sugar

¾ cup hazelnuts, chopped

⅓ cup almonds, chopped

½ cup all-purpose flour

¼ teaspoon salt

4 ounces bittersweet chocolate

4 ounces white chocolate

½ teaspoon mint extract

½ cup peppermint hard candies,
  crushed

Peppermint Florentine Lace Cookies

Type of cookie: Drop wafer

24 cookies

Here wafer-thin Florentines are sandwiched with minty dark chocolate in the center, then dipped halfway in white chocolate. While the white chocolate is still wet it is inscribed with patterns and the edges are dipped in peppermint candy.

1. Preheat the oven to 350°F. Butter 2 cookie sheets. Ready 2 double boilers.

2. Combine the butter, cream, and superfine sugar in a small saucepan and bring to a boil. Remove from the heat and let cool for 3 to 5 minutes.

3. Add the hazelnuts and almonds and stir until combined. Stir in the flour and salt.

4. Drop 1-teaspoon mounds of the dough 3 inches apart on the cookie sheets. Flatten with a wet fork.

5. Bake for 8 to 10 minutes, until golden. Let cool on the pans for 5 minutes. Transfer to a rack to cool completely.

6. For the filling and topping, melt the bittersweet and white chocolates separately in double boilers.

7. Add the mint extract to the bittersweet chocolate and spoon it onto half of the cookies. Top with the remaining cookies. Let harden.

8. Dip the sandwiches halfway in the white chocolate. While the chocolate is soft, create a texture by dragging a fork over the white chocolate in a zigzag pattern. Dip the edges in the crushed candies and place on parchment paper. Let harden.

Pignoli Cookies

Type of cookie: Drop

20 cookies

12 ounces almond paste
½ cup granulated sugar
4 large egg whites
1 teaspoon almond extract
1 cup plus 2 tablespoons
  confectioners' sugar
1½ cups pine nuts

Because I'm an Italian American, pignoli cookies share the stage with American favorites at Christmastime in my household. The moist, chewy texture comes from the almond paste. The pignoli (pine nuts) that coat the top are toasted as the cookies bake, adding to the sweet, nutty flavor. To make sure the pine nuts don't burn, keep the balls of dough smaller than 1 inch in diameter and keep your eye on the cookies, checking them frequently as they bake.

1. Preheat the oven to 300°F. Line 2 cookie sheets with parchment paper.

2. Combine the almond paste and granulated sugar in a food processor or blender until smooth.

3. Add 2 of the egg whites and the almond extract, and pulse until blended. Gradually add 1 cup confectioners' sugar and process until smooth; set aside.

4. Lightly beat the remaining 2 egg whites in a small bowl. Spread the pine nuts on a plate. Form the dough into

Above: Pignoli Cookies.

¾- to 1-inch balls with floured hands. Dip the balls in the egg whites; then roll them in pine nuts, pressing them into the dough. Place the balls on the cookie sheets 2 inches apart. Press to flatten a bit. Bake for 15 to 18 minutes, until the pine nuts are toasted and the cookies are light golden.

5. Let cool on the pans for 3 minutes. Transfer to a rack to cool completely. Lightly sprinkle with confectioners' sugar.

Variations

Chocolate Pignoli Cookies: Add 3 tablespoons cocoa powder to the dry ingredients.

Cherry Pignoli Cookies: After placing the balls on the cookie sheets, press a candied cherry into the center of each cookie.

Orange Pignoli Cookies: Replace the almond extract with orange juice. Add 1 teaspoon grated orange zest along with the juice.

SPRITZ COOKIES

If you have never made spritz cookies, you have a little catching up to do. Try them once, and you'll be hooked. These traditional Scandinavian cookies had spread all over Europe by the 1500s, and they are so simple and there are so many varieties of them that I decided to give them a section of their own. Top them with cherries, dip them in chocolate, or make them into finger-shaped sandwich cookies. I received a spritz gun for my tenth birthday and another when I got married, and having two of them to use at once comes in very handy when working with different colored doughs. Spritz cookie doughs can also be piped out of a pastry bag.

Spritz Butter Cookies

Type of cookie: Pressed

36 cookies

A spritz gun was my first kitchen tool, and the cookies that were extruded from it became a fascination. This is one of the most

2¼ cups all-purpose flour
½ teaspoon baking powder
¼ teaspoon salt
1 cup (2 sticks) butter, softened
¾ cup granulated sugar
1 large egg
1 teaspoon vanilla extract

basic butter cookie recipes you can make for a spritz gun. The dough can be dyed with food coloring and shaped into wreaths, stars, flowers, and dozens of other shapes. Top with candied cherries or sprinkle with colored sugar.

1. Preheat the oven to 350°F. Line 2 cookie sheets with parchment paper.

2. Combine the flour, baking powder, and salt in a medium bowl; set aside.

3. Cream the butter and sugar until light and fluffy. Beat in the egg and vanilla.

4. Gradually stir in the flour mixture.

5. Put the dough in a cookie press and press into shapes on the cookie sheets 1½ inches apart. Bake for 7 to 8 minutes, until golden. Transfer to a rack to cool.

Variation

Almond Spritz: Reduce the flour to 2 cups. Add ½ cup ground almonds to the dry ingredients. Replace the vanilla extract with almond extract.

Left: Spritz Butter Cookies.

Cookies

2 cups all-purpose flour
3 tablespoons cocoa powder
¼ teaspoon salt
⅔ cup butter, softened
1 cup sugar
2 large eggs
1 teaspoon vanilla extract

Filling

Raspberry Glaze (page 277),
  Coffee Cream (page 277), Mint
  Cream (page 71), or Orange
  Cream (page 277)

Chocolate Jam-Filled Fingers

Type of cookie: Pressed

20 sandwiches

These simple filled finger cookies can be made with a cookie press or a pastry bag. I like to pile a serving plate high with a selection of cookies containing different fillings.

1. Preheat the oven to 350°F. Butter 2 cookie sheets. Fit a cookie press with a large star disk or a pastry bag with a large star tip.

2. Combine the flour, cocoa powder, and salt in a medium bowl; set aside.

3. Beat the butter and sugar until creamy. Beat in the eggs and vanilla.

4. Gradually stir in the flour mixture.

5. Fill the cookie press or pastry bag half full. Press 2-inch lengths on cookie sheets 1 inch apart. Bake for 10 to 12 minutes, until lightly browned around the edges. Let cool on the pans for 5 minutes. Transfer to a rack to cool completely.

6. Spread filling on the flat side of half of the cookies and top with the remaining cookies.

2½ cups all-purpose flour
½ teaspoon baking powder
1 cup (2 sticks) butter, softened
3 ounces cream cheese, softened
1 cup sugar
1 large egg yolk
½ teaspoon vanilla extract
Lemon Icing (page 176)
2 tablespoons poppy seeds

Cream Cheese Poppy-Seed Spritz Cookies

Type of cookie: Pressed

30 cookies

Prepare these cookies with the flower-shaped tip and add Lemon Icing and poppy seeds to the center of each flower.

1. Preheat the oven to 325°F. Butter 3 cookie sheets. Fit a cookie press with the flower disk.

2. Combine the flour and baking powder in a medium bowl; set aside.

3. Cream the butter, cream cheese, and sugar until light and fluffy. Beat in the egg yolk and vanilla.

4. Stir in the flour mixture.

5. Put the dough in a cookie press and press into shapes on the cookie sheets 2 inches apart. Bake for 10 to 12 minutes, until golden but not browned around the edges. Let cool on the pans for 5 minutes. Transfer to a rack to cool completely.

6. Put ½ teaspoon icing in the center of each flower and sprinkle with poppy seeds.

Variations

Chocolate Cream Cheese Spritz Cookies: Spread Chocolate Glaze (page 277) on the flat sides of half of the cookies and top with the remaining cookies.

Jam Cream Cheese Spritz Cookies: Spread jam on the flat sides of half of the cookies and top with the remaining cookies.

COOKIE EXCHANGE COOKIES

Ever had a cookie-swap party for the holidays? Invite your friends over to make all of their favorite cookies. Offer a selection of cookie tins so that everyone can take some of each kind of cookie home with them. An even easier way to do it is to have your friends bring already-baked cookies and trade them for other varieties. Here is an assortment of holiday cookies that are perfect for cookie exchange parties: There are unusual treats and classic favorites, some very easy to make and some more involved recipes.

Fruitcake Cookies

Type of cookie: Drop molded

18 large cookies

Fruitcake flavors have been a sweet part of holiday baking for centuries. These chunky fruit cookies packed with dried fruit have a touch of rum in the dough and are soaked with a rum-infused

2 cups all-purpose flour

½ teaspoon baking soda

½ teaspoon ground cinnamon

1 cup rolled oats (not instant)

1 cup (2 sticks) butter, softened

1½ cups light brown sugar

2 large eggs

¼ cup unsulfured molasses

2 tablespoons dark rum

1 cup pecans, chopped

½ cup almonds, chopped

1 cup dried cranberries, chopped

½ cup raisins

½ cup dried apricots, chopped

¼ cup dried pineapple, chopped

¼ cup candied ginger, chopped

Rum Glaze (page 277)

¼ cup sugar

1 vanilla bean, crushed and
   broken into chunks

½ cup toffee pieces

1 cup (2 sticks) butter, cubed

2⅓ cups all-purpose flour

2 large egg whites, lightly beaten

1 cup slivered almonds, chopped

*Left: Cookie Exchange. Note Almond Toffee
Crescent in upper left of tin.*

glaze after baking. For a more traditional fruitcake flavor, substitute candied fruits and peels for the dried fruits.

1. Preheat the oven to 300°F. Set a 3-inch hemisphere silicone mold on a cookie sheet.

2. Combine the flour, baking soda, cinnamon, and oats in a medium bowl; set aside.

3. Cream the butter and brown sugar until blended. Beat in the eggs, molasses, and rum until smooth.

4. Stir in the flour mixture. Stir in the pecans, almonds, dried fruit and candied ginger.

5. Drop 2 rounded tablespoons of the dough into each mold and bake for 20 to 22 minutes, until firm. Let cool in the molds for 10 minutes. Pop out the cookies and transfer to a rack to cool completely.

6. Brush the glaze over the cookies.

Almond Toffee Crescents

Type of cookie: Rolled cutout
36 cookies

I love the endearing qualities of old-fashioned cookies like these, which combine two of my favorite buttery treats, almond toffee and vanilla crescents.

1. Put the sugar, vanilla bean, and toffee in a food processor or blender and pulse until finely ground. Add the butter and flour and pulse until the dough is blended. Form into a ball, wrap in plastic wrap, and refrigerate for 20 minutes to harden.

2. Preheat the oven to 350°F. Ready 2 ungreased cookie sheets.

3. Roll the dough out on a floured work surface to ¼ inch thick. Cut with a crescent-shaped cookie cutter. Place

the shapes on the cookie sheets about 1 inch apart. Brush with the egg whites and top with the almonds.

4. Bake for 10 to 12 minutes, until golden. Transfer to a rack to cool.

Variation

Butterscotch Vanilla Crescents: Replace the toffee with butterscotch chips. Melt 1 cup butterscotch chips and 2 tablespoons butter in a double boiler. Dip the cooled cookies in the butterscotch and set on parchment to harden.

Rolled Cutout Butter Cookie Dough (page 275)
Royal Icing (page 274)
1½ cups mint hard candies, crushed

Mint Candy Butter Cookies

Type of cookie: Rolled cutout
24 cookies

Mint is the flavor of the holiday season. Wintermint, spearmint, and peppermint—we all like different kinds. For the cookie exchange, top simple butter cookies with your favorite.

1. Preheat the oven to 350°F. Ready 2 ungreased cookie sheets.

2. Roll the dough out on a floured work surface to ¼ inch thick. Cut into 3-inch squares. Place the squares on the cookie sheets and bake for 15 to 18 minutes, until the edges begin to turn golden. Transfer to a rack to cool completely.

3. Cover with icing. While the icing is still wet, top with the crushed candies.

Linzer Cookies

Type of cookie Rolled cutout
24 cookies

These lemony butter cookies are a bit zestier than traditional Austrian Christmas linzer cookies. Although simple to make, they are quite sophisticated. When cut in this shape with a round

1 cup (2 sticks) butter, softened
1 cup granulated sugar
1 teaspoon grated lemon zest
2 large eggs
1 teaspoon lemon juice
4 cups all-purpose flour
Raspberry Glaze (page 277)
Confectioners' sugar

hole in the middle they are known as "linzer eyes." You can use this same recipe to create other celebration cookies by varying the external shape, cutout, and filling. I prepared these for my husband for Valentine's Day, which is also the anniversary of the day we met.

1. Beat the butter, granulated sugar, and lemon zest with an electric mixer until smooth and creamy. Beat in the eggs and lemon juice.

2. Gradually stir in the flour.

3. Form the dough into a ball, wrap in plastic wrap, and refrigerate for 45 minutes, until firm but not hard.

4. Preheat the oven to 350°F. Line 2 cookie sheets with parchment paper.

5. Roll the dough out on a floured work surface to ¼ inch thick. Cut the dough into 2-inch rounds with a fluted cookie cutter. Cut smaller circles out of the middle of half of the rounds. Place the rounds on the cookie sheets 1½ inches apart and bake for 12 to 15 minutes, until golden brown around the edges. Transfer to a rack to cool completely.

6. Place 1 teaspoon of the glaze in the center of the solid round cookies. Top with the rounds with cutouts to create a sandwich. Sprinkle with confectioners' sugar.

Variations

Valentine's Day Linzer Cookies: Cut a heart shape in the center of each cookie.

Thanksgiving Linzer Cookies: Cut a maple-leaf shape in the center of each cookie. Replace the Raspberry Glaze with apricot jam.

Christmas Linzer Cookies: Cut the cookies with Christmas tree cookie cutters. Replace the Raspberry Glaze with green mint jelly.

Easter Linzer Cookies: Cut a bunny shape in the center of each cookie. Replace the Raspberry Glaze with lemon curd.

Gingerbread Truffles

Type of cookie: Drop

48 cookies

Honey Gingerbread Cookie
Dough (page 275)
3 large egg whites, lightly beaten
White nonpareils
Rainbow nonpareils
Chocolate sprinkles

Gingerbread cookie dough does not lose its shape while baking, so I like to use the leftover dough from making houses to make these ball-shaped truffle cookies. They are super-simple cookies to add to your cookie-exchange collection.

1. Preheat the oven to 350°F. Line 2 cookie sheets with parchment paper.

2. Form the dough into 1-inch balls. Dip in the egg whites and coat with nonpareils or chocolate sprinkles.

3. Place the balls on the cookie sheets 1 inch apart and bake for 15 to 18 minutes, until cooked through in the center. You may want to break one open to see whether it is baked on the inside. Let cool on the pans.

Amaretto Amaretti Cookies

Type of cookie: Drop, sandwich

30 cookies, 15 sandwiches

2 large egg whites
2 teaspoons amaretto liqueur plus
    ¼ cup
1 teaspoon almond extract
2 cups almonds, ground
1 cup shredded sweetened coconut
1¾ cups confectioners' sugar
1 cup apricot preserves

These Italian favorites, made with amaretto, coconut, and almonds, have a nutty sweetness that cannot be matched. For extra amaretto flavor, spray some of the liqueur on with a spritzer after the cookies are baked.

1. Preheat the oven to 325°F. Line 2 cookie sheets with parchment paper.

2. Lightly beat the egg whites, 2 teaspoons of the amaretto, and the almond extract in a small bowl; set aside.

3. Combine the almonds, coconut, and 1½ cups of the confectioners' sugar and mix well.

4. Make a well in the center and pour in the egg-white mixture, stirring to make a paste.

5. Shape the dough into 1-inch balls. Place the balls on the cookie sheets 2 inches apart and bake for 12 to 15 minutes, until lightly browned.

6. Remove from the oven. Spray the remaining ¼ cup amaretto on the cookies with a spritzer and let sit for 5 minutes. Assemble into sandwiches with preserves as the filling.

Variation

Amaretto Orange Cookies: Add 1 tablespoon orange zest and 1½ teaspoons orange juice along with the amaretto and almond extract to the dough.

Nonpareil Cookies

Type of cookie: Rolled cutout

24 cookies

1 cup all-purpose flour

¼ cup cornmeal

⅛ teaspoon salt

½ cup (1 stick) butter, softened

½ cup plus 1 tablespoon granulated sugar

4 ounces cream cheese

2 large egg whites

Nonpareils

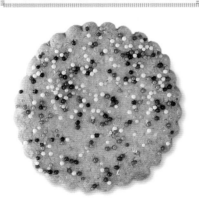

Simple and easy to make, these cream cheese–butter cookies are a tasty addition to the cookie exchange. For variety, cut them into different shapes and top with colored sugars and candies before baking.

1. Combine the flour, cornmeal, and salt in a medium bowl; set aside.

2. Beat the butter, ½ cup of the sugar, and the cream cheese until blended.

3. Gradually stir in the flour mixture to make a soft dough.

4. Form the dough into a disk, wrap in plastic wrap, and refrigerate for 30 minutes.

5. Preheat the oven to 350°F. Line 2 cookie sheets with parchment paper.

6. Roll the dough out on a floured work surface to ⅛ inch thick. Cut the dough with a 3-inch fluted round cookie

cutter. Place the shapes on the cookie sheets 1½ inches apart.

7. Combine the egg whites and remaining 1 tablespoon sugar in a small bowl. Brush on the cookies and top with nonpareils. Bake for 15 to 18 minutes, until golden. Transfer to a rack to cool completely.

Eggnog Cookies

Type of cookie: Drop

24 cookies

Eggnog spices up the tender texture of these seasonal favorites. The eggnog cream filling gives them even more of that holiday flavor.

1. Preheat the oven to 300°F. Ready 2 ungreased cookie sheets.

2. Make the eggnog cookies: Combine the flour, baking powder, salt, cinnamon, and ½ teaspoon of the nutmeg in a medium bowl; set aside.

3. Cream the butter and granulated sugar until fluffy. Beat in the eggnog, vanilla, and egg yolks until smooth.

4. Gradually stir in the flour mixture until just blended. Drop rounded-teaspoon mounds of the dough on the cookie sheets 2 inches apart.

5. Combine the remaining 2 teaspoons nutmeg and the coarse sugar in a small bowl. Sprinkle the nutmeg-sugar onto the cookies. Bake for 15 to 20 minutes, until light brown. Transfer to a rack to cool completely.

6. Make the eggnog cream filling: Beat the butter, confectioners' sugar, cinnamon, and nutmeg with an electric mixer until fluffy. Beat in the eggnog. Refrigerate for 20 minutes to make the filling firm.

7. Spread the filling on half of the cookies. Top with the remaining cookies to create sandwiches.

Eggnog Cookies

2¼ cups all-purpose flour

1 teaspoon baking powder

¼ teaspoon salt

½ teaspoon ground cinnamon

2½ teaspoons freshly grated nutmeg

¾ cup (1½ sticks) butter, softened

1¼ cups granulated sugar

½ cup eggnog

1 teaspoon vanilla extract

2 large egg yolks

2 tablespoons coarse sugar

Eggnog Cream Filling

¼ cup (½ stick) butter

1 cup confectioners' sugar

¼ teaspoon ground cinnamon

¼ teaspoon freshly grated nutmeg

3 tablespoons eggnog

Basics

COOKIE DOUGHS

Chocolate Cookie Dough

> 20 (2-inch) cookies
> 1¾ cups all-purpose flour
> 1 teaspoon baking soda
> ½ cup Dutch-process cocoa
>   powder
> ½ cup (1 stick) butter
> 1 cup sugar
> 2 large eggs
> 1½ teaspoons vanilla extract

1. Combine the flour, baking soda, and cocoa powder in a medium bowl; set aside.

2. Cream the butter and sugar until fluffy. Beat in the eggs and vanilla.

3. Gradually stir in the flour mixture.

4. Form the dough into a flat disk, wrap in plastic wrap, and refrigerate for 30 minutes. Follow individual recipes for rolling, cutting, and baking.

Shortbread Butter Cookie Dough

> 24 (3-inch) cookies
> 4 cups all-purpose flour
> 1 teaspoon salt
> 2¼ cups (4½ sticks) butter
> 1½ cups confectioners' sugar
> 2 teaspoons vanilla extract

1. Combine the flour and salt in a medium bowl; set aside.

2. Cream the butter and confectioners' sugar until light. Beat in the vanilla.

3. Gradually stir in the flour mixture. Form the dough into a flat disk, wrap in plastic wrap, and refrigerate for 3 to 4 hours. Follow individual recipes for rolling, cutting, and baking.

Orange Butter Cookie Dough

> 20 (2-inch) cookies
> 3 cups all-purpose flour
> 1½ teaspoons baking powder
> 1 teaspoon salt
> 1 cup (2 sticks) butter
> 1½ cups granulated sugar
> 2 large eggs
> 1 teaspoon vanilla extract
> 1 tablespoon orange juice

1. Combine the flour, baking powder, and salt in a medium bowl; set aside.

2. Beat the butter and sugar until fluffy. Beat in the eggs, vanilla, and orange juice.

3. Gradually stir in the flour mixture.

4. Form the dough into a flat disk, wrap in plastic wrap, and refrigerate for 1 hour. Follow individual recipes for rolling, cutting, and baking.

Rolled Cutout Butter Cookie Dough

> 20 (2-inch) cookies
> 1 cup (2 sticks) butter
> 1 cup superfine sugar
> 1 large egg yolk
> 1 large egg
> ½ teaspoon salt
> 2 teaspoons vanilla extract
> 3½ cups all-purpose flour

1. Beat the butter and superfine sugar until light and fluffy. Beat in the egg yolk. Add the whole egg, salt, and vanilla and stir to combine.

2. Gradually stir in the flour. Form the dough into a flat disk, wrap in plastic wrap, and refrigerate for 30 minutes. Follow individual recipes for rolling, cutting, and baking.

Variations

Rolled Butterscotch Cookie Dough: Substitute brown sugar for the superfine sugar.

Rolled Sugar and Spice Cookie Dough: Add ½ teaspoon ground cinnamon, ½ teaspoon ground ginger, and ¼ teaspoon ground allspice with the flour.

Rolled Nutty Cookie Dough: Add ⅔ cup peanut butter and ½ cup chopped peanuts to the dough after the butter and sugar are combined. Increase the flour by ¼ cup.

Molasses Gingerbread Cookie Dough

36 (2-inch) cookies

5 cups all-purpose flour

½ teaspoon salt

1 teaspoon baking powder

2 teaspoons ground ginger

1 teaspoon ground cinnamon

1 teaspoon freshly grated nutmeg

¼ teaspoon ground cloves

1 cup (2 sticks) butter, softened

1 cup dark brown sugar

⅔ cup unsulfured molasses

1 large egg

1 teaspoon cider vinegar

1. Combine the flour, salt, baking powder, ginger, cinnamon, nutmeg, and cloves in a large bowl; set aside.

2. Cream the butter and brown sugar until light and fluffy. Beat in the molasses, egg, and vinegar.

3. Gradually stir in the flour mixture. Form the dough into a flat disk, divide and wrap in plastic wrap, and refrigerate for 30 minutes. Follow individual recipes for rolling, cutting, and baking.

Honey Gingerbread Cookie Dough

48 (2-inch cookies)

7½ cups all-purpose flour

1 tablespoon baking soda

½ teaspoon salt

2 tablespoons ground cinnamon

1½ tablespoons ground ginger

1½ teaspoons freshly grated nutmeg

1½ cups (3 sticks) butter

1½ cups dark brown sugar

¾ cup honey

3 large eggs

1. Combine the flour, baking soda, salt, cinnamon, ginger, and nutmeg in a large bowl; set aside.

2. Beat the butter and brown sugar until light. Beat in the honey, then the eggs.

3. Gradually stir in the flour mixture. Divide into 2 flat disks, wrap in plastic wrap, and refrigerate for 2 hours. Follow individual recipes for rolling, cutting, and baking.

FROSTINGS, FILLINGS, AND ICINGS

Royal Icing with Fresh Egg Whites

3 large egg whites

4 cups confectioners' sugar

1 tablespoon vanilla extract

1 tablespoon water

1. Beat the egg whites, confectioners' sugar, vanilla, and water with an electric mixer on low speed until blended.

2. Increase the speed to high and beat until stiff, glossy peaks form. Add more confectioners' sugar or water to achieve the desired consistency.

Variation

Lemon Royal Icing: Replace the vanilla and water with juice of 1 freshly squeezed lemon.

Royal Icing with Powdered Egg Whites

1 cup, enough for 12 2-inch cookies

2 cups confectioners' sugar

1 teaspoon powdered egg whites

1 tablespoon vanilla extract

3 tablespoons water

Combine the confectioners' sugar, powdered egg whites, vanilla, and water until blended. Add more water or confectioners' sugar until thick and stiff.

Royal Icing with Meringue Powder

2 cups confectioners' sugar

4 teaspoons meringue powder

1 tablespoon vanilla extract

3 tablespoons water

Combine the confectioners' sugar, meringue powder, vanilla, and water until blended. Add more water or confectioners' sugar until thick and stiff.

White Buttercream Frosting

¾ cup vegetable shortening

¾ cup (1½ sticks) butter, at room temperature

1 tablespoon vanilla extract

4½ cups confectioners' sugar

Beat the shortening and butter until combined. Beat in the vanilla. Gradually stir in the confectioners' sugar. Add a bit of water to achieve the desired consistency.

Variations

All-Butter Buttercream: Replace the shortening with butter.

Chocolate Buttercream: Add 3 tablespoons milk along with the vanilla and ⅓ cup cocoa powder along with the sugar.

Coffee Buttercream: Dissolve 2 tablespoons instant coffee in 2 tablespoons water. Add to the buttercream along with the vanilla.

Mint Buttercream: Replace the vanilla extract with mint extract.

Orange Buttercream: Add the grated zest of 1 orange and 2 tablespoons orange juice along with the vanilla.

Almond Buttercream: Replace the vanilla with 1 teaspoon almond extract. Add ¼ cup ground almonds

Whipped Cream

1 ½ cups heavy cream
1 teaspoon vanilla extract
1 cup granulated sugar

Combine the cream, vanilla, and sugar in a large bowl. Beat with an electric mixer until thick.

Cream Cheese Icing

4 ounces cream cheese
½ cup (1 stick) butter
1 cup confectioners' sugar
1 teaspoon vanilla extract
4 tablespoons milk

Beat the cream cheese and butter until creamy. Stir in the confectioners' sugar, vanilla, and milk to make a thin glaze.

Variations

Cream Cheese Filling: Add 1 ½ cups confectioners' sugar to the icing

Strawberry Cream Cheese Filling: Add 1 cup sliced strawberries and 1 ½ cup confectioners' sugar to the icing after the milk is added.

Sugar-Free Cream Cheese Filling

8 ounces cream cheese
½ cup (1 stick) butter
2 teaspoons vanilla

Beat the cream cheese, butter, and vanilla until creamy.

Vegan Cream Cheese Frosting

½ cup soy margarine, at room temperature
8 ounces tofu cream cheese, at room temperature
2 tablespoons soy or rice milk
4 cups confectioners' sugar
1 tablespoon lemon juice
1 teaspoon vanilla extract

1. Cream the margarine, cream cheese, and milk. Add the sugar slowly, beating constantly until combined. Add the lemon juice and vanilla and beat until light and fluffy. If necessary add more sugar or milk to reach consistency.

Variations

Vegan Berry Icing: Add ¼ cups mashed fresh or frozen berries.

Rosewater Icing

Place all the ingredients in a medium bowl and mix.

½ lb cups confectioners' sugar
4 teaspoons rosewater
Juice of 1 lemon
2 large egg whites

Lemon Icing

4 cups confectioners' sugar
½ cup (1 stick) butter
3 tablespoons grated lemon zest
½ cup freshly squeezed lemon juice
   from 3–4 large lemons

1. Cream the confectioners' sugar and butter until smooth.

2. Beat in the lemon zest and juice. Add more lemon juice or confectioners' sugar to achieve the desired consistency.

Vanilla Cream Frosting

3 cups confectioners' sugar
½ cup (1 stick) butter, softened
2 teaspoons vanilla extract
2 tablespoons milk

Cream the confectioners' sugar and butter until light and fluffy. Beat in the vanilla and milk until smooth and of spreading consistency.

Variations

Coffee Cream: Replace the vanilla and milk with 3 tablespoon double strength espresso. Add 1 teaspoon ground espresso beans.
Orange Cream: Replace the vanilla and milk with 3 tablespoons orange juice. Add 1 teaspoon orange zest.

Marshmallow Frosting

2 tablespoons milk
6 tablespoons sugar
minimarshmallows
2 tablespoons boiling water
½ teaspoon vanilla, extract

1. In a saucepan over medium-low heat, heat the milk and sugar for 6 minutes without stirring.

2. In a double boiler heat the marshmallows. When they are very soft add boiling water, stirring until smooth.

3. Remove from heat. Add the vanilla. With an electric mixer on medium speed beat in the hot sugar, keep beating until partly cool. Use at once.

Chocolate Glaze

1½ cups chocolate chips
3 tablespoons butter

Heat the chocolate and butter in a double boiler over simmering water, stirring until smooth.

Chocolate Icing

3 tablespoons boiling water
1½ ounces unsweetened chocolate
3 tablespoons butter
1 teaspoon vanilla extract
¾ cup confectioners' sugar

Heat the boiling water, chocolate, and butter in a double boiler over simmering water, stirring until melted. Remove from the heat and stir in the vanilla. Gradually stir in enough confectioners' sugar to make a thick but pourable icing.

Raspberry Glaze

½ cup raspberry jam
3 tablespoons lemon juice

Combine the jam with the lemon juice in a saucepan and cook over low heat until thickened. Remove from the heat and let cool.

Rum Glaze

¼ cup sugar
¼ cup water
¼ cup dark rum

Dissolve the sugar in the water in a small saucepan over low heat. Remove from the heat and stir in the rum.

Candied Rose Petals

Petals from two large roses
2 large egg white, beaten
¼ cup superfine sugar

1. Using a small brush lightly coat the top and underneath each petal with the egg whites.

2. Sprinkle sugar on the top and bottom of each petal

3. Place flowers on wax paper or parchment paper. Set until firm, about 1 hour.

Variation

Sugared flowers: Press the flowers in a flower press for 4 hours before covering with egg whites and sugar.

Edible flowers: dandelions, chamomile, chrysanthemums, lavender, mint, primrose, pansies, roses, scented geraniums, violets.

PUDDING

Rocky Road Milk Chocolate Pudding

1 cup granulated sugar
¼ cup Dutch-process cocoa
   powder
¾ cup cornstarch
¼ teaspoon salt
4 cups milk
¾ cup milk chocolate chips
¼ cup (½ stick) butter
2 teaspoons vanilla extract
¾ cup minimarshmallows
¾ cup chopped walnuts

1. Make the pudding: Combine the granulated sugar, cocoa powder, cornstarch, and salt in a saucepan.

2. Add the milk and bring to a boil over medium heat, stirring constantly or 5 to 7 minutes until the mixture thickens. Remove from the heat and let cool.

3. Stir in the chocolate chips, butter, and vanilla. Refrigerate for 30 minutes before serving.

4. To assemble the parfait, put ⅓ cup of the pudding in parfait glasses; then layer marshmallows and some of the nuts on top. Add more pudding and top with more nuts. Add cookies and serve (see photo, page 65).

Templates for Cookie Construction

To view full-scale templates, baking tips and more fun, creative ideas, visit http://www.crazyaboutcookiesbook.com.

Stained-Glass Ornament Cookies (page 240)

Fondant Snow Globe Cookies (page 241)

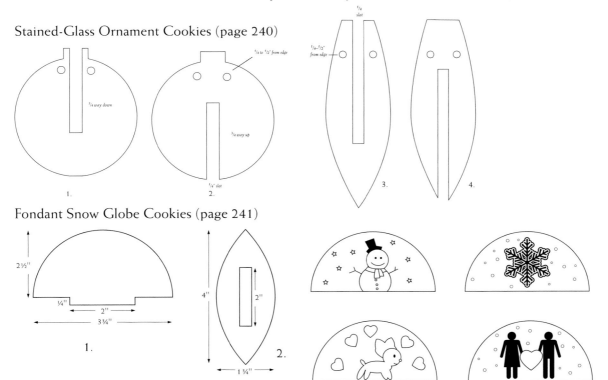

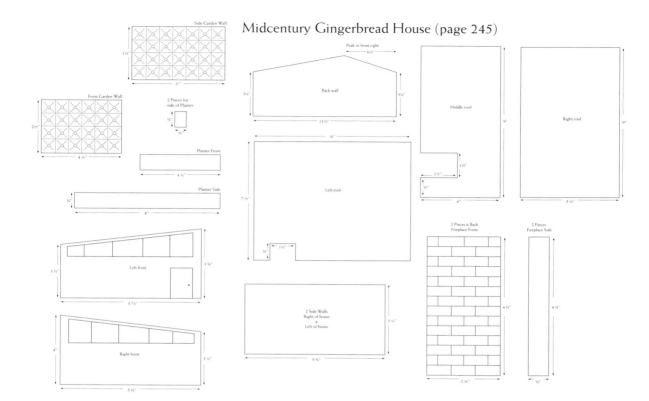

Midcentury Gingerbread House (page 245)

Side Garden Wall

2 ½"

5"

Front Garden Wall

2 ½"

4 ½"

2 Pieces for
side of Planter

½"

¼"

Planter Front

4 ½"

Planter Side

¾"

8"

Peak in front right

4 ½"

Back wall

3 ½"

3 ¼"

12 ½"

9"

Left roof

7 ½"

1 ½"

¾"

Left front

3 ½"

3 ¾"

5 ½"

Right front

4"

3 ¼"

5 ¾"

2 Side Walls
Right of house
&
Left of house

3 ¼"

5 ¾"

Middle roof

9"

2 ½"

1 ½"

¼"

4"

Right roof

9"

5 ½"

2 Pieces & Back
Fireplace Front

4 ¾"

2 ¾"

2 Pieces
Fireplace Side

4 ¾"

¾"

Fifth-Wheel Trailer (page 248)

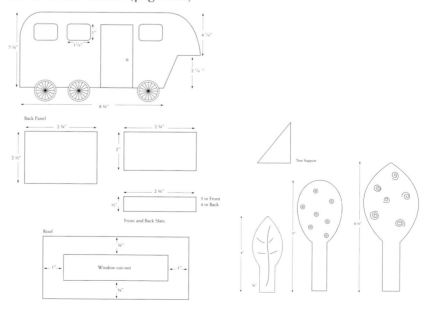

1"

1 ⅛"

4 ⅛"

7 ½"

2 ¼"

8 ¾"

Back Panel

2 ¾"

2 ½"

2 ¾"

2"

2 ¾"

5 in Front
4 in Back

½"

Front and Back Slats

Roof

¾"

1"

Window cut-out

1"

¾"

Tree Support

5"

6 ½"

4"

¾"

Mini-Gingerbread Houses (page 250)

Roof

1 ¾"

3 ¼"

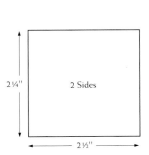

2 Sides

2 ¼"

2 ½"

Front & Back

2 ¼"

2 ³/₈ "

Gingerbread Dollhouse (page 252)

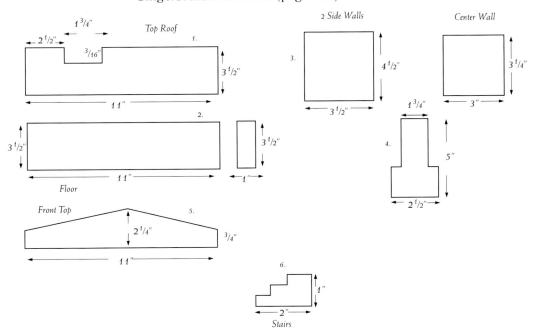

Top Roof

1 ³/₄"

2 ¹/₂"

³/₁₆"

3 ¹/₂"

1 1"

1.

2.

3 ¹/₂"

1 1"

Floor

3 ¹/₂"

1"

Front Top

2 ¹/₄"

³/₄"

1 1"

5.

2 Side Walls

3.

4 ¹/₂"

3 ¹/₂"

Center Wall

3 ¹/₄"

3"

1 ³/₄"

4.

5"

2 ¹/₂"

6.

1"

2"

Stairs

Index

About the Author

KRYSTINA CASTELLA is obsessed with playing in the kitchen and sharing her tasty and beautiful discoveries with others. Krystina is the author of *Crazy about Cupcakes* (Sterling 2006), *Pops! Icy Treats for Everyone* (Quirk Books 2008), *A World of Cake* (Storey Publishing 2010), and co-author of *Booze Cakes* (Quirk Books 2010). She is also co-author/photographer of the children's book *Discovering Nature's Alphabet* (Heyday 2006). She lives and works near Los Angeles as a writer, industrial designer, and professor at Art Center College of Design.